PHILOSOPHY AND
POST-STRUCTURALIST THEORY

PHILOSOPHY AND POST-STRUCTURALIST THEORY

From Kant to Deleuze

Claire Colebrook

EDINBURGH
University Press

© Claire Colebrook, 1999, 2005
Published in hardback as *Ethics and Representation:
From Kant to Poststructuralism* in 1999 by
Edinburgh University Press

Edinburgh University Press Ltd
22 George Square, Edinburgh

Typeset in Palatino Light
by Pioneer Associates, Perthshire, and
printed and bound in Spain by
GraphyCems

A CIP record for this book is available from the
British Library

ISBN 0 7486 2227 6 (paperback)

The right of Claire Colebrook to be identified as
author of this work has been asserted in
accordance with the Copyright, Designs and
Patents Act 1988.

CONTENTS

ACKNOWLEDGEMENTS

Despite the fact that this book was written after my departure from the inspiring environment of Murdoch University's school of Humanities, my motivation for thinking about these issues arose from my interaction with both the students and staff of the school. In particular I need to thank Horst Ruthrof, whose support and enthusiasm encouraged me to begin this and many other projects, as well as Wendy Parkins, Robyn Barnacle, Monika Kilian and Abigail Bray. I have been extremely fortunate to have finished this book at Monash University where I have benefited from the lively and stimulating postgraduate community. I owe special thanks to Jacinta Kerin, Valerie Hazel, Experience Bryon and Terri Bird. David Neil provided his typically meticulous and intelligent feedback on the final chapter. Lee Spinks was kind enough to work through and correct the Derrida and Foucault chapters. I am also grateful to Elizabeth Grosz who has provided me with valuable advice, support, and comments on the Irigaray chapter. The friendship of Alexander Garcia Duttmann made my first year at Monash truly worthwhile; his scholarship, integrity and wit have inspired whatever is of value in this book. Finally, and most importantly, I need to thank Lubica Ucnik, for her inspiration and energy.

INTRODUCTION

REPRESENTATION AS THE THRESHOLD OF MODERNITY

Within the self-understanding of the history of ideas representation is seen to constitute the threshold of modernity: and this sense of the threshold is deployed in two senses. On the one hand, modernity is inaugurated by representation: the demand that one's law no longer be given from without but that law should emerge through self-representation.[1] Representation, in this sense, is intertwined with democracy, autonomy, rights, enlightenment and identity. The passage to self-representation is the passage to modernity. Modernity, at least as an idea or telos, opens with this demand for representation, a demand given in both Kant's definition of enlightenment (Kant [1785] 1959: 185) as well as in liberal theories of representative democracy (Rawls 1996: 47–88).

On the other hand, the threshold of representation not only marks modernity off from its darker past (when law was imposed from without); the threshold of representation scars modernity itself, occurring as a limit within the possibility of modernity. Turning against the speculative reflections on substance and essence, modern philosophy situates itself within the representational limits of the subject. Representation is a condition of finitude. Because knowledge is received from without it must be taken up and re-presented. What can be known is therefore determined and delimited by the representational powers of the subject. This idea of representation as an internal limit is most clearly articulated in Kant's 'Copernican turn'. If what is known is experienced or *given*, then the conditions of experience mark the

1

object of knowledge. There can be no knowledge of things in themselves. To be known or experienced a thing must be other than the knower; it must be *given* to the knower. As *known*, things are only as they are re-presented to a subject.[2] Modernity occurs with this 'turn' to the subject and the recognition of knowledge's position, limit, point of view and, most importantly, its *separation*. There can be no immediate knowledge, for knowledge is, by definition, received or given, and therefore mediated.

If representation in the first (political) sense occurs with a demand for identity, recognition, autonomy and self-determination, representation in the second (epistemological) sense is intertwined with mediation, finitude, anti-foundationalism and separation. On the one hand the subject is instituted through representation, and demands a continuity or identity with political representation. On the other hand, the subject is separate from any represented thing, for the subject is the process of objectification. In both senses we deal with a threshold. The demand for democratic representation is a demand that modernity break free from its heteronomous past, that it emerge freely into a domain or space of non-interference, communication, recognition and inclusion. On the other hand, and in tension with this demand for representation as self-recognition, is the recognition of representation as a threshold that limits thought. Representation marks a limit, a point beyond which knowledge cannot go: a recognition of the point of view of knowledge. For knowledge's very possibility lies in perspective, point of view, position and finitude: the necessary consequence of the fact that if thought is to *know some thing* then it must be placed in a position in relation to that thing. Because knowledge relates to what is other than itself, it is situated in a relation, such that what it knows is not immediately present but must be re-presented. This recognition of the threshold of representation separates knowledge, reduces its claims and precludes any *ec-static* knowledge (knowledge that would step outside itself and be at one with what is known). Knowledge can no longer rest its claims on the pure revelation or participation with an outside. It is in this separation that knowledge becomes responsible. Because there are now (representational) limits to the knowable, there can no longer be appeals to some absolute or infinite ground that would justify human law. What is known is given only through the human subject's conditions of knowing, and so human law must become self-grounding – aware that its ground is nothing other than its self. In this regard, the representational condition or threshold separates the subject from the world, in a conditioned position of finitude.

On the other hand, the modern democratic demand that the subject be represented and become self-determining also means that the subject should accept no external threshold as simply given. The demand of representative democracy and enlightenment is precisely this: that any putatively 'given' external law be recognised as internal to human representation. What appears as divine law, ancient right, tradition or heavenly fiat is actually a human intention that has forgotten its status as human. To recognise external law as human representation, to internalise all those spectral illusions that have haunted man is the first step to enlightenment, and is at one with the striving for democracy.

REPRESENTATION AND DEMOCRACY

Central to the demands of liberal theory is the capacity and duty to represent oneself. According to Louis Dumont (1977), the specific feature of modern ideology is the rejection of any external, transcendent or hierarchical form of order. Order is not imposed from without. Rather, order is generated from the interaction among social units – the social units in liberal democracies being individuals. It is this secular and non-hierarchical principle of immanence which, according to Dumont, defines modern man as 'homo economicus'; and this also defines modern societies as economical. Economy is used here in both a literal and a figurative sense. At the literal level, the rejection of an external mode of legitimation or hierarchy is at one with capitalist modes of production. Only if value is determined by the free exchange of a uniformly quantifiable material can order be immanent: generated from the relation between units rather than imposed as a transcendent principle or law. Human individuals emerge as independent social units only in this 'equalitarian'[3] relation to capital; it is the capacity to sell one's labour that both defines one's social position and determines the social as such (Dumont 1977: 84). The resulting principles – of protection of property, non-interference and individual rights – assume that social order results from the interaction of rational and labouring individuals.

However, as Dumont and a series of twentieth-century theorists of modernity have made clear, this literal sense of economy is exceeded by economy in a figural sense. Modern societies are 'economic' not just because their mode of production is capitalist and determined by exchange value. Modernity is economic or 'mathematical' precisely because *all* being is thought according to a quantitative or calculative way of thinking (Dumont 1977: 33).[4] It is this more general sense of modern economism as mathematical – concerned with equivalence, exchange and quantification – that is crucial to the predominance of representation (Colebrook 1997). If it is the case that the world holds no inherent order, and if the world is a uniform and meaningless domain of exchangeable matter, then the world can be determined mathematically; it can be measured, exchanged, ordered and determined in advance. The socio-political individual is, furthermore, nothing other than this capacity for exchange (MacPherson 1962). This is what characterises the modern political subject. He no longer bears a moral nature, or what has been described as the transcendence-in-immanence of the soul (such that he partakes in some more divine nature or lawful cosmos [Gilson 1961: 72]). The subject is not determined beforehand by an absolute law or order. As the capacity for labour the individual is defined economically, in his relation *as* labour *to* property. But the individual is also defined in relation to labouring others, as a will whose law and determination is not already given but must be arrived at through negotiation and interaction. Law is determined through social representation, but this process of representation takes place through the medium of exchange value, the quantifiable and the calculable.

The idea that modernity is mathematical or economic in this broad sense is more often than not accompanied by a definite nostalgia (especially in Marxist accounts of the transition from use value to exchange value or in Jean Baudrillard's account of the loss of symbolic exchange [Baudrillard 1993]). What modern society has lost, it is argued, is any sense of a natural order, any sense of the meaning of the world, or continuity with the cosmos. Representation is situated in a domain of arbitrary exchange and meaningless equivalence. The world is reduced to representable matter, and politics achieves order only through processes of representation. In the absence of any meaning or law in the world itself, representation will have to re-invent order through social processes. But this generation of law through representation will also be the fulfilment of modern 'economism'. No external order will impede the free exchange of self-determining individuals. Subjects must not only overthrow external law, they must also recognise their rational capacity to represent a law to themselves. Only in a rational representational process can the *absence* of order be recognised as man's very possibility, his liberation into autonomy and freedom from dictated authority. According to the earliest theorists of modern representational democracy, the idea that one has been freed from the imposed constraints of external law can only reach its fulfilment in representation (Paine [1791–2] 1985: 176–7). Subjects may have overthrown the past and its spectres of ordained or divine hierarchy, but subjects only truly enter the present when they become self-representing. In speaking for themselves, and by contracting a social whole with others who also represent themselves, subjects move from a domain of exploitation, illusion and heteronomy to a spontaneous order of equal and self-determining individuals.

It is this logic of representation that motivates Rousseau's criticism of the bourgeoisie, and is sustained in twentieth-century liberal theory. By the time Rousseau was lamenting man's fall it was not enslavement to the *ancien regime* that was at issue so much as the self-enslavement of man to the very principle of exchange that had promised his freedom (Manent 1994: 67). Society had rid itself of the illegitimate order of ancient privilege and divine right, and in so doing had placed itself in a position where individuals could interact as free and self-determining. But the very principle of free exchange that had liberated man – capital – had now become his new master. Thus Rousseau describes a typical and repeated motif in theories of modernity: economism and representation are the necessary conditions for liberation, but too often result in man's self-enslavement. One can only become self-determining in the absence of any imposed law; freedom demands the removal of any transcendent order and the capacity for individuals to represent themselves. Representation, therefore, depends upon an absence of law. True democratic order cannot be given in advance or determined from some ground, but must be *open to determination*. The process that arrives at the democratic order is thus not extrinsic to that order. Democracy is as much a form of procedure – of deliberation, representation and reason – as it is a way of life.

However, while the absence of external law is the necessary condition for free determination, it is also the possibility for an abnegation of freedom. If no law is given and subjects must represent themselves, and if this self-representation depends upon free, equivalent and inter-acting individuals, then it is possible that individuals can *misrecognise* their duty and take the condition of free exchange as law itself. For Rousseau, when individuals allow their representational duty to pass over into an external representative they once again become enslaved and non-autonomous: 'The moment a people adopts representatives it is no longer free; it no longer exists' (Rousseau [1762] 1968: 143). When critics of modernity, from Rousseau to the present, lament the modern enslavement to capital, they do so precisely because what was originally a representation is reified into a presence or law in itself. The system of exchange takes on a being of its own, and is externalised and hypostatised as an imposed order.

This is how capitalism is diagnosed as the crisis of liberalism; the procedure of unimpeded exchange is fetishised and supplants rational representation. Economy is taken as an end or law in itself (rather than a condition through which law might be determined). In many of the lamentations surrounding the fall of the enlightenment into capitalism, society is criticised as being enslaved or dominated by a principle of exchange. The principle no longer functions as a relation between individuals but becomes externalised into an alien law to which indi-viduals submit. No longer in the service of reason and liberation, exchange functions as a false representation of reason. Reason fails to be self-representing and once more falls under the illusion of one of its own representations: the spectre, allure or image of capital. From Marx's theory of commodity fetishism to Adorno and Horkheimer's *Dialectic of Enlightenment* reason is diagnosed as bearing the continual capacity to fall under the spell of its own representations.

But it is important to note that this inherent dialectic of reason is described in the earliest demands for democratic representation.[5] The ideal of democratic representation is the ideal of an immanent order, an order not imposed from without but generated through the social process itself. Democratic representation occurs when, freed from the determination of any prior or given law, subjects represent themselves. The condition of this act of self-representation is the absence of any transcendent law. The law is not given but needs to be determined through acts of social interaction and exchange. But this absence of law can also allow that realm of exchange to appear itself as imposed law, as the law of capital, the invisible hand of the market or economic rationalism – as a logic imposed on existence rather than the very *logos* or self-movement of existence. The therapy for this always possible fall, whereby subjects misrecognise the principle of their freedom – exchange – as an external law, is participation in representation. Modernity is only fully achieved when the passage from values given from without to values generated from within is thoroughly internalised, and not separated from life by the external images, illusions or lures of capital and commodities. What must be recognised is not just that there are no values beyond the world that can determine the system of exchange, but that exchange itself is also a human representation. Democratic representation, in its political sense, can only be achieved in a thorough-going representationalism in the epistemological sense. For what appears as an external order or law – whether that be reason, nature, man or economy – must, in a fully democratic and enlightened world, be recognised as the outcome of man's own representations. Reason is a representational capacity, and not a thing to be represented that could replace God or nature as one more moral foundation.

This self-recognition of reason as a representational procedure extends beyond Kant's 'Copernican turn' and characterises many of the late eighteenth-century criticisms of rationalism that had replaced the image of God with one more imposed image of reason. Kant's criticism of rationalism was directed at the hypostatisation of reason's own laws into external values. But the idea that man is a representational animal, whose capacity for representation was *both* the promise of his freedom as well as the risk of his enslavement, is a familiar eighteenth-century motif. Revolution needs to take two stages (at least). The first is economic in the narrow sense: the removal of ancient privilege and the self-determination of individuals through their own capacity for labour. And this leads to processes of political representation. No longer ordered from without, subjects become free individuals capable of representing their will alongside other individuals. But this move to free exchange and representation needs to be extended to a more radical sense of representation. Once reason accepts *itself* as self-legislating and self-representing, it needs to avoid any representation *of* reason. At the very least, any representation must be recognised *as* representation (and not as an image or norm to which reason ought to submit).

If modern societies risk falling into an indiscriminate economism, where the quantifiable comes to govern human life, then this can only be overcome through the retrieval of representation: all those external systems, orders and reified structures must be seen as human representations and reunited with the domain of responsible and intentional constitution. This is where the political demand for democratic representation intersects with the epistemological demand for enlightenment. Subjects have the power to represent themselves as free individuals because they are rational; but rationality is also the responsibility of recognising man as a representational animal. His order and law is not imposed from without but is represented through the law-giving power of reason.

REPRESENTATION AND AUTONOMY

Representation is also both the condition and consequence of autonomy. In the absence of any given law or authority subjects are compelled to give the law to themselves. Consequently, subjects have the *right* to representation precisely because of their autonomous nature as rational individuals. Political representation is grounded on this autonomy. Subjects take part in the constitution of a polity because the polity ought to be *nothing other than* this taking part. Subjects must be a law for themselves, and represent this law for themselves. At the same time, while their right to representation draws upon their status as autonomous, autonomy is also an effect of man as a representing being. Whereas natural being is determined, man's reason endows him with a capacity to think or desire what is not given. He can represent the world *as a world*, and in so doing become other than a naturally determined thing. It is because subjects are not merely determined by necessary natural law, but can represent a law that is other than nature, that they can become self-determining. It is this very possibility of representing something other than a natural law that renders subjects necessarily autonomous. The possibility to act other than by mere compulsion follows from the capacity to represent one's compulsions – to be other than, or in a position of judgment in relation to, one's nature. It is this separation of the representing self from the self that is represented that leads to autonomy as an unavoidable duty. Autonomy follows from the subject's capacity – as a subject – to imagine or represent what is not given. It is the self-separation through representation that obliges subjects to decide in relation to their being, and to be placed in the responsible position of autonomous judgement.

This may sound like a strictly Kantian argument, but it is not confined to Kant's specific theory of transcendental freedom. Two examples can make this point clearly. In early forms of liberal and modern ethics it is the separation of 'ought' from 'is' that opens the burden of autonomy. Law no longer resides in the world as an already present meaning. In fact, modernity – according to the majority of definitions – is constituted precisely in this break. Once it is recognised that *man represents*, he constitutes a separate domain of value; and it is because of this separation that he is forced to decide for himself. In early liberal theory this separation through representation is defined through the distinction between nature and law. Man's capacity to represent a law to himself separates him from any given decree. As autonomous, he must represent himself (politically). But man is autonomous precisely because he can represent (epistemologically); his world is a represented world and so man is not immediately determined. The inextricably intertwined motifs of autonomy and representation are the promise of modernity. Man becomes autonomous when he recognises that all external injunctions are human representations; and democratic representation is possible only for an autonomous self. Further, subjects become autonomous selves, and institute their autonomy, through democratic representation.

REPRESENTATION AND IDENTITY

What the foregoing accounts of representation's relation to autonomy, democracy and enlightenment indicate is the inextricable connection of all these motifs with identity. It is a commonplace of social theory and the history of ideas to locate the emergence of individualism and subjectivism at the origin of modernity. Whether modernity is inaugurated through Descartes's *cogito*, Hobbes's method of beginning analysis from individual social units or Kant's 'Copernican turn', there is generally recognised to be a significant historical 'shift'. This is so much the case that those theories critical of modernity – from German idealism onwards – tend to appeal to pre- or supra-individual formations in order to overcome the alienation regarded to be constitutive of contemporary subjectivism. These formations would include notions of community, public sphere, culture, polity, embodiment or lifeworld.[6] The critical force of such notions lies in their ability to explain the division or alienation of the individual from some pre-individual unity or totality.

Criticisms of the autonomous modern subject frequently extend rather than reject the modern demand for representation, a demand that order not be opposed from without but be representative of the subject's own self-formation. Both enlightenment individualism and subsequent critics of rampant capitalist individualism are critical of any separation of order from individual will. Rousseau, for example, is at once critical of any alienated individualism at the same time as he insists that the social whole ought to be *nothing more* than the individual. In the ideal formation of society,

> [T]here is no associate over whom he does not gain the same rights as others gain over him, each man recovers the equivalent of everything he loses, and in the bargain he acquires more power to preserve what he has. . . . Immediately, in place of the individual person of each contracting party, this act of association creates an artificial and corporate body composed of as many members as there are voters in the assembly, and by this same act that body acquires its unity, its common *ego*, its life and its will. The public person thus formed by the union of all other persons was once called the *city*, and is now known as the *republic* or the *body politic*. (Rousseau [1762] 1968: 61)

Thomas Paine also saw the ideal polity as a unity that stemmed directly from the being of its members, rather than being an imposed or external order; and this unity between individual and the social whole was achieved through representation:

> That which is called government, or rather that which we ought to conceive government to be, is no more than some common centre, in which all the parts of society unite. This cannot be accomplished by any method so conducive to the various interests of the community, as by the representative system. . . . It admits not of a separation between knowledge and power, and is superior, as government always ought to be, to all the accidents of

individual man, and is therefore superior to what is called monarchy.

A nation is not a body, the figure of which is to be represented by the human body; but is like a body contained within a circle, having a common centre, in which every radius meets; and that centre is formed by representation. To connect representation with what is called monarch is eccentric government. Representation is of itself the delegated monarchy of a nation, and cannot debase itself by dividing it with another. (Paine [1791–2] 1985: 181)

This idea of the social whole as representative of its individuals was not only an inaugurating ideal of the enlightenment. Like Paine and Rousseau, many contemporary theorists appeal to such a unity or integration through a critique of modernity and an appeal to pre-modern or pre-individual societies. Unlike capitalist individualism, which is based on competitiveness, quantification and the ruthless extension of individual reason, pre-modern social wholes were charac-terised by an identification between the self and its irreducibly social role. Consider the standard description of the Athenian polis that has been deployed by neo-Aristotelians to criticise the limits of modernity. On this picture, the polis is nothing other than the shared represen-tation of individuals; the individual exists only in so far as he or she is a member of the community, or takes part in the self-representation of the public sphere. The individual is not a 'private' or 'interior' mental space: one's identity is nothing other than the expression of one's social role.

And so we might conclude that both contemporary identity politics and communitarianism regard individual self-identity as fully formed only through representation, as ideally *at one* with its manifestation. Any gap, separation or distance between the self and its representation would be the error of political exclusion where a self is belied by stereotypes (for identity politics) or an alienated State (for communi-tarians). This is why there is an implicit (and occasionally explicit) criticism of modernity, both in contemporary identity politics and communitarianism. For the former, modernity has alienated the self from the means of representation: global capitalism, mass media and patriarchy impose unifying norms. For the latter, it is the modern fiction of the Cartesian subject that leads us to conceive of any supra-individual values as impositions on our personal being. What separates these two models is the status of the subject: on the one hand there is a demand for the proliferation of subjective representations in identity politics; on the other hand there is an appeal to the overcoming of the subject by tying the individual back to processes of representation. But for both it is the separation between the subject's identity and representation that is the ill of modernity.

In the case of Jurgen Habermas's public sphere – which is defined by Habermas as the fulfilment of modernity and enlightenment – there is still a nostalgic sense of historical loss, a loss to be overcome through the *integration* of the individual and communication 'back into' the life-world. (Habermas describes certain practices in modernity such as the natural sciences as having become disengaged from the life-world; their grounding in human interests is no longer recognised. The cure of this separation or disengagement is re-inclusion. No science should be seen as a set of rules to govern human life, but should be re-included *within life*.[Habermas: 1987]) Habermas's own ideal of modernity – where legitimation is achieved through the unimpeded communication of participants – is the fulfilment of democratic representation, and he is explicit that modernity does offer this self-critique (Habermas 1985). While being the fulfilment of modern demands for representation, the public sphere is also, no less, a critical tool directed against the specifically modern alienation of the means of representation. This is why Habermas speaks of *returning* certain practices to the life-world (the *Lebenswelt* or domain of social meaning [Habermas 1971]). Indeed, it is the postmodern loss of the goal of unity, consensus and integration that Habermas's theory of communicative action has as its target. What Habermas's project manifests is the sustained demand for individual representation alongside a criticism of individualist separation. No less than the popular demands for individual fulfilment and identity politics, communitarian approaches remain critical of individual separation – the idea that the individual is submitted to or subject to a logic, system or order imposed from without. On both accounts identity is ideally achieved through representation, whether that be collective or individual, rather than representation being an external system.

If both identity politics and communitarianism depend upon a sustained or invigorated enlightenment demand for representation, how do we negotiate the manifestly anti-humanist and postmodern criticisms of identity? Once again, what appears to be a clear opposition

is muddied by a consideration of the role of the concept of representation. On the one hand, for both identity politics and communitarians,
representation is deemed to be the fulfilment of identity. Against the
alienation of modernity, identity politics demands that one's identity
not be an external or reified representation, but that one represent
oneself. Communitarianism in its fullest sense is seen as an arena of
mutual self-representation, set against the modern atomisation or
separation of the individual from some alien or imposed order. Both
these currents are expressed in Chandra Talpade Mohanty's exemplary
account of the critical threshold of representation. For Mohanty, critical
movements, such as feminism, achieve their force by elucidating the
gap or break between representational norms and those identities that
are supposedly being represented:

> The relationship between 'Woman' – a cultural and ideological
> composite Other constructed through representational discourses
> (scientific, literary, juridical, linguistic, cinematic etc.) – and
> 'women' – real, material subjects of their collective histories – is
> one of the central questions the practice of feminist scholarship
> seeks to address. (Mohanty 1991: 60)

In this regard the postmodern critique of essential identities unites
with the enlightenment demand for the expression *of* identity. Talpade,
like Catharine MacKinnon (1987: 22–3) and Drucilla Cornell (1991:
78), does not grant women an essential identity, but does insist that
women cannot be reduced to some imposed representation of
'Woman'. Rather than appeal to women's identity these forms of
contemporary feminism demand that the process of representation be
intensified and that the singularity of a stereotype be resisted by the
proliferation of representations.

REPRESENTATION AND MODERNITY

The idea of modernity as representational is expressed with varying
degrees of approval and complicity by a number of thinkers from a
number of traditions. The simplest form of the thesis argues that the
seventeenth century gives birth to the notion of the idea – as a picture
or representation of the world – and that it is this invention of a

mental or subjective entity that enables the modern problems of philosophy as theory of knowledge, mind or language (Hacking 1975;
Rorty 1980). More complex accounts of modernity as representational
suggest that the modern emphasis on representation is merely an
intensification of a tendency of Western thought in general.[7] Western
thought has been grounded on an appeal to presence, a presence that
would then be doubled, represented or ordered through a *logos* or
logic. Modernity merely intensifies this representationalism by locating
the *logos* as a 'logic,' 'ratio' or reason within a separate subject who is
set over against the being of the world.

Representation in its political or democratic sense is also proclaimed
as the essence of modernity.[8] While this notion of representation was
defined in the eighteenth century by reference to the Ancient Greek
polis, it was also seen at the time as peculiarly modern. The re-invigoration of the Greek polity could only be achieved, it was argued, in an
enlightened age. The ancient mode of representation was bound to
self-destruct precisely because the original polis depended upon the
contingent locality and manageable homeliness of the Greek community. According to Rousseau, 'Among the Greeks, all that the people
had to do, it did itself; it was continually assembled in the market
place' (Rousseau [1762] 1968: 142). As such, then, the ancient mode of
representation – in which there was no separation between the individual citizen and the social whole – depended upon having a social
whole sufficiently limited for all individuals to recognise their will and
freedom in each other. The social whole could be thoroughly representative only if the whole did not exceed the direct participation of
its members; the relation was one of an *identity* between individual
and collective will, rather than the social whole being *representative* of
collective will. Because the ancient polity depended on identity it was
always threatened by the risk of tyranny: no space or separation was
allowed between individual will and collective law.[9]

Modern democracy, on the other hand, through the device of representation, overcomes the need for a strict identity between individual
and collective will. It does this by seeing collective will *as representative*.
There are individual wills that are separate from the state, and can
perceive and live themselves as such. But individual wills are also capable
of abstracting from their particular and private being and generating a
collective will that is representative. The difference between identity

and representation is crucial here. In pre-modern societies such as the Greek polis self-identity is nothing other than social role or political being. In modern representative democracies the representational process is answerable to and effected from individual wills; it must be representative of those wills even though, *as general or collective,* identity with individual will is impossible. The social whole is what all individuals would ideally will; it is representative. It must therefore operate not on the idea of a *collection* of wills – the direct participation of the idealised polis – but a will that would be representative of any individual.

In order to have this shift in meaning between representation as political *participation,* to representation as what is representative, ostensibly there needs to be a strong normative conception of the subject. And this is where the first (epistemological) sense of representation connects with the second (political) sense. If the human subject is understood as a contingent and socially determined collection of attributes and desires who might then enter an aggregate of individuals, the social whole will also be a contingent formation of those desires. However, if I have a sense of the philosophical *subject* – not as a thing within the world but a way in which the world is represented – then I can think of a human being as a representational relation: a being that has no positive properties but is defined as a form of self-representation, autonomy, self-determination, pure freedom and so forth. The two senses of representation are tied to this 'emptying out' of the philosophical subject. The Cartesian subject is defined as nothing other than the relation of self-certainty, and this relation is definitively separated from causally determined and empirical matter. And it is only because we can think of an 'empty' human subject that representative democracy can work: democracy is not just the collection of self-seeking interests and the expressed desires of competing individuals. In representative democracy the will expressed is that of an individual adopting the 'universal standpoint'; this is not what the individual in particular wants, but what the very structure of individual being demands: freedom, self-determination and autonomy. The political ideal of Athenian democracy – of a social whole that is representative of its members – can only be fulfilled through an enlightenment conception of the subject, a subject who is nothing other than a capacity for (self) representation.

It is this direct relation between the two senses of representation which constitutes the systemic unity of Kant's philosophy: a philosophy that can develop a theory of freedom from the basis of the question of knowledge alone (Allison 1990). Not only does Kant's theory of knowledge – as a representation of the world, rather than the world itself – lead directly to the idea of a free human subject; his theory of knowledge is also articulated through a moral and political language of legitimation, justification, assent and agreement (O'Neill 1989). What enables this intimate link between theory of knowledge and politics is the idea of representation. It is because the world is not immediately given as a thing in itself but is represented that we have to assume a separation between appearances and things in themselves. From this separation we also have to assume a subjective domain of knowledge or representations; it is this separateness of the subjective that directly underpins the notion of freedom. Because the world is represented – and because the conditions of representation reside in the domain of knowledge rather than the world itself – it is possible for the subject to imagine what is not given. It is this capacity to represent that separates the subject from the world as given and opens the site of subjective freedom. From the very structure of knowledge as a representation of the world, we are led to the idea of a self-determining subject. And it is this notion of subjective self-determination that underlies the notion of representation in the political sense. But the relation of representation in its epistemological and political senses also works the other way around. If we can derive a theory of freedom from Kant's theory of knowledge it is also the case that his theory of knowledge is articulated through the model and metaphorics of a democratic republic (O'Neill 1989). This is what opens the project of reason's inherent *self*-vindication.

By arguing that enlightened knowledge is possible only when subjects are aware of themselves as autonomous, Kant articulates one of the key eighteenth-century motifs of representative democracy. The link between representation and modernity neither emerges with Kant nor can be contained within the Kantian problematic. Consider one of the central images of the 'age of reason': the French revolution with all its promise of liberty, equality and fraternity followed soon after by the Terror. How do we explain this self-enslavement of what is, ideally, a self-legislating reason? The problem had been encountered a century earlier in the English revolution and its subsequent reversion to monarchy. Not surprisingly, the appeals to democracy that followed both failures of reason were similar. It is not sufficient to offer individuals the political opportunity for representation if they are not yet enlightened. And what is enlightenment? It is the recognition of the very capacity for self-determination or representation. If individuals are not aware of themselves as free and self-determining, then the opportunity for freedom will be just submission to another authority. What needs to be realised is not that it is possible to choose another authority, but that there is no authority other than reason itself. It is not enough to behead the king; the very position of kingship or external authority itself needs to be abolished. When John Milton lamented the failure of the English revolution what he lamented was not that power had fallen into the wrong hands, nor that the English had chosen the wrong authority, but that reason was still not self-authoring. Only by recognising themselves as free could the English have a reasoned, or representative, government (Milton 1982: 190). A century later, when the English were responding to the Terror, the failure to develop a truly representative democracy was also interpreted as a failure to recognise the self-representing character of reason. In fact, both sides of the argument – those for and against the French revolution – held this to be the case: as long as men were not self-determining there was no point in giving them the political right to representation. The dispute concerned whether reason was such that it was essentially capable of recognising itself as self-determining, despite a history of subordination (Paine [1791–2] 1985; Godwin [1793] 1985; Wollstonecraft [1792] 1985); or, whether the capacity for true self-representation eluded the grasp of modern individuals (Burke 1910).

The right to political representation is therefore definitive of the modern subject. It is not that there are subjects who may or may not engage in the process of self-representation; subjectivity is nothing other than a procedure of representation. This is an idea that marks the first expressions of the enlightenment as well as theories of the enlightenment and critiques of modernity. The self-enslavement of reason is seen as a problem of self-representation. Valid and legitimate political representation is only possible if individuals recognise themselves as self-determining. But the capacity for self-determination can only be realised in an enlightened or modern representative democracy. How does the passage to representation get instituted? How does

modernity come to represent itself? One of the necessary, if not
sufficient conditions is, of course, through the idea of the pre-modern
as the pre-representational.

In order to consider this question we might turn back to the self-
definition of enlightenment maturity and its own reference to a
pre-representational past. The simplest definitions of the enlightenment
regard the eighteenth century as a violent 'presentism' (White 1973).
Enlightenment would be the annihilation of all past superstition, all
historical debt and all relation to tradition (Descombes 1993: 146). Not
surprisingly, then, the enlightenment was expressed through a series
of metaphors of apocalypse, where the structures and veils of the past
would be torn away to reveal the clarity of the present (Goldsmith
1993). But it also needs to be considered that the enlightenment was
also critical of apocalyptic revelation, and this for several reasons. As
Kant asserted, the minute a philosophy adopts an apocalyptic tone it
has forgotten the responsibility of its own representational position
(Kant 1993b). There can be no knowledge of the absolute, no apocalypse
and certainly not *now*, because knowledge is necessarily temporally and
spatially located. There can be no knowledge or experience of that which
exceeds the very conditions of knowledge. So the enlightenment – and
not just for Kant – was at once a reaction against a past characterised
by superstition, prejudice and submission to external authorities, at the
same time as it constantly warned against the threat of resurrecting its
own force as yet another authority. We might define this enlightenment
relation to the process of *becoming enlightened* as the problem of *spectrality*. Kant gives a particularly clear example of this problem. Reason
must act as a critical force and must act for itself and not submit to
external authority. To this extent reason acts as an apocalyptic unveiling
of man's hitherto unrecognised submission to external forces; all those
representations and demonstrations of the absolute are *reason*'s representations. They cannot provide reason with a method, for method is
nothing other than reason's own activity. However, if we were to go on
and accept reason as an already given system, and fail to see that any
such system must be built or constructed, then reason would become
yet one more dogmatically asserted external authority. Reason becomes
spectral – haunted or dominated by an image of its own making. For
Kant, the proper use of reason would be anti-spectral; reason is not
an image to which thought ought to submit but a continual critical

capacity of all such images and symbols. To this extent reason is also anti-apocalyptic: any final or absolute revelation that claims to present the world beyond the finitude of human knowledge belies its own act of representation. There can be no knowledge of the unconditioned; any proclaimed apocalyptic revelation of the unconditioned is at one with a tyranny that exempts itself from the procedure of reasoned demonstration.

One of the clearest articulations of this logic of spectrality is given in the works of Jacques Derrida. For Derrida, philosophy in general, and not just Kantianism, is the aim for logocentric closure – the aim that knowledge be its own father, its own point of origin. Indeed, according to Derrida, this figure of self-fathering or 'autoinsemination' drives the very project of logic and concepts: 'The conception of the concept is an autoinsemination' (Derrida 1981a: 48). However, this aim for self-origination is necessarily haunted by all those spectres that it seeks to eradicate. Reason's eradication of all external authorities, for example, has to proceed by way of some image or representation of reason. Pure self-presence will always be haunted by some spectre or double, some image or text that re-presents the present *as present*. Thus the aim of philosophical autonomy and responsibility – the aim to not be determined from without – will necessarily be haunted by that which resists all autonomy: the writing, textuality or representation that enable presence to be thought as pre-inscriptional. Apart from Derrida's frequent use of metaphors of haunting, spirit and spectres to describe the problem of philosophical autonomy, the motif of the spectre and its relation to modernity goes back to the enlightenment. Consider the late eighteenth-century English poet William Blake's use of the spectre. For Blake a spectre emerges when an activity of the imagination is hypostatised and then seen as an authority to which human beings ought to submit.[10] His most famous description of this process is in *The Marriage of Heaven and Hell*:

The ancient poets animated all sensible objects with Gods or Geniuses, calling them by the names and adorning them with the properties of woods, rivers, mountains, lakes, cities, nations, and whatever their enlarged & numerous senses could perceive.
And particularly they studied the genius of each city and country, placing it under its mental deity;

Till a system was formed, which some took advantage of, &
enslav'd the vulgar by attempting to realize or abstract the mental
deities from their objects: thus began Priesthood;
Choosing forms of worship from poetic tales.
And at length they pronounc'd that the Gods had order'd such
things.
Thus men forgot that All deities reside in the human breast. (Blake
[1793] 1966: 153)[11]

This account is typical of earlier eighteenth-century explanations
(and demystifications) of human enslavement through religion. It also
sounds remarkably similar to later nineteenth-century Nietzschean
accounts of religion as the self-enslavement by human beings to their
own created myths. What makes Blake interesting is that he sees
institutionalised religion, as did Voltaire, as the self-alienation of the
imagination; but he also attributes a similar spectrality to human reason.
The critical spirit which has torn down the structures of state religion
itself becomes an external authority. This explains why Blake's poems
always take the form of a never-ending and unashamedly violent
apocalypse. The very force of life that violently destroys the spectre of
external authority *by that very action* inaugurates itself as another violent
authority. The very demand of human life is such that it must respond
or act in relation to its world, but in any reflection on that action it is
also capable of taking the force or event of action as an external thing
or object. Life enslaves itself by taking its own activity as an external
foundation.

Once reason is recognised as a capacity to represent then it is
definitively separated from that which it represents. Representations
must be recognised *as representations*, and not hypostatised into alien
authorities which present reason with an external foundation; it is
through representation that reason becomes self-grounding. Reason's
faith must be in nothing other than itself and its own limits. In order to
emerge as a process of self-representation, as a continual disengagement
from external authority, reason must understand itself as a critical
relation. Reason is not a given law but the capacity for law-giving; and
such law can only be defined against any positive, given or empirical
determination. Reason's autonomy is therefore given as a counter-
heteronomy: a recognition that in representing the conditioned I have

the capacity to be *other than* conditioned. The unconditioned cannot be presented but only used critically against any attempt to reduce reason to a fact within given conditions. In Kant, reason not only directs itself against the superstitions of revealed religion and the past; reason's autonomy is also asserted against reason's *own* natural illusions.

Kant established his own enlightenment philosophy by being critical of all those previous forms of metaphysics that were not aware of their own point of view. By introducing the problem of point of view into philosophy Kant raised the question of representation. Knowledge is not the immediacy of pure presence – only a divine intuition is at one with what it intuits. Knowledge is *essentially* received or given. What is known is, therefore, not the immediacy of presence but re-presentation. Philosophy is therefore compelled to address the position, point or ground of representation:

> [R]eason shows such a pure spontaneity in the case of ideas that it far transcends everything that sensibility can give to conscious- ness and shows its chief occupation in distinguishing the world of sense from the world of understanding, thereby prescribing limits to the understanding itself.
>
> For this reason a rational being must regard himself as intelli- gence (and not from the side of his lower powers), as belonging to the world of understanding and not to that of the senses. Thus he has two standpoints from which he can consider himself and recognize the laws of the employment of his powers and conse- quently of his actions: first, as belonging to the world of sense under laws of nature (heteronomy), and, second, as belonging to the intelligible world under laws which, independent of nature are not empirical but founded only on reason. (Kant [1785] 1959: 71)

The problem of autonomy is, therefore, directly connected to the representational antinomy. On the one hand, the world is given through representation. Whether representation is located in the subject, logic or structure it becomes a site of separation and autonomy. The process of representation is not a direct mirror but must recognise its contribution to what is known. Thus, there is an imperative to recognise represen- tation as autonomous, as not determined directly by its world. On the other hand, any recognition of representation could not exempt itself from the representational process; it, too, would be a representation. This antinomy plays itself out in the post-Kantian attacks on subjectivism, humanism and anthropologism. Any recognition of the representational process as, say, subjective, cultural, or linguistic, offers one representation as the ground of representation in general. However, if one does *not* recognise the domain of representation one precludes autonomy and responsibility. It is only in realising that there is no direct participation in the world, or that our experience of the world is conditioned by a logic, that we are thrown back upon the site of that condition. We are separated from the world, even if we are not quite sure just where this separation leaves us. This sense of separation was, of course, crucial for the enlightenment. Because the world did not itself ordain a natural hierarchy, and because reason is a capacity to determine nature rather than being determined, human life can separate itself from a history of illusion, myth and domination by nature. But it is just this autonomy of the subject and the loss of a 'prose of the world' that has also led to a perceived crisis of representation. Is enlightenment the fulfilment of the *subject*'s representation or, is it only when representation is freed from any idea of what a subject *is* that autonomy is truly achieved?

NOTES

1. Apart from the more general discussions of representative democracy, the more complex issues surrounding modernity and political representation are discussed by Ernesto Laclau in 'Representation and Power' (Laclau 1996).
2. The idea of modernity as representational in this second, epistemological sense is criticised in Richard Rorty's *Philosophy and the Mirror of Nature* (1980), where Rorty laments the Cartesian problem of the representation of the world in mind. Ian Hacking also describes modern philosophy as being concerned with mental representations or ideas (1975). The most complex account and critique of modernity and representation is given in Michel Foucault's *The Order of Things* (1970). This account will be discussed in detail in Chapter 7.
3. Dumont refers to modern society as 'equalitarian' in so far as it seeks to maintain the ontological sameness of its members; the term 'egalitarian' is the distribution of rights and benefits that would follow.
4. Following Martin Heidegger (whose concept of modernity as mathe-

matical will be explored in Chapter 3), Adorno and Horkheimer also employ the notion of a modern 'mathematicisation' of being. In *Dialectic of Enlightenment* the progress of reason through history is linked to a process of domination and loss of meaning where the 'multiplicity of forms is reduced to position and arrangement, history to fact, things to matter'. This process of enlightenment, which has its origins in Platonic thought but becomes modern with Bacon's 'scientific attitude' is, they argue, mathematical in character: 'The same equations dominate bourgeois justice and commodity exchange. [Adorno and Horkheimer then quote from Bacon's *Advancement of Learning*:] Is not the rule, "Si inaequalibus aequalia addas, omnia erunt inaequalia," an axiom of justice as well as of mathematics? And is there not a true coincidence between commutative and distributive justice, and arithmetical and geometrical proportion? Bourgeois society is ruled by equivalence. It makes the dissimilar comparable by reducing it to abstract quantities' (Adorno and Horkheimer [1944] 1979: 7).
5. The very power or reason that overthrows order can also come to function as one more external rule or dogma. This is clearly expressed in writers as early as Rousseau who argued that representation had to remain immediate and at one with the body of the people, and not alienated into any external power: 'It is what is common to those different interests which yields the social bond; if there were no point on which separate interests coincided, then society could not conceivably exist. And it is precisely on the basis of this common interest that society must be governed . . . the sovereign, which is simply a collective being, cannot be represented by anyone but itself – power may be delegated, but the will cannot be' (Rousseau [1762] 1968: 69).
6. The most persuasive argument for the importance of the public sphere, lifeworld and intersubjectivity is given by Jurgen Habermas and contemporary critical theory (Habermas 1989). Notions such as community, culture and polity are used more widely, but are specifically employed by neo-Aristotelian philosophers, such as Alastair MacIntyre (1990) and Martha Nussbaum (1994), or holists such as Charles Taylor (1995), all of whom are critical of modernity and post-modernity for its inability to see the positive value of social, collective or shared goods.
7. The idea of Western thought as representational *in general*, with modernity acting as an intensification of representationalism, is expressed most explicitly by Martin Heidegger. Heidegger's anti-representationalism will be discussed at length in Chapter 3.
8. For Rousseau, 'The idea of representation is a modern one. It comes to us from feudal government, from that iniquitous and absurd system

under which the human system is degraded and which dishonours the name of man. In the republics and even in the monarchies of the ancient world, the people never had representatives; the very word was unknown' (Rousseau [1762] 1968: 141).

9. According to Thomas Paine, 'Representation was a thing unknown in the ancient democracies. In those the mass of the people met and enacted laws (grammatically speaking) in the first person. Simple democracy was no other than the common-hall of the ancients. . . . As these democracies increased in population, and the territory extended, the simple democratical form became unwieldy and impracticable; and as the system of representation was not known, the consequence was, they either degenerated convulsively into monarchies, or became absorbed into such as then existed. Had the system of representation been then understood as it now is, there is no reason to believe that those forms of government, now called monarchical or aristocratical, would ever have taken place' (Paine [1791–2] 1985: 176–7).

10. The most clear example of spectrality in Blake concerns the very image of Enlightenment reason. Frequently Blake describes the liberating destruction of the images or personifications of reason, only to have this moment of imagination subsequently reified into yet another image or 'spectre'. The 'rational' opposition to religion itself becomes one more religion or 'Newtonian Phantasm' (Blake 1966: 532).

11. Compare a similar account given by Mary Wollstonecraft: 'In the infancy of society, when men were just emerging out of barbarism, chiefs and priests, touching the most powerful springs of savage conduct, hope and fear, must have had unbounded sway. An aristocracy of course, is naturally the first form of government. But, clashing interests soon losing their equipoise, a monarchy and hierarchy break out of the confusion of ambitious struggles, and the foundation of both is secured by feudal tenures. This appears to be the origin of monarchical and priestly powers and the dawn of civilization' (Wollstonecraft [1792] 1985: 98).

1

KANT AND ENLIGHTENMENT
RECOGNITION

———◦——

[M]etaphysics actually exists, if not as a science, yet still as a natural disposition (metaphysica naturalis). For human reason, without being moved merely by the idle desire for extent and variety of knowledge, proceeds impetuously, driven on by an inward need, to questions such as cannot be answered by any empirical employment of reason, or by principles thence derived. Thus in all men, as soon as their reason has become ripe for speculation, there has always existed and will always continue to exist some kind of metaphysics. (Kant [1787] 1933: 59)

THE COPERNICAN TURN

Modern philosophy, it might be argued, is inaugurated with the question of point of view: the problem of the appropriate position, point or site of the philosophical question. This is what distinguishes the 'subject' from earlier theories of 'man'. Man was a being *within* the world with a certain nature and certain attributes. But the subject is that being for whom the world is represented. The world is, then, not just a collection of things, or all that is; the world is what is represented. And if the world is seen as what is represented to a subject, then it makes sense to question the relation between the representing subject and what is represented. This 'epistemological' turn in philosophy is frequently seen as a shift in perspective or way of seeing. Man no longer subordinates himself to some larger totality, hierarchy or order. Rather the question of order must be generated from man himself.

However, in many ways this idea of a 'shift in perspective' begs the question. The idea of modernity as a subject-centred way of seeing presupposes the highly subjectivist notion of a 'way of seeing'. We have to assume that the world is determined according to certain viewpoints in order to mark modernity off as that point in history where the idea of viewpoint emerges. And, in fact, theories of modernity do tend to work in this question-begging way. The clearest example comes from Hegel. According to Hegel, ancient Greece was thoroughly at home with itself. The ancient Greek world was experienced in the immediacy of its presence; it was not considered as a represented world for a knowing subject (Hegel [1825] 1995: 151). Rather, the world was given without any sense of the modes of givenness or knowledge interrupting the relation to the world. We might say, then, that the Greek world was not yet a 'world'. It was not a separate totality of representations but the lived plenitude, proximity and immediacy of being. This might be referred to as the pre-epistemological myth of Greece: the idea of an experience that was characterised by a wondrous reception of presence, without the intrusive epistemological question of how that world was represented.

Lest this myth of ancient Greek unity – in which the world was experienced without reflection upon the separation of the experiencing subject who 'has' a world – be dismissed as excessive Hegelian origin-positing, we need only think of the contemporary theories of anti-modern anti-representationalism. Both Jean-Pierre Vernant and Pierre Hadot, in different ways, argue that Greek philosophy was lived as a way of life (Hadot 1995), or as the dazzling openness to presence, prior to an objectification of the body (Vernant 1991: 28). According to Vernant, not only did the Greeks live a world that was not yet ruptured by a division between the divine and the corporeal (47), the Greeks were also unburdened by any sense of interiority or subjectivity. Indeed, the unity between the Greek individual and being is, Vernant insists, *existential* – where experience is at one with its world and not yet incarcerated within the Cartesian *cogito*: 'Existence is prior to the consciousness of existing. As has been often noted, the *cogito ergo sum*, I think therefore I am, has no meaning for a Greek' (328).[1] Marcel Detienne, like Foucault, also argues that the Greeks did not live truth as a set of ordered rules and representations; rather truth was nothing other than the force or effect of lived speech (Detienne 1996: 17; 37).[2] The idea that the world appears as a separate representation is, Richard

Rorty argues, a legacy of Cartesian dualism and modern subjectivism (Rorty 1980). Only with the peculiarly modern way of seeing do we need to posit a subject who then represents an outside world. Rorty's argument about the pernicious effects of modern representationalism, like so many others, is, however, caught within the malaise he is attempting to diagnose. In order to reject the idea of the world as mentally represented Rorty attributes this representationalist 'way of seeing' to a peculiarly modern perspective. But Rorty's quite common procedure itself draws upon the modern idea of a way of seeing: an idea that, by his own account, would not have been possible for the ancient way of seeing. The ancient 'way of seeing' had no notion of a 'way of seeing'. Pre-modernity is thought of, or represented, as a world prior to representation or perspective: as a world so at home with itself that it has no sense of world, no sense of the specificity, limit or locatedness of its location. Modernity, by contrast, is marked by separation and the problem of location. Modernity is not at one with its world, does not just dwell within its own ground, but demands a legitimation, grounding or systematisation of its own ground. The question raised by the widespread criticism of the modern way of seeing as representationalist is whether a pre- or non-representational position is possible. Could we, by an act of philosophical Luddism, return to a point where our world was lived and we were no longer burdened by some sense of justification in relation to a real? Or, could we overcome our Cartesian location and separation by moving forward to a point where the world and representing subject dissolve in a post-human realm of difference in general?

KANT AND TRANSCENDENTAL SUBJECTIVITY

According to Kant, any reflection on experience necessarily leads to the burden of metaphysical separation. The idea of the subject or point of view is not a purely philosophical idea, and certainly not one limited to modernity, but is a necessary presupposition for any experience. To have an experience at all demands some a priori sense of point of view and one's own subjectivity. Thus in Kant there is a metaphysical imperative at the heart of even the most 'naive' experiences. Knowledge of the world is only possible with the presupposition of the difference between a subject and an object.

As Kant made clear, the system of formal logic from Aristotle to his own enlightenment present, had remained as a rigorous, necessary and universal order of judgements. Only this aspect of philosophy – logic – possessed the same rigour as the sciences (Kant [1787] 1933: 17). Metaphysics, on the other hand, had wallowed in speculation, refutation and conjecture, and had made no progress. Progress could only be made, Kant insisted, if the ideal of logic could be transposed into questions of the world, and not just questions of judgement. In order to achieve this aim Kant has to undertake the modern representationalist turn. Logic can apply to the world – indeed, the world can itself appear as a logical system – if the world is a representation for a subject. That is, it makes no sense to ask questions about the world prior to the ordering judgements of experience, for the very idea of a *world* as an experienced and ordered spatio-temporal object, presupposes a *transcendental logic*: categories that apply not just to what we say about the world but also to how the world is experienced. Experience is inherently representational; it is a forming, synthesising and unifying activity. Thus, with Kant, the status of logic and system is relocated: no longer a feature of statements or judgements, logic defines the very form of experience. Logic is the way in which the world is given. Logic is the ordering and unifying power of the subject and not an order that can be intuited in the outside world.

The turn to perspective or the transcendental point of view involves stepping back from the experience of things as real, and asking how such a real is possible. According to Kant, I do not just 'live' my world; I have a world in so far as I represent a world to myself. I have a world through certain conditions of representation – time, space, concepts, the categories and so on. This *epistemological* foundationalism is not the straightforward appeal to some external ground. Indeed, external grounding, according to Kant, is the error of all previous metaphysics that have simply taken flight from the empirical world into some putatively timeless and absolute ground where all truths are given (Kant [1787] 1933: 561). If the ground of knowledge were to be known it would have to partake in all those features of any intuited, received, represented and therefore grounded object. Any grounding of knowledge takes place *from knowledge itself* and is, Kant insists, a self-grounding. The ground of philosophy is not some supersensible realm to which we can enthusiastically or fanatically take flight. Rather, the supersensible that we necessarily assume (but cannot know) must be seen as a consequence of reason's own activity of ground-laying.

A proper philosophical system does not, therefore, assume or assert a foundation. System-building begins with the recognition that our world does not offer itself as grounded but demands an act of grounding. This is the task of reason. Given the experienced order of the world, reason extends its ordering power to the ultimate question of a grounding condition. For Kant, then, experience *per se* is not at home with itself; it possesses certain natural illusions which take it beyond what is given empirically to the idea of some non-empirical ground. It is because the world is a represented world, given to us in a certain way and according to transcendental logic, that our experience of the world is always more than the world itself. In knowing the world as a representation we are separated from the world. We order the world *through* concepts but can never intuit those concepts themselves in the world. (Causality, for example, is not something we know or experience; it is the form of knowledge.) Far from this separation of our concepts from the world being the cause of sceptical despair, it produces the possibility of legitimating or grounding knowledge. Once we recognise the proper home of rational concepts, in the human subject, then we need no longer take flight from the given world and leap into some irrational absolute. We no longer look for God, freedom or immortality as given objects of knowledge, for such ideas are effects of reason's own power to extend itself beyond the given. Consequently, the ultimate ground or foundation is not outside us; the ground is nothing other than reason's own striving for foundations. This is why Kant insists on the distinction between those concepts of the understanding which we apply to our experienced world, and those ideas of reason, through which reason strives to think what lies beyond experience. Recognising this distinction brings the foundation of metaphysics back into reason's own domain:

> Since all illusion consists in holding the subjective ground of our judgments to be objective, a self-knowledge of pure reason in its transcendent (presumptuous) use is the sole preservative from the aberrations into which reason falls when it mistakes its calling and transcendently refers to the object that which concerns only its own subject and its guidance in all immanent use.
>
> The distinction of Ideas – that is, of pure concepts of reason – from categories, or pure concepts of the understanding, as cognitions of a quite distinct species, origin and use, is so important in

founding a science which is to contain the system of all these *a priori* cognitions that, without this distinction, metaphysics is absolutely impossible or is at best a random, bungling attempt to build a castle in the air without a knowledge of the materials or of their fitness for this or any purpose. (Kant [1783] 1950: 76–7)

Through this relocation of grounding concepts in the subject, representation becomes both the bridge and the gulf of Kant's transcendental idealism. Recognising that the world is a represented world separates man from the given and compels him to seek the supersensible in terms of reason's own striving. Kant insists then on the 'gulf' that separates the concepts of the reason from what can be given, and this stems from the fact that in order to experience a world I must already receive that world in terms of reason's own logical order. But representation is also the bridge between subject and world. As Kant insists, the very idea of mind (and a separate world) already presupposes certain representational forms; we can only think of a mind relating to a world if we deploy notions of time, space and relation. These notions are transcendentally ideal; they must be in place before we even ask about the relation between mind, world and mental representations. The very question of scepticism – is the world I know a real world? – has to use the concept of world, of mind and the notion of the real. We only have a world – even in this minimal sceptical sense – in so far as we have certain representational conditions (notions of time, space, identity, substance.) Kant's grounding of thought, therefore, takes place through a recognition of thought's own conditions; the ground of thought is not 'in' the world. The world is only possible because there is already the ground of a unifying or representing subject. This turn to the subject is, according to Kant, not just one more philosophical assertion of some ultimate ground; for it changes the very concept and possibility of grounding. The ground of thought is no longer an object for knowledge, but is given only in the reflection upon knowledge's own procedures.

Consequently, Kant's description of his own philosophy as a 'Copernican turn' presents itself not as another theory of what is, nor as another (more accurate) description of the world. It is a shift in the very modality of metaphysics. The failure of metaphysics, according to Kant, has been that it has not asked this question: the question of the position or ground of the philosophical question. There have been no shortage of answers and ultimate grounds offered to explain the world, but we have not asked how it is possible that reason is not at home in its world, nor how it is that reason *can* be metaphysical and *can* think a supersensible ground. Rather than undertake another departure from the given, Kant's philosophy begins by asking how it is that reason goes beyond itself into unanswerable questions. The sciences have progressed steadily but reason has continually offered one groundless metaphysical theory after another. How is it that philosophy's questions have met with no answers and why does reason undertake the sort of questions that lead it so astray? The answer lies in reason's inherent capacity for misrecognition: those things that are in fact an outcome of reason's own striving – the idea of ground, absolute, supersensible and so on – are mistakenly taken to be things that reason might intuit. Kant's Copernican turn begins with the recognition that the world is *reason*'s own world. Any account of the world must be in terms of reason's way of seeing.

Kant will therefore begin with the same idea that motivates later nostalgic accounts of the nature of modernity, although he does so in opposition to the pre-modern. Kant also depicts pre-modern philosophy as a way of seeing that had no sense of itself *as a way of seeing*. Plato begins philosophy as a form of fanaticism. Kant continually refers to Platonism as an irresponsible or groundless 'leap' or 'flight' into a higher real; for the assumption of Plato's philosophy is that reason can know a non-empirical realm: 'It was this enthusiasm that lifted Plato above empirical concepts to ideas that he thought could be explained only by an intellectual community [between ourselves and] the origin of all beings' (Kant [1790] 1987: 240). And this enthusiasm is a consequence of reason's natural illusions: reason represents the world in terms of its own a priori concepts. Once it perceives the world in this way, it makes the mistake of assuming that a priori grounds lie in the world itself, outside reason. It locates reason's own concepts for representing the real world *in* a world beyond reason. Philosophy has imagined that it might intuit the absolute, know a first cause, or cognise freedom, but these supersensible notions are the effect of reason's own extension beyond the sensible. Only the sensible can be known or given; the supersensible is not given but only thought (Kant [1787] 1933: 28). Kant's idea that enlightenment is an overcoming of the naive belief in the immediate community with the supersensible is merely an approving description of what later theorists will define as modernity's malaise. In both cases the Ancient Greek origin of philosophy is deemed to be an unselfconscious, pre-subjective, pre-representational and immediate harmony with the truth of the world. Whereas Kant regards the modern separation of the subject as a liberating autonomy, those after him will judge it as a divide, alienation or gulf to be bridged.

Kant's critique of pre-modern forms of metaphysics proceeds by demonstrating that experience or knowledge is *given*. If this is the case, if we are finite beings to whom the world is given, then any account of experience will also need to establish the character and specificity of the site of knowledge. Previous philosophy has sought a theory of what 'is' and offered definitions of being as though being itself were immediate and self-present, forgetting that what is experienced is given. For Kant, however, philosophy should be aware of itself as a point of view: aware that if the world is given it is never *in itself* but always given *to*. Experience is not the thing itself; it is, rather, an encounter with what is other than ourselves. The problem of the mode of givenness, the form of experience and the conditions of objectivity establish critical philosophy as a self-conscious position. Kant's critique of reason is a reflection on the site of experience itself, a turn towards the point of view from which the world is experienced. For it is only with the *location* of the philosophical question, only with a recognition that metaphysics or a theory of existence always *takes place for a subject* who experiences, that knowledge might find a ground.

Thus Kantian critique turns quite explicitly against the Platonic opening of philosophy. Plato, according to Kant, in attempting to account for the given or experience, departs from the field of experience but fails to establish or build another site. Rather than turn to the point to which experience is given, Platonic philosophy leaps into a non-place beyond all possible experience. Like so many metaphysical theories of totality that will follow, experience and the given are abandoned by Plato and some absolute condition is established *as real*: as simply there, in itself and independent of the subject of knowledge. Against this perpetual temptation to what he describes as transcendental realism (Kant [1787] 1933: 347), Kant establishes critical philosophy as a *location* of the transcendental. Kant's transcendental idealism is a recognition that the conditions of the given, the foundations of experience, are nothing other than our own point of view. The transcendental manoeuvre that will account for existence is not a shift of location – a move into the domain of the supersensible – but a description of the territory we already inhabit. To have an experience of the empirical – what is given as real – demands certain transcendental conditions: ways in which this real is represented *as real*. The transcendental, or what exceeds the empirical, is therefore not another realm or territory, but simply a critical *recognition* of the forms and conditions that the empirical presupposes.

Essential to Kant's distinction between the transcendental and the empirical is the very notion of the world; in so far as we have or experience a world we are already other than that world. The world, *as a world*, is not ourselves and must therefore be viewed, received or encountered by a subject. The question of point of view, as the necessary representation or essential non-immediacy of the world, opens the question of the self-grounding of philosophy. If the world is not given in itself but is represented through a certain logic then philosophy must ask the location or ground of this logic. From Kant, through German idealism to structuralism and post-structuralism, it is the *site* of this grounding logic that occupies thought. On the one hand, there is no shortage of modern representationalisms that accept that the world is only viewed as a representation, and that the logic of this representational system is just the final ground of knowledge. Ideas of structure, discourse, semiotics, culture, and so on present the world as an effect of a representational system. On the other hand, this representational system can be questioned according to its logic. How is it that structure is generated? Where is this logic located? Jacques Derrida will therefore ask the question of the 'structurality of structure' and define philosophy as a logocentrism (as an attempt to comprehend experience within a logic without asking how that logic is written or traced) (Derrida 1978: 278). Michel Foucault and Gilles Deleuze will also, in different ways, attempt to think the condition of existence as a logic that exceeds the subject. In contemporary post-structuralism (and its opponents) we see the continuation of the Kantian question: if it is possible to have a system of logic that expresses the universally true, what is the site and possibility of this logic? Such a system cannot, Kant insists, be explained *within* the world. As universally true, logic must be the very ground of the world. And for Kant this ground is nothing other than the point of view of the finite subject.

Accordingly, Kant's transcendental logic is nothing other than an inquiry into the site, architectonic and system of the source, birthplace or origin of logical concepts (Kant [1787] 1933: 103). It is only through the pure concepts of reason that anything like an external world is possible. This is the thrust of Kant's refutation of idealism. In order to argue that the world is only subjective appearances, the idealist has to already adopt the notion of a subject; and this already demands the thought of an inner, mental region. But if that is the case and we have already presupposed the subject as a persisting identity then we are already assuming time (persistence), space (the subject's mind) *and objectivity*: to speak of appearances 'inside me' presupposes the 'outside' of the world. Thus, idealism has not explained the possibility of the world or objectivity, for it has merely taken one object – mind – as the explanation of all other objects (Kant [1787] 1933: 244). Thus a subject or mind cannot be presupposed as it was by Descartes; we have to ask how the very idea of subject is possible. The subject is only possible through a transcendental logic: categories that enable the order and coherence of an external and persisting world. Only with a transcendental or ordering logic are ideas of subjectivity and objectivity possible; the subject is revealed reflectively as a presupposition of experience and not as one more experienced thing.

In this idea of a transcendental logic the meaning of *logos* changes. Logic is not just a system of language or representations (formal logic); any such system depends upon a *transcendental* logic: an ordering that enables the world in general. Logic is not a representational system applied or imposed upon the world. Any experience of the world is *already systemic* and, when considered from the transcendental viewpoint, demands the recognition of the subject's ideal and logical contribution. If the world is perceived *as a world*, this means that it is not given immediately but is logically ordered. The very idea of a world presupposes the subject as a world-representing power and the world as a possible representation. To establish philosophy as transcendental logic is a *separation* of the representing subject: for the aim of knowledge is now not the unintuitable world-in-itself. We can only legitimately know what our point of view or position will allow. We cannot *know* an absolute or unconditioned origin beyond the categories that form experience. Nevertheless, transcendental logic is an extension as well as a separation of the subject: the world is always given to us and given *as* a world. There is, therefore, a site of intelligibility – the ground of representation – that is not exhausted by the given. This is the site of transcendental logic and is philosophy's proper and legitimate home. Kant's critical philosophy departs from the naivety of transcendental realism: the idea that we know the world immediately. Experience, as *experience*, cannot be immediate but must be given. But his critical philosophy also departs from empirical idealism: the idea that structures of the given are 'inside our heads' as ideas or mental events. There would be no possibility of the empirical object of mind if there were not already transcendental categories that enabled entities like 'mind' to be thought. The system that renders experience possible is not 'inside' consciousness or mind; any such entity (like mind or consciousness) is already given through the transcendental categories or system. This constitutes Kant's anti-Cartesianism. We cannot posit a substance like *res cogitans* as the ground of the world (Kant [1787] 1933: 332). Any such substance itself has to be known. Only a transcendental power that can think notions like 'substance' can explain Descartes's subject. Like Husserl after him, Kant will criticise Descartes for an empirical idealism (Kant [1783] 1950: 85); the subject is still perceived by Descartes as a 'tag end of the world' and not the origin of the world as such (Husserl [1931] 1960: 24).

The empirically real – the world as experienced by a being called 'man' – has as its transcendental possibility the system of the categories. Considered transcendentally, we are nothing other than this system. Transcendental logic is, therefore, a responsibility for our own point of view, a turning back to our contribution, and a demystification of the illusion that there is an immediate correspondence between ourselves and our world. For if it is our *world* (and hence other than us and therefore encountered), it is also *our* world (we contribute to this encounter). Critical philosophy is a responsibility for *where we are*, and transcendental logic is a reflection on this site. This ground or point of origin of philosophy is neither given nor self-evident. Rather, philosophy's proper site can only be achieved through an autonomous and reflective act of system building (Kant [1787] 1933: 573).

This system must, on the one hand, recognise the necessary position of knowledge. It must be a system, not of some absolute, but of located and finite knowledge. On the other hand, this location must not be conflated with an object within the world, such as man. This is what unites Kant's transcendental logic and the enlightenment ethic of autonomy. If the world is given, then the conditions of its givenness can be described as a logic. The *transcendental* nature of this logic means that philosophy can ask questions that exceed the immediate givenness of the world – questions that concern the subject to whom the world is given. The subject is not fully determined by the world but, as a logical power, contributes to the determination of the world.

As such, then, the subject can be discerned as an autonomous power. And once the subject is defined non-substantively, as an autonomous power, morality is opened as a possibility. Only an autonomous power – and not a causally determined being – can be the proper beginning of an inquiry into morals. A moral action cannot be explained according to what man is as an object; this would be the error of anthropologism. To be moral an act must be undertaken freely and thus not determined by any given cause. The determining power of the subject, as a conditioning and representing capacity, enables us to think of an action as moral: as undertaken from a point of view that is not within the world, but that grounds the world. The possibility of morality, for Kant, is at one with the possibility of thinking the unconditioned spontaneity of the representing subject: an unconditioned ground that can be thought but not known. To claim to *know* such a ground would locate the ground within the world, as a thing that could be intuited; but if this were so it would not be a true ground. Concomitantly, to not recognise the world as *grounded* – as given through a representational condition or logic – would preclude the separate site of moral freedom. It is between these two possibilities that Kant charts the passage of morality, system, representation and ground. Between the error of locating man as nothing more than an animal within the world and the error of positing a second world or supersensible realm that can be known or intuited, Kant locates the subject as the limit of the representable that can also think, if not intuit, the unrepresentable.

ANTHROPOLOGISM

Kant describes his 'Copernican turn' in the first *Critique* in a number of ways and presents the achievements of his critical method in opposition to a host of metaphysical misdemeanours. One of the targets of Kant's critical process is *anthropologism*, an error that needs to be distinguished from the legitimate, though limited, task of practical anthropology. Whereas a practical anthropology has its place alongside a metaphysics of morals, anthropologism is one of reason's natural, inevitable but infelicitous illusions. As Kant argues in the *Groundwork*, practical anthropology is the 'empirical part' of ethics. Anthropology can borrow from knowledge of man and can consider what ought to happen with regard to man's nature (Kant [1785] 1959: 4–5). But this practical anthropology must be preceded by a metaphysics of morals which considers *law in general*. Only a 'pure moral philosophy which is completely freed from everything which may be only empirical' can possess absolute necessity – a necessity that essentially lies beyond any anthropological determination (Kant [1785] 1959: 5).

The error of anthropologism, therefore, lies in the confusion of the very nature of law which, *as law*, cannot depend on the contingency of any particular empirical nature. Law cannot be *given*: it cannot be *encountered* by experience, for it would then be contingent (Kant [1788] 1993a: 19). Law must transcend the given (what is known through experience). As law, moral rules must possess a necessity that exceeds the contingency of empirical determination. Law could not then be derived from or determined by any fact of anthropology. Knowledge of man according to his nature has its proper, yet subordinate, place within ethics, but ought not be confused with 'morals proper' (Kant [1785] 1959: 4). A theory of man, as an object within the world, cannot justify a moral *law*. Any such anthropological determination is an *effect* of judgement and not its ground. What precedes the determination of man as an anthropological being is the purely formal structure of law itself. Critical procedure steps back from the prescription of any anthropological norm and asks the question of how such normativity is possible. What is man such that he *can* give a law to himself?

Kant's anti-anthropologism locates law in the structures of reason, rather than in an external world. Anthropology is thereby given its proper place: man as a being within the world is always determined according to reason's own law-giving power. No notion of man can prescribe or explain that power. Anthropology, then, is not an error of reason *per se*. Anthropology is a legitimate activity of a pre-anthropo-logical *autonomy*. The error of anthropolo*gism* lies in extending the knowledge of man as an empirical being to an explanatory ground. A theory of man that seeks to explain experience forgets that any described 'man' is itself an experienced thing and must be regarded as empirically conditioned. 'Man' cannot act as a legislating ground precisely because man as an experienced anthropological being is already grounded. As empirically real, or encountered through experience, man cannot provide a law. Only the turn to a transcendental point of view – asking *how* man appears *as man* – can ground a moral law. Anthropology cannot legislate; for any anthropology depends upon a prior judging power. The character of such a power can only be revealed in the Copernican turn to the transcendental point of view:

> So far, then, as regards this empirical character there is no freedom; and yet it is only in the light of this character that man can be studied – if, that is to say, we are simply observing, and in the manner of anthropology seeking to institute a psychological investigation into the motive causes of his actions.
>
> But when we consider these actions in their relation to reason – I do not mean speculative reason, by which we endeavour *to explain* their coming into being, but reason in so far as it is itself the cause *producing* them – if, that is to say, we compare them with [the standards of] reason in its *practical* bearing, we find a rule and order altogether different from the order of nature. (Kant [1787] 1933: 474)

Anthropologism, therefore, commits the error of locating law within the world, within man as an empirical being. Law is thereby seen as an object of empirical knowledge and not as the purely formal structure of any possible knowledge. Appropriately considered, law is not given in a particular experience but can be known only as that which makes experience possible. But Kant is also insistent that anthropologism's misrecognition of reason is no accident; it stems from reason's very nature: '[R]eason restlessly seeks the unconditionally necessary and sees itself compelled to assume it, though it has no means by which to make it comprehensible and is happy enough if it can only discover the concept which is consistent with this presupposition' (Kant [1785] 1959: 83).

Reason is not a thing to be known but a power to represent the world in terms of ordered and conditioned events. Reason, as an ordering power, thinks all experiences as conditioned. Indeed, it is this very representation of conditions that renders our empirical experience of a causal world possible. But it is also this possibility of thinking the Idea of a condition that leads reason to strive for an ultimate condition, an unconditioned cause. Reason can therefore lead itself into illusion by seeking to represent, intuit or know the unconditioned (Kant [1787] 1933: 25). In its correct usage this striving for the unconditioned allows reason to conceive the moral law: if it is possible to think a cause not given in the empirical series of causes then reason can, through this representational capacity, give itself a law. But in order to think the unconditioned as a moral law, reason has to recognise that the Idea of an unconditioned is its own. If it looks for the unconditioned outside itself – in an absolute, supersensible or God – or if it locates the law within man as an empirical being, then rather than reason being a law-giving power, the law will be offered as a thing or object. To be *known* as a thing, however, would locate the law within time and space (and within causality). A *moral* law, beyond determination, can be neither in the world, nor 'in' man. As pure freedom and the capacity to give a law to itself, morality must stem from the transcendental power of thinking in terms of conditions and not itself be conditioned. Law here is defined precisely through its distinction from empirical givenness. Because law is not *given to* reason, but is derived from the structure of any possible reason, law bears its proper universality. The error of anthropologism misses the lawfulness of law; if law were derived from a given feature of man or the world, it would not be properly lawful. To be a law it must be conditioning rather than conditioned. It must be that which enables any possible representation, rather than one representation among others:

> Only the concept of freedom enables us to find the unconditioned for the conditioned and the intelligible for the sensible without going outside ourselves. For it is our reason itself which through the supreme and unconditioned practical law recognizes itself, and the being which knows this law (our own person) as belonging to the pure world of the understanding and indeed defines the way in which it can be active as such a being. Thus it can be seen why in the entire faculty of reason only the practical can lift us above the world of sense and furnish cognitions of a supersensible order and connection, though these cognitions can be extended only as far as needed for pure practical purposes. (Kant [1788] 1993a: 111)

The moral law that follows from reason's own Idea of an unconditioned cause is therefore grounded on the recognition of the subject as
a representational capacity. The idea of man as a being within the
world is appropriate for anthropology. But morality must view man
from a different point of view – not as an object of knowledge but as a
subject who can judge. If the world is given as a coherent temporal and
spatial order, with causal connections and laws of appearance, this is
precisely because of the representational condition of the subject as a
finite being with a point of view. Law is not given from this or that
point of view, and certainly not from an absolute position beyond point
of view or perspective altogether. The transcendental turn is not a step
outside man, to an absolute viewpoint, but is a consideration of the
very possibility of viewpoint. For if we consider the subject as a point
of view (and not a viewed thing) then we recognise the subject's
capacity to order, judge and represent. This then means that the site of
law is not a domain beyond the given, but the subjective point that
allows the given to be synthesised or represented as given. We move
beyond the given – man as anthropological entity – not by claiming
to *know* some non-empirical soul, but by realising that man as an
empirical being is the effect of a representing point of view (Kant
[1787] 1933: 88). The possibility of representing *man* depends upon
representation in general. Representation is not a human capacity –
this is the error of anthropologism. Representation is the condition for
thinking of any being, including the human. The moral law depends,
then, on a step back from any anthropology of man to thinking how
man is given. It is in the failure to think of the representational condition of any theory of man, that law is displaced from its universal and
transcendental position and becomes a feature of man.

    Anthropologism might be aligned, then, with the error of empirical
idealism. Empirical idealism recognises the 'subjective' quality of lawfulness – order, time, morality and so on are seen, rightfully, as ideal.
But the error comes when ideality is located *within* an empirical entity:
mind, mental space or the human. Kant's transcendental idealism sets
itself against this (Cartesian) anthropologistic error: the ideal is not
within the human – it is not a mental event. The ideal is the possibility
of the human. Only through the ideal conditions of time and space is
anything like the human given.

ANTHROPOMORPHISM

If anthropologism extends the position of man to an explanatory ground, anthropomorphism commits the contrasting error of forgetting man's *position* altogether. Alongside anthropologism one of the most important errors targeted by Kant's critical project is the striving to know a world in itself, for it is this paradoxical and impossible striving of transcendental realism that can only lead to sceptical despair. If knowledge is defined not as the representation of the world through reason's categories, but as some grasp of pure presence independent of reason, then what is sought is some absolute real: a transcendental real undetermined and unconditioned by the categories of reason. But we need only reflect on the very meaning of *knowledge*, as the reception or givenness of what is 'outside me', to recognise that knowledge as such entails receptivity (Kant [1787] 1933: 68). And if this is so then knowledge entails that experience be given *to* some finite being. Anthropomorphism, however, forgets this necessary *relation* of givenness. In anthropomorphism, reason's own concepts that enable experience – concepts of totality, causality, magnitude, conditions and order – are sought in a world in itself. Anthropomorphism theorises an absolute or supersensible realm – as though true knowledge were beyond experience (Kant [1787] 1933: 563). But when we reflect upon the descriptions of this absolute – say, as an unconditioned cause, as an infinite extension of space, or as an eternal extension of time – we recognise reason's own forming power (such as the synthesising representations of time and space). The absolute, properly considered, is not a world beyond reason but is the effect of reason extending its own representations beyond experience. The idea of the universe as infinitely extended in space takes the concept of a spatial magnitude – a concept that orders experience for a finite subject – and then extends this concept to what exceeds all possible experience and finitude. To argue that this absolute exceeds knowledge commits the anthropomorphic error of not recognising that such an absolute is only an effect of the extension of concepts of experience. With reflection, however, the subject realises that the supersensible realm that appears as reason's absolute other is an effect of reason's own striving.

While anthropologism locates law within man, and sees reason or logic as a collection of empirical features, anthropomorphism fails to consider the position of man altogether. Rather than acknowledge that the world *as given* must be subject to, and conditioned by, its mode of givenness, anthropomorphism projects reason's own strivings and achievements onto the world itself. Anthropomorphism is therefore at one with transcendental realism: those pure concepts of the understanding that enable finite human reason to experience an object world are seen as outside us, as transcendentally real (Kant [1787] 1933: 584). Anthropomorphism, therefore, looks for laws *in* nature, looks for a first cause to the world, tries to determine the limit of the world in space or its beginning in time, strives to answer questions of temporality, spatiality, law, totality, freedom and causality: and does all this by trying to find such *objects* outside experience (as transcendentally real). In so doing, reason forgets that the objects of its striving – law, causality, totality and so on – are reason's own formations and cannot be found as present, outside us, beyond experience. Such concepts *are concepts* and as such cannot be transcendentally real. They are empirically real – given as experienced – but transcendentally ideal: ways in which the world is given, and not independent of the finite experience of a given world.

Kant's transcendental idealism is, therefore, also an anti-anthropomorphism. It reminds us that the world is *given*. If the world is not *immediately* at one with or absolutely correspondent to our reason – if the world has to be experienced – then it requires us to recognise thought's place in experience. This is nothing other than an imperative to think the representational conditions of experience. To *not* consider such conditions leads reason into the inevitable errors of locating those conditions in some putative absolute (transcendental realism) or some human entity (empirical idealism).

PHILOSOPHY AND POINT OF VIEW

In dealing with those *concepts* and *principles* which we adopt a priori, all that we can do is to contrive that they be used for viewing objects from two different points of view – on the one hand, in connection with experience, as objects of the senses and of the understanding, and on the other hand, for the isolated reason that strives to transcend all limits of experience, as objects which are thought merely. If, when things are viewed from this twofold standpoint, we find that there is agreement with the principle of pure reason, but that when we regard them only from a single point of view reason is involved in unavoidable self-conflict, the experiment decides in favour of the correctness of this distinction. (Kant [1787] 1933: 23)

The task of Kant's transcendental logic is, therefore, one of recognition, autonomy and responsibility: we cannot find any present or external object in the world that will correspond to reason's own pure concepts. Reason's pure concepts, such as the Idea of a condition, are what makes the representation of a world possible. To locate such concepts *in* the world is an infelicity of anthropomorphism – seeing the world not *as given* but as directly correspondent to thought (Kant [1787] 1933: 434). To think of the world as *in itself* lawful and ordered forgets reason's contribution, as the power which represents the world *as a world*. This is the classic and frequently identified error of anthropomorphism: projecting the features of one's point of view onto the world, and forgetting point of view as such.

According to Kant, such projection is the irresponsibility of an ungrounded or homeless philosophy. If we want to strive beyond the empirical, Kant argues, we must know where we are. We cannot simply leap from the empirical and dogmatically assert a realm of ideas, pure law or absolute totality: we have to build the intelligible on a secure foundation (Kant [1787] 1933: 573). For Kant, the only proper place for such a foundation begins with a recognition of the empirically real – the experience of the world as outside us – and then turns to the point of view of the transcendentally ideal – how this experience of an outside, or object, is possible:

High towers and metaphysically great men resembling them, round both of which there is commonly much wind, are not for me. My place is the fruitful bathos of experience; and the word 'transcendental,' . . . does not signify something passing beyond all experience but something that indeed precedes it *a priori*, but that is intended simply to make knowledge of experience possible. (Kant [1783] 1950: 122–3)

Kant's transcendental perspective is not, therefore, another domain or position separated from the empirical: it is the empirical considered transcendentally. Critical philosophy begins with the question of how a world is given *as empirically real*, and from there discovers transcendental conditions (Kant [1787] 1933: 325). The error of anthropologism lies in failing to consider the transcendental point of view – the conditions for the empirical. For anthropologism merely uses one more empirical thing – man, mind or *res cogitans* – to explain things in general. Anthropologism remains *within* a worldly point of view and does not ask how a world, in general, is possible. The error of anthropomorphism, on the other hand, is to have no awareness of point of view at all; it is a failure to acknowledge that experience, *as experience*, is given. Any explanation of 'what is' will only be responsible if it accounts for the receptivity or knowability of what is. Anthropomorphism, however, leaps or takes flight from the knowable – only to project its own human strivings onto a putative supersensible realm (Kant [1787] 1933: 500; 524). Whereas Kant attacked the anthropologism of modernity that had attempted to reduce all knowledge and morality to man as an empirical being, anthropomorphism was the feature of all those pre-modern philosophies that had not yet turned to the subject as the site of representation. Kant's clearest attack on pre-modern anthropomorphism was directed at Platonic metaphysics, a metaphysics that located truth beyond the finitude of experience:

> The light dove, cleaving the air in her free flight, and feeling its resistance, might imagine that its flight would be still easier in empty space. It was thus that Plato left the world of the senses, as setting too narrow limits to the understanding, and ventured out beyond it on the wings of the ideas, in the empty space of the pure understanding. He did not observe that with all his efforts he made no advance – meeting no resistance that might, as it were, serve as a support upon which he could take a stand, to which he could apply his powers, and so set his understanding in motion. (Kant [1787] 1933: 47)

Anthropomorphism takes what we contribute to the world as existing in itself. It therefore believes that one could find truth by departing from the locatedness of experience. Kant, adopting the transcendental perspective, insists that concepts of reason such as law, totality and order are *ours* and therefore need to be considered in terms of finitude. This results in the idea of a transcendental logic. Categories are neither in the mind nor in the real; they are the ordering forms that enable the distinction between mind and reality to be thought. Transcendental logic describes a procedure of representation, and not a thing to be known or intuited. The *logos* – the necessary truth of the world – is not 'in' the world as a thing to be discovered, nor 'in' the mind of an inner worldly being. Logic is the relation or mode of givenness of the world in general. It is from this logic that certain beings can be known – such as man, world, the real, or mind. None of these beings can be the ground or home of logic. The transcendental subject is, then, nothing other than a representational or logical power.

It is only in granting logic a transcendental status that the subject is rightfully established as philosophy's proper locale. On the one hand Kant must extend the traditional position of logic. Aristotle had already given the categories as the possible forms of judgement. But this raises the problem of how such pure – or, for Kant, analytic – truth could relate to a given world. Is logic just a way of picturing an external world, a world that in itself remains outside our logical representations? Certainly it was this separation of the world from the ordered representations of reason that motivated Hume's scepticism. Kant, as all the standard readings remind us, recognises the validity of Hume's empiricism: if we look for causality *in* the world we will come to grief. Causality itself is not experienced; it is a certain form given to experience. Rather than saying, as Hume does, that causality is a fiction imposed on experience – and thereby exacerbating the gulf between logic and the world – Kant argues that concepts like causality are the condition for experience (Kant [1787] 1933: 127). It is not that we are given a world in itself that we then order or represent. The very meaning of the world – as an experienced, ordered and coherent object – depends upon the conditions of subjective representation (Kant [1787] 1933: 393). This is what makes logic transcendental. The reason why the logic of judgements, or formal logic, can apply legitimately to the world is because the world, as given, is already logically conditioned. Man's representations are not subjective fictions imposed on the world; both subject and world depend upon the transcendental logic that generates the meaningful experience of a world and the subject.

So, just as transcendental critique attacks the Humean error of stepping from the recognition that causality is not in the world 'in itself' to the idea that that causality is a contingently imposed fiction, so Kant also attacks the scepticism regarding the subject. Again, Kant agrees with Hume's anti-(Cartesian)subjectivism: when I examine experiences all I am aware of is this or that impression; I do not actually experience the subject, and certainly not as an identical or simple substance (or *res cogitans*). But the error of Hume's inquiry lay in looking for the subject *within experience*. The subject is not given as a thing within the world, but must be presupposed (as ideal) in order to think a world; the subject is nothing other than the unity of ordered experiences to whom a world is given (Kant [1787] 1933: 368). Transcendental logic is therefore a recognition of the separation and autonomy of human reason: pure concepts cannot be found in the world but must be located in the transcendental logic that renders the world possible. This transcendental logic is located neither within man (anthropologism) nor in the world (anthropomorphism); transcendental logic is what enables both man and world to be given. The universality of transcendental logic cannot be given through experience, but is the very lawfulness of experience. Law is not given from outside but is reason's own formal structure. In recognising that the lawful status of transcendental logic stems from the necessary separation and finitude of an experiencing being, Kant is able to define a pure autonomy of law. Reason is nothing other than the possibility of law-giving.

At the same time that transcendental logic is formed through a recognition of reason's separation and autonomy, the *transcendental* status of logic also internalises the world. Reason must be aware of its autonomy, and this stems from its nature as finite, but this also means that any world is also *reason*'s world. The idea of some absolute ground or law entirely outside the domain of reason cannot meet with any possible object. Further, the striving for such an unconditioned object must be recognised as an effect of reason's own representational power. The very idea of a world outside us – the idea of the real which we do in fact experience – can only be explained from the position of reason considered transcendentally. The idea of a world 'outside me' already uses reason's own temporal and spatial representations. The possibility of the empirical – an experienced world – depends upon transcendental ideality: those ordering categories that allow the subject to represent a world.

ENLIGHTENMENT REASON AND ANTI-ANTHROPOLOGISM

The idea that logic is not a representation imposed on the world but is a condition of the world, depends upon a radically reoriented sense of 'world' (Nancy 1997). And it is this radical reorientation of sense that ties Kant's transcendental idealism to the representational demands of modernity. The demand of enlightenment in its revolutionary and political manifestations began as an internalisation of law: authority ought not be seen as imposed from without but should be generated from human reason itself. Reason demands that it represent itself. This takes the form both of representative democracy as well as a rethinking of what the self that demands representation is. My individual being is fulfilled, not by accepting some already given position in a social whole, but by being allowed to represent myself. It is this capacity for self-representation, or autonomy, that establishes the enlightenment as a continual task of internalisation. If the authority of reason is used to overthrow the external authority of divine law, monarchy or traditional right, then reason itself must not become yet one more external or enslaving authority. Defining reason as a substance within the world that has certain features from which law can be derived is the error of anthropologism: an error in which the representing power of reason enslaves itself to one of its own representations. The only way of overcoming this self-enslavement of reason is not by offering yet another representation of reason – as possessing this or that attribute – but by seeing reason as the transcendental capacity of representation as such (Kant [1787] 1933: 331). Only in this radical internalisation, where laws are not only reason's laws but where reason is nothing other than a law-giving power, is man freed from anthropologism. The individual whose represented will generates the enlightened political whole, must be a rational individual: an individual not enslaved to any already determined representation of what it is to be human.

We have already seen that for Kant the subject is not defined as a subject within the world. The world, as an ordered and experienced totality, is only possible through the transcendental logic of the subject. Logic, then, is not a set of representations or external and contingent rules invented by man and applied to the world. Logic is the way in which the world is given, as a determined and conceptually ordered objectivity. The Kantian idea of the subject is therefore tied to the notion of transcendental logic. The very possibility of the world demands some ordering power that constitutes the world as given. The subject is not given as an experience but is the condition for the possibility of experience. Further, the given does not exhaust what is, for the very idea of givenness presupposes some ground or condition *to which* the world is given (Kant [1787] 1933: 156). When Kant then explains the necessary freedom of the subject he does so in terms of its non-given-ness. It is because the subject is not an object of knowledge that it makes no sense to see it as causally determined. Causality is the way in which knowable objects are experienced; but this category does not apply to the subject considered transcendentally (that is, the sub-ject considered as that which represents a world rather than what is represented). The subject is not experienced as a thing within the world but only 'knows' itself by recognising the transcendental logic which orders all experience. This is not knowledge strictly speaking for Kant. Only an intuition subsumed by concepts can give us knowledge. But the pure concept of cause itself is what sets reason to the task of seeking a cause for every event. This striving also leads reason to go beyond the givenness of events and think a first cause. It is because I *can* think an unconditioned cause that I can represent myself as a law-giving power. I cannot legitimately attribute causal determination to the subject, for causality applies to experienced objects; it is the way experience is ordered. To argue that the experiencing subject is also causally deter-mined applies an empirical concept to what lies beyond empirical determination. If the subject is a representing power then it cannot itself be determined according to representational conditions. We cannot know the subject as either free or determined, as the subject is not a possible object of experience. It is at least therefore possible to think (but not know) an uncaused power. From this possibility or idea of freedom I am capable of generating a moral law. I can think of my decisions as not determined. If I *can* think in this way, from the tran-scendental viewpoint, then I can no longer exhaust the possibilities of reason through empirical determination. I can no longer attribute my decisions to a causally determined will because there is at least the possibility that I can give a law to myself. And it is this possibility, rather than any determined knowledge of the self, that establishes the moral law. Indeed, according to Kant, this recognition of the transcen-dental nature of the subject (as determining rather than determined) opens the idea of freedom but in no way 'gives to pure theoretical reason . . . the least encouragement to run riot into the transcendent' (Kant [1788] 1993a: 59). For a *transcendental* subject is a world-representing power, while the *transcendent* is what transcends, or is represented by subjects. To recognise the pure concepts as our own provides, Kant argues, an 'accession' to a moral domain. We cannot *know* the supersensible, as though it were part of the world; our speculation about freedom, God and immortality that extends beyond the given can yield no object. But the concept of the supersensible can be used *immanently* – as reason's own – and therefore can open the possibility of morality:

> It was therefore no extension of knowledge of given supersensible objects, but still an extension of theoretical reason and of its knowledge with respect to the supersensible in general, inasmuch as knowledge is compelled to concede that there are such objects without more exactly defining them, and thus without being able to extend this knowledge of objects given to it on only practical grounds and only for practical use. For this accession, pure theoretical reason has thus to thank its pure practical faculty, for all these Ideas are to it transcendent and without objects. Here they become immanent and constitutive, since they are the grounds of the possibility of realizing the necessary object of pure practical reason (the highest good); otherwise they are transcendent and merely regulative principles of speculative reason, which is charged with the task not of assuming a new object beyond experience but only of approaching perfection in its employment within experience. Once in possession of this accession, for the security of its practical employment it will set to work as speculative reason with these Ideas in a negative manner, i.e., not broadening but purifying, in order to ward of anthropomorphism as the source of superstition (apparent extension of those concepts through alleged experience) and fanaticism which promises such an extension through supersensuous intuition or feelings. (Kant [1788] 1993a: 142–3)

Kant's second critique therefore establishes the freedom of the subject through its unknowability. The separation of the subject from the determined world is what establishes human freedom. I *can* represent a pure moral law to myself. I am able to think an uncaused cause. In so doing I render myself responsible, for I have now established a procedure of decision making that acts independent of any given or empirical cause. The very *idea* of a moral law that is undetermined by empirical causes separates the subject from the world. The idea of this separation is the ground of morality. If I imagine myself (transcendentally) as an autonomous and law-giving subject, then I at once represent myself in terms of subjectivity in general. It is then possible to act morally: not as a determined being within the world but as the power of self-determination. Once this separation of the subject is thought as an ideal possibility the domain of moral responsibility and legitimation is inaugurated. Only with this possibility of not being empirically determined can I view actions as justifiable or condemnable, and only this recognition of one's 'personality' can disclose the non-sensuous origin or 'root' of any sensuous human being:

> This root cannot be less than something that elevates man above himself as a part of the world of sense, something which connects him with an order of things which only the understanding can think and which has under it the entire world of sense, including the empirically determinable existence of man in time, and the whole system of all ends which is alone suitable to such unconditional practical laws as the moral. It is nothing else than *personality*, i.e., the freedom and independence from the mechanism of nature regarded as a capacity of a being subject to special laws (pure practical laws given by its own reason), so that the person belonging to the world of sense is subject to his own personality so far as he belongs to the intelligible world. For it is then not to be wondered at that man, as belonging to two worlds, must regard his own being in relation to his second and higher vocation with reverence, and the laws of this vocation with the deepest respect. (Kant [1788] 1993a: 90)

If the world we perceive is always a represented world then it makes no sense to strive to *know* a pre-representational presence. At the same time, there must be a subject who represents this world as a world, and it makes no sense to regard this subject in terms of those representations it enables. We are left with the critical division that isolates a subject who must not regard itself as a representable thing (for this would be the error of anthropologism that precludes freedom). This subject is also set over against a world that must not be regarded as a thing in itself independent of its representation. (This would be an error of anthropomorphism that would preclude synthetic a priori knowledge; for we can only know the world as lawful if these laws are necessary and not contingently experienced.)

What is *thought* such that it can question or think beyond its own ground? For Kant the possibility of such a question placed a duty upon thought. If I can think a law that is not grounded in the world then I must do so. The very thought of such a law generates a feeling of respect. And this is what renders morality radically autonomous: the thought of what exceeds all given grounds liberates thought from any idea of a grounded morality (a morality that is the *effect* of feeling, rules, authority or nature). Any morality figured as an effect – such as a morality derived from aesthetic feeling or moral sense – would have to deny this possibility of reason: the ability to think the supersensible, to think beyond any present or representable ground.

Following Kant this supersensible unity might be thought in two ways (at least). The first is to regard the supersensible as more than an idea, and certainly as more than an idea or substrate *of humanity*. Thus we might follow the path of German idealism. Once we recognise that our world is always a represented world how might we think the unrepresentable? How does the absolute come to represent itself? This response would take seriously the critique of anthropologism: what is (or the world) cannot exhaustively be explained by referring to a thing within the world (man). Beyond representations of what is there must be a pre-representational presence. The challenge would not be, as Kant and the enlightenment did, to separate and recognise the representing subject. Rather, the imperative would be to recognise what exceeds subjective determination. This is manifestly the path of German idealism, a project of thinking the unrepresentable or absolute. But this path also has its contemporary manifestation not only in current re-invigorations of the German Romantic tradition (Bowie 1990), but in many anti-anthropologistic projects of post-modernism: projects that think beyond the human, beyond thought and beyond representation. But if this path takes the critique of man as an explanatory horizon seriously, how does it fare against the critique of anthropomorphism?

How could any *thought* of the absolute or the unrepresentable not partake of thought's own conditions?

Another path from Kant would, therefore, intensify the critique of anthropomorphism. Here, Kant's idea of a supersensible substrate might be regarded as still too speculative; for such a supposedly indeterminate substrate must always be referred to determinately. Any presupposed unity would nevertheless be a *presupposed* unity. Rather than thinking an unrepresentable unity one might see such a unity as always effected from the domain of representation. This is clearly the path taken by Habermas's self-proclaimed 'post-metaphysical' theory (Habermas 1992). Habermas's ideal speech situation is the fulfilment of eighteenth-century demands for self-representation. The ideal of the public sphere is a domain of universal *validation*: the consensus is not given in fact but is an ideal that generates a procedure of communication. There is no given unity from which representation takes place, nor towards which representation proceeds. Unity is an ideal of representation. It is in the very *thought* of universal agreement, rather than its achieved existence, that speech is directed toward an ideal of consensus and intersubjective unity.

In both the German idealist tradition and in Habermasian notions of consensus the form of Kant's presupposed unity is sustained. On the one hand, for idealism, there is an ongoing commitment to a necessarily unrepresentable absolute (despite the risk of anthropomorphism). On the other hand, for critical theory, there is an insistence that such an unrepresentable is an effect of thought, and that one must remain within the domain of thought and legitimation (despite the risk of anthropological parochialism).

Is there a way of thinking unity other than these two paths? Perhaps the problem lies with unity itself, and a different path is only thinkable by questioning the necessity of unity or ground. In his list of 'symbolic hypotyposes' Kant lists such 'words' as 'substance' and 'ground': empirically intuitable concepts whose principle of application can be transferred by analogy to non-intuitable concepts:

Our language is replete with such indirect exhibitions according to an analogy, where the expression does not contain the actual schema for the concept but contains merely a symbol for our reflection. Thus the words *foundation* (support, basis), to *depend* (to be held from above), to *flow* (instead of to follow) from something, *substance* (the support of accidents, as *Locke* puts it), and countless others are not schematic but symbolic hypotyposes; they express concepts not by means of a direct intuition but only according to an analogy with one, i.e., a transfer of our reflection on an object of intuition to an entirely different concept, to which perhaps no intuition can ever correspond. If a mere way of presenting [something] may ever be called cognition (which I think is permissible if this cognition is a principle not for determining the object theoretically, as to what it is in itself, but for determining it practically, as to what the idea of the object ought to become for us and the purposive employment of it), then all our cognition of God is merely symbolic. Whoever regards it as schematic – while including in it the properties of understanding, will, etc., whose objective reality is proved only in worldly beings – falls into anthropomorphism . . . (Kant [1790] 1987: 228–9)

In the case of substance (which is not intuitable) one thinks in terms of a thing that supports or holds certain (intuitable) accidents or properties; but this sense of substance is a symbol and the relation between substance and accidents is only analogous to one thing that supports another. Substance and ground, *in their metaphysical sense*, are not *things* that exceed our knowledge. They are thought only by analogy with things. What then are substance, ground and foundation in their metaphysical sense if they are only analogous to things? If German idealism is the attempt to think the ground and modern critical theory is the insistence that the ground is nothing other than thought, is there a way of questioning the analogous or symbolic character of such words: neither as unknowable things nor as self-adequate thoughts but as 'indirect exhibitions'?

Not only was Martin Heidegger's response to Kant avowedly opposed to German idealism, it was also directed against what Heidegger diagnosed as a persistent representationalism in Western metaphysics. Furthermore, Heidegger's response to Kant and representationalism in general also entailed a rethinking of the notion of ground and its relation to *logos* and logic. According to Heidegger the history of Western metaphysics had been determined by the way in which it had asked the question of being. The question that opens philosophy is a *grounding* question: what is the being of being? But the question had been asked through a certain idea of the *logos*. The being of being was sought as some underlying foundation, ground or presence – a ground that provides a prior logic through which being appears. Thus the tradition of Western thought had already determined being *logically*: as though its appearing was the appearance *of* and *through* some present substrate or grounding *logos*. For the most part this *logos* was determined ontotheologically: as though the ground of being were some higher being that thought might disclose to itself. From Descartes, however, the *logos* becomes ego-logical: the ground of being is the representing subject. And so the shift to the subject and the Copernican turn are, Heidegger insists, different forms of the same representationalism; in all cases being is the manifestation of some grounding presence. What has been foreclosed in this history is the *question* of being: how is it that the experience of being leads beyond itself to the issue of its ground? And what is it that leads thought to the idea of the *logos* as that ever-present unity, ground or substrate?

NOTES

1. 'There is no introspection. The subject does not make up a closed, interior world he must penetrate in order to find himself. The subject is extroverted. . . . His self-consciousness is not reflexive, folded in on itself, and contained. It is not internal, face-to-face with itself: it is existential' (Vernant 1991: 328).
2. Detienne and Foucault, however, locate the fall into 'logic' and the external verification of truth within the Greek period. For Detienne it is in the Greek period that 'efficacious speech conveying truth gradually became obsolete' (Detienne 1996: 17). For Foucault the rupture occurs between Hesiod and Plato (Foucault 1972a: 218).

2

HEIDEGGER:
PROXIMITY AND DISPERSION

—◦⊂—

Anthropology is no longer just the name for a discipline, nor has it been such for some time. Instead, the word describes a fundamental tendency of man's contemporary position with respect to himself and the totality of beings. (Heidegger 1990: 143)

KANT AND THE QUESTION OF METAPHYSICS

Metaphysics, according to Heidegger, has been a history of forgetting the original question. A series of grounds have been offered: grounds that thought would merely find, discover or re-present. What is not considered is the crucial function of the question in any disclosure of such grounds. The very fact that thought *can* posit a ground of being demonstrates that thought can go beyond the present and question what grounds the present. The present therefore exceeds itself. By focusing on the metaphysical question Heidegger will both extend and 'destroy' the Kantian project of transcendental logic. Any given presence raises the question of the *giving* of that presence, the question of how the given is given or how the present is 'presenced'. But to assume that this question of presencing ought to be grounded on another present site – that of the transcendental subject – is to once again subordinate the metaphysical question to a being within the world. The difference between Heidegger's phenomenology and Kantianism lies precisely in the understanding of the site of the world and the position of thought in relation to the world.

55

Heidegger's critique of Kant's transcendental idealism can be seen, on the one hand, as an intensification of Kant's own attack on anthropologism. Kant *locates* transcendental logic within the domain of reason. Kant's pure concepts, as transcendentally ideal, are not things in the world but ways in which the world is given. Similarly, Heidegger will be critical of any attempt to answer the question of being in general through an appeal to an experienced or present being. Just as Kant had demonstrated that there were certain Ideas that were an effect of reason's own striving and not possible objects of knowledge, so Heidegger will insist that many answers to the question of being posit an ultimate ground without recognising that any such ground is the effect of a ground-laying. Any unity or totality, any higher being or God, cannot act as the ground for the world, for any such ground would itself be given through the world. The attempt to ground the world on a higher or present being is described by Heidegger as an ontotheology: being in general is grounded on a higher being (*on*) or god (*theos*) (Heidegger 1988: 126). What the positing of such a ground forgets, or fails to question, is how this ground or present is disclosed, grounded or presented.

Kant's refusal to see the ground of the world as a *given* logic or system, but as transcendental, therefore enables a departure from all those anthropomorphisms that had projected their own categories onto the world and all those anthropologisms that located those categories within the mind of man. The ground of thought, for Kant, is not an intuited object or possible perception but must be thought from the point of view of the subject reflecting upon how its position as subject is possible. Thus, from the question of the conditions for the possibility of experience Kant posits *a transcendentally ideal subject*. Unlike the Cartesian ego, this subject is not a being within the world. This subject is nothing other than the logic, or *logos*, through which the world is given. While the transcendental status of this subject resists anthropomorphism – by locating the *logos* or system within the subject rather than 'finding' a logic in the world – it runs the risk of an anthropologism. For the Heidegger of *Being and Time* the 'subjective' status of Kant's transcendental logic presents two problems. Firstly, Kant's way of questioning is still too Cartesian, too subjectivist or (in short) too human. The judging subject of transcendental logic is presupposed by Kant as a type of entity which must then be related to an outside

world. Understanding (thought) and intuition (receptivity) are presented as two faculties which unite to explain experience. At this stage,
for Heidegger, Kant's transcendental logic sustains an anthropologism;
it may locate transcendental logic as a *condition* for experience but it
still locates this logic or condition *in* a judging subject (Heidegger 1996:
189–90). The second problem of Kant's approach, for Heidegger, is
related to the first error of anthropologism but this time takes the form
of an anthropomorphism: Kant too readily accepts the structures of
judgement and assertion as *general* conditions of experience. That is,
while Kant relocates the system of thought from an external set of rules
or logic to the very form of the subject, he does not question the very
character of the logical categories themselves. Kant explains the status
of logic as a ground (or transcendental logic) but does not question
how this ground is given. Indeed, the entire Kantian project is set
against those forms of metaphysical speculation that would question
any condition or ground beyond the limits of the subject. Such a
'supersensible' must be presupposed, but cannot be a legitimate object
of philosophical inquiry.

For Heidegger, however, the logic that Kant takes to be transcendental is really the projection of a particular (representational) way of
relating to the world. Kant's categories are transcendental forms of the
Aristotelian categories of judgements. For Heidegger this means that
Kant's grounding of the world is derived from the way in which the
world has been represented in propositions. In Kant's transcendental
logic the structures of judgement determine *in advance* the character of
the world. Transcendental logic defines experience in general according
to the form of judgement or assertion (Heidegger 1996: 148). (And the
synthesis of judgement is defined as the bringing together of the terms
of an assertion.) But this conceals, Heidegger argues, a 'more primordial'
understanding of *logos*. Prior to *logos* as judgement of some outside
world there must first be the disclosure of that world. *Logos* is, for
Heidegger, not judging or asserting but, *originally*, a relatedness-
towards, a speaking about, a way of revealing the world *as world*, a
synthesis in the sense of a bringing-together: not just in the form of
judgement but also in the pre-ontological directedness of *involvement*.
Logos for Heidegger has this sense of a *pre-ontological* directedness,
precisely because the world is not given immediately as 'objectively
present'. Rather, any 'objectivity' of the world follows on from presencing;

and this presencing takes place through the always located *logos*. Thus, prior to any objective presence that is then re-presented, Heidegger argues that there is a specific movement of presencing, disclosure, dwelling or gathering. This is the more original meaning of *logos*: not a 'logic' employed by a subject to re-present the world, but a 'saying-gathering' that discloses the world as a world (Heidegger 1996: 30–1). *Logos* is not a present ground but the movement of presencing. And this mode of presencing is determined by the particular relation towards the world, the specific comportment or way of dwelling that discloses the world.

For Heidegger, then, the *logos* is not given once and for all as a transcendental condition or ground. The *mode* of *logos* or presencing is inextricably tied to the factical existence of that being who discloses. To employ the terminology of *Being and Time*: being-in-the-world begins as a concerned involvement in terms of actual projects. The positing of an 'objective' world to be judged by a subject presupposes a prior disclosure of the world in terms of specific actions and involvements. Being-in-the-world is described by Heidegger as *pre-ontological* in two senses. Pre-ontological being-in-the-world is not yet ontological – not yet a subject judging an objective world. But pre-ontological existence is also on its way to being ontological; it is an ontology or understanding of being – a metaphysics – that has not recognised itself as such. First, before there is any judged positing of the world as objective being, the world is *lived*. It is not yet lived as a separate object standing over against a subject, but as a totality of involvements. Secondly, this world is pre-ontological not just because it is prior to a general ontological thesis; it is also pre-ontological because it already presupposes a certain positing of being. It is on its way to being ontological.

In order to 'have' a world I must implicitly have some idea of being; I must already have understood the world in a certain way. If I 'have' a world this means that I do not just experience random perceptive data but *already interpret* experience as experience *of* some existing thing. I *posit* a world, and must therefore have a notion of being. The very character of worldly existence thus presupposes an implicit metaphysics. But this pre-ontological character of being-in-the-world means that an understanding of being is not an objective and merely philosophical argument. Rather, an understanding of being is inextricably intertwined with any mode of existence.

The question of being cannot be asked without considering the existence through which being is disclosed. This is why Heidegger avoids *substantive* terms like consciousness, mind, man or subjectivity. There is no consciousness or subject who subsequently encounters a separate and already present world. Rather, 'there is' presencing or disclosure. And it is from this disclosure that specific differentiations take place, such as subject and matter, or thought and world. Thus in *Being and Time* Heidegger analyses pre-ontological modes of existence: ways in which the world is lived prior to its 'objective' positing. And Heidegger also gives historical examples of differing modes of world-disclosure. If, for Descartes, the world was so much representable objectivity, the world for the Ancient Greeks was a truth to be disclosed. The world is not an already given objective presence, but a continually disclosed presence. As such, then, the world will *be* in the way in which it is disclosed. The ground of the world is given through this disclosure; there is no ground in general but a continual grounding.

This argument is more than a history of ideas or culturalist way of understanding existence. Heidegger is not just saying that understanding of what the world is differs according to various historical epochs and cultures. In fact Heidegger was strongly opposed to notions like a 'world-picture': the idea that the world is always a particular representation or way of seeing for a subject. By arguing that existence *is metaphysical*, Heidegger insists that in order to experience a world there must already be some understanding of being. In modernity this understanding is representational. The world is understood as what is represented for a viewing subject. The idea of world is then grounded in a representational schema or logic. But Heidegger's argument is not a perspectivism. How is it, he asks, that we can think of the world as presence for a re-presenting subject? How is the subject as viewpoint or representational ground possible? Heidegger examines the conditions or transcendental possibilities of the subject. In order to have the idea of a subject I must also think an objective world. But an objective world is only possible, as Kant also argued, through the synthesis of perceptions. Unlike Kant, however, Heidegger refuses to see the 'synthesis' that assembles the perceptions of being into an objective world as an 'ideal' or purely logical formal power. It is true, he argues, that we cannot understand what a thing or being would be without the forms of time and space that connect our apprehension of the thing. But time and space for Heidegger are not ways of seeing or subjective perspectives; they are forms of *comportment* [*Verhalten*]. Time is not a mental or 'subjective' form in which the world is represented; it is an event of existence.

In *Being and Time*, Heidegger demonstrates that time is always the time of specific projects. The presencing, revealing or disclosure of the world does not take place in terms of a perspective, system of present conditions or transcendental logic. The givenness of the world occurs through an *intentional* temporality; the world is always disclosed *as* this or that specific thing according to a way of Being-in-the-world. The way in which the world is 'gathered', lived, or given differs according to one's Being-in-the-world. And Being-in-the-world is *both logos* and temporality. It is temporality because the world is never a given self-presence but always a lived world, through ongoing projects and historical situation. It is *logos* because Being-in-the-world is continual world *disclosure*. The world is not a presence to be represented by a grounding subject who 'has' a logic. (This is only one mode of Being-in-the-world, a mode that has forgotten or 'passed over' the world's disclosure [Heidegger 1991: 109].) The *logos*, or the mode of the world's revealing is originally accomplished, not as a 'logic' or representational scheme, but as a comportment, or a way of relating. *Logos* for Heidegger is the disclosure of a specific and determined 'there'. Only when a 'there' is disclosed is it possible for an object to emerge as present, and for a subject to be disclosed as one who judges.

For Heidegger, then, the Aristotelian and Kantian definitions of the *logos*, as the general truth of judgement and assertion, follow on from, and are derivative of, the located, determined and factical disclosure of some specific existence. Before any 'subject' there must have been a *Dasein*: the disclosure of a certain 'there' *as being*. What this means is that subjectivism, perspectivism or the grounding of the world as a representation is only one form of world disclosure. But before the world can be grounded in the logic of a subject the world must have been revealed through a specific comportment. This means, firstly, that the representational 'ground' of thought is the effect of a certain way of being-in-the-world. Secondly, it also suggests that there might be other modalities of *logos* or Being-in-the world: modes of comportment that do not 'ground' being in some particular being (such as a subject or logic) but think being *in its revealing*. This second possibility is the one pursued by Heidegger's project of overcoming metaphysics. Here, being would not be thought as a present ground which thought then re-presents. Rather than ask how thought encounters being, Heidegger will ask that we think how the difference between thought and being comes about. This would be the question of the *logos*: the movement of disclosure that allows something like a subject or thought to be differentiated from a world or presence.

This project is avowedly anti-anthropologistic and anti-anthropo- morphic. We can neither explain the world according to a subject within the world who re-presents the world (anthropologism). Nor can we see the world as a given system or order that is present independent of its specific disclosure (anthropomorphism). For Heidegger truth is neither a subjective representation nor the objectivity of the world; truth is the unveiling of the world as a world. Truth is an event of revealing, neither subjective nor objective. It is through this revealing that a subject and object are then capable of being thought (Heidegger 1996: 205).

THE DISPERSION OF POINT OF VIEW

If Kant calls metaphysics away from its anthropomorphism back to its *own* point of view, he is still able to determine point of view in general (transcendental logic) and sustain this point of view as a *point*: a point upon which his Copernican turn can be centred. If the world is always given *as* a world then it must be possible to reflect upon that point, ground or condition of givenness in general. By locating logic within the subject Kant is able to turn the philosophical question of truth away from some misguided notion of a world in itself. The philosoph- ical gaze becomes reflective through a recognition of the necessary subjective *position* of knowledge. Kant's critical point of view is (as he continually insists) not a departure from the empirically real but a reflection on the specific point of empiricism's own condition. If the world is experienced *as real* then it must be possible to isolate the very categories of what it means to be real: magnitude, cause, extension, and so on. The empirically real world is always empirically real *for* a subject; this is the very meaning of the real. The transcendental point of view thus explicitly posits what is presupposed in the empirical point of view. The transcendental viewpoint does not depart to another world – as did Platonism – but considers this world *as if* there were two worlds: the world of appearances and the world of supersensible conditions for experience.

Heidegger, on the other hand, refers the possibility of a point of view (or the temporal comportment towards being) not to the *point* of the subject but to the *dispersed* disclosure of a 'there' (Heidegger 1996: 53). The 'there' from which any judgement takes place is, for Heidegger, not a point of view, position, perspective or representational world-picture that *then* encounters a world: for all such points are derived from a *located existence*, or a being-in-the-world (Heidegger 1996: 58). This is the very meaning of *Dasein*. The site for being, the way in which being is disclosed, does not take place 'in' a subject receiving an object. Prior to any subject/object distinction there is a dispersion or distribution of a 'there'. *Dasein* is neither a subject nor an object but a comportment: a 'going-out-towards' that lives a world. Accordingly, prior to any transcendental logic or form of judgement or knowledge in general, Heidegger affirms *existential* categories. These categories cannot be reduced to present conditions, for Heidegger insists on their *equi-primordiality*. There is not a subjective synthesis of time and space that then enables a world, as in Kant. For Heidegger time and space are not forms of intuition (for this implies that time and space exist within the subject). Rather, we might say that 'there is' the existence of a specific spatial and temporal dispersion, with neither being the ground of the either. From this dispersion it is then possible to think the point of view of a subject.

Prior to any transcendental subject/object distinction there is a specific and factical directedness towards a world, or a 'sending' of being. The 'existential' categories of *Being and Time* seek to uncover the essential *possibilities* of ontology: how it is that being is thought *as being*. The 'existential' categories are, therefore, *pre*-ontological and inquire into the essential structures of existence that enable any metaphysical questions (or questions of being) to emerge. Heidegger therefore refers the formality of metaphysics and the positing of a transcendental logic back to the locatedness of existence. *Logos* for Heidegger is therefore not a logic – a system of conditions for encountering any possible world – but is firstly disclosure through lived existence. *Being and Time* 'steps back' from the overly Cartesian and 'too human' point of view of transcendental logic to the facticity of existence, *returning* any logic of judgement to a more primordial 'there' of existence. On the one hand, this means that Heidegger is critical of the explanation or grounding of the world in a subject. On the other hand, Heidegger also argues that if the world is always disclosed *through existence* then it will not be possible to think an objective world *in general*; the world is always disclosed to a particular being-in-the-world. If Heidegger's thought is a stringent anti-subjectivism in its refusal of the rhetoric of mind or consciousness, he nevertheless sustains the importance of *Dasein*. Even in the later 'turn' to being, Heidegger will still stress the historicity and locatedness of any disclosure of being. Neither the world nor presence can be thought beyond the event of its disclosure. To what extent, then, does the point, position, '*Da*', or site of disclosure act as a ground for being? And what precludes this ground from being interpreted as a self or subject?

HEIDEGGER'S READING OF KANT AND THE QUESTION OF ANTHROPOLOGISM

That presence is achieved through self-constitution is an integral guiding idea in Heidegger's reading of Kant. The self, for Kant, is not some pre-existent, ontic or substantive thing; rather, the self is the possibility of the thing. In order for an object to exist as an object (and not a thing in itself) it is necessary that it be received. The receptivity of the thing *as object*, or as something present, depends upon the transcendental imagination's apperception. The thing as a given *object* occurs within the horizon of a connectedness of representations and therefore depends upon the pure intuition of time. Time, as the condition for an object's coming to presence, is not itself an object. On the contrary, as a pure intuition time is the imagination's mode of receiving that which it also produces. The giving of some present thing has as its condition the subject's self-affectation (Heidegger 1990: 48). Further, the self is *nothing other than* this relatedness to some presence. The very possibility of the presence of being is at the same time the subject's self-constitution through the pure intuition of time. For it is only through time that the 'opposition' of 'objectivity' is connected and set over against a 'subjectivity'. Heidegger concludes from this reading of Kant that our finitude, the fact that we have to receive beings as given to us, means that we dwell metaphysically. To posit a thing as a separately existing thing, we also have to posit its *existence* above and beyond the set of appearances; we sustain the presence of being:

> Thus it is time, as given a priori, which in advance bestows upon the horizon of transcendence the character of the perceivable offer. But not only that. As the unique pure universal image, it gives a preliminary enclosedness to the horizon of transcendence. The single and pure ontological horizon is the condition for the possibility that the being given within it can have this or that particular, revealed, indeed ontic horizon. But time does not give just the preliminary, unified coherence to transcendence. Rather, as the pure self-giving it simply offers to it, in general, something like a check. It makes perceivable to a finite creature the 'Being-in-opposition-to' of objectivity, which belongs to the finitude of the transcending-toward. (Heidegger 1990: 74)

What Heidegger's reading of Kant serves to emphasise is that the first *Critique* is not just a theory of knowledge but has as its task an investigation into the *question* of being or the possibility of metaphysics. To ask how metaphysics is possible is not to ask about any particular being, or even the 'highest' being, but to ask how it is that being at all, in general, comes to be understood. The very idea of experience or knowledge (the idea of the given) means that there is already some understanding of being. According to Heidegger, Kant's question about the possibility of knowledge is therefore also a question about the possibility of metaphysics. To experience a thing entails that there be some idea of existence. Kant shows that in order to see a thing *as existing* it must be synthesised by the imagination. By locating the possibility of being in the transcendental imagination Kant shows that prior to any particular thing, or any ontic determination, there must be a structure of receptivity. This structure is defined as the pure intuition of time. Only with the transcendental imagination can an object – as some given, present and existing thing – be set against the horizon of receptivity. The presencing of being therefore depends upon the subject's relatedness to what is given. At the same time, the subject is produced as a subject only in this relating. Subjectivity is, then, nothing other than a relatedness:

The human being could not be the thrown being as a self if in general it *could* not *let* the being as such *be*. . . . On the grounds of the understanding of Being, man is the there [*das Da*], with the Being of which occurs the opening irruption into being so that it can show itself as such for a self. *More original than man is the finitude of the Dasein in him.* (Heidegger 1990: 156)

The subject's experience of itself, *as a self*, is at once an act of self-constitution and an effect of receptivity. In this regard the subject is no longer a subject, as a ground, site or presence, but is more appropriately described as *Dasein*.

To ask the question of metaphysics, the question of being, is to ask about this possibility of receptivity in general. Transcendence – the experience of the object in its objectivity – presupposes the *presencing* of being. To exist as a subject is, therefore, to have ontological knowledge, to posit some thing *as being*. Metaphysics, the thought of being, is not just a part of philosophical inquiry, but the condition for the possibility of subjectivity: 'Ontological knowledge has proven itself to be that which forms transcendence' (Heidegger 1990: 82). 'We' are produced or effected in the ways in which we understand the world to be; the question we direct towards the world is not an academic activity added on to existence, but the very way in which we are. In the 'passing beyond' to existence or objectivity the subject as transcendence also *anticipates* the being of the essent; the object is received through a horizon that posits in advance, prior to the particular (ontic) being of the essent, the (ontological) idea of objectivity in general.

In *Kant and the Problem of Metaphysics* Heidegger places a great deal of emphasis on Kant's transcendental object. The transcendental object is what all experience anticipates in order to have a world. Because the world is given through a synthesis of appearances, or a gathering, I must already have some idea of existence or of a separate being in order to form my experiences into an object world. Thus experience 'goes out toward' or anticipates a 'transcendental object = X'. To have experience means then that we already have some idea of being. Kant recognised that some understanding of an external object (object = X) had to already be in place for experiences to be organised as experiences *of* some outside world (Kant [1787] 1933: 137). Experience is only *of* an object if what is experienced is synthesised (or gathered) into the idea of an external given. Heidegger interprets this as an argument for an originary and pre-subjective transcendence: before any 'thing' there is a 'going-out-towards' or an anticipation of a thing in general. Being is anticipated in order for a world to be:

> Indeed, in general [experience] must give something in advance which has the character of a standing-against in general in order to form the horizon within which original beings can be encountered. This terminus [*Woraufzu*] of the preliminary turning-toward, therefore, can no longer be intuited by us in the sense of empirical intuition. . . . This terminus of the preliminary turning-toward, therefore, can 'be termed the non-empirical object = X'. (Heidegger 1990: 83)

The positing of a transcendental object = X is the positing of being. Being is not a philosophical supplement or fiction; its understanding is essential to existence in general. Furthermore, this object = X is non-empirical; it is the condition for the possibility of empiricity, of the essential otherness of the thing. For Heidegger, the directedness towards this transcendental object = X is *transcendence*: a horizon that is 'unthematic' in so far as it anticipates not a particular object, but objectivity as such. Transcendence is 'nothing other than the holding-open of the horizon within which the Being of the being becomes discernable in a preliminary way' (Heidegger 1990: 84). Prior to the encounter of any particular being or any determinate essent there is, then, this *general (ontological) comportment towards existence*. This act of transcendence is both temporality – a connectedness of representations to produce the thing as thing – and subjectivity – a 'passing beyond' the self to an anticipation of existence in general. Kant's metaphysics, for Heidegger, asks how this 'passing beyond' to being in general is possible.

Heidegger's own argument is that once we have recognised, with Kant, that having a world demands an anticipation of being or an idea of what it means to exist, then we can ask about the *ways* in which being is anticipated or approached. This would be the very character of the *logos*: the saying-gathering or synthesis that brings the world to presence. To think of the subject as an effect of the transcendental imagination's receptivity, as Kant did, already overcomes a certain subjectivism. Time, as pure intuition, is, Heidegger insists, already more primordial than any experienced or thematised self. Heidegger's rejection of the language of consciousness, the emphasis on *Dasein*'s 'ec-stasis' and projection and, finally, his favouring of being's presencing and revealing (rather than its comprehension) indicates a radical intensification of the Kantian *Critique*'s argument that the subject and object's presence depend upon time.

According to Heidegger, the very possibility of the ontic (of any being) has as its condition the *ontological* possibility of transcendence – the 'going beyond' or projection of synthesis. For Heidegger, this means that the Kantian *Critique* marks an opening into a more authentic understanding of time in the history of Western metaphysics. The fundamental role granted to the imagination in the first edition of the first *Critique* demonstrates an essential connection between the presence of being and temporality. For it is in the passing beyond, or the projection to the thing, that both subject and object can be said to exist or be present. Time is not a thing but the originary horizon within which subjectivity and objectivity take place. The thing is constituted in its presence only by being said to sustain itself through time. The uncovering of temporality is also a more originary uncovering of being – no longer conceived of as a particular present being but as the possibility of being in general.

In *Kant and the Problem of Metaphysics* Heidegger directed his attention away from Kant's transcendental logic – the focus of *Being and Time* – and found an opening of metaphysics in the suggested power of the imagination. (This forming power of the imagination is also what will provide a way of thinking unity or the absolute for post-Kantian German Romanticism [Heidegger 1990: 135]. For Heidegger, however, far from being a unity or ground, Kant's projective imagination suggests an 'original' ungrounding, dispersion or disunification.) As a fundamental 'power' Kant's theory of imagination suggests that prior to the *relation* between concepts and the intuitions to which they are applied, there is an originary 'looking' (Heidegger 1990: 132): an openness to the world that does not determine this or that particular thing but is a 'going-out-towards' a thing in general: 'This going-beyond to the "wholly other," however, requires a Being-in-there [*Darinnensein*], in a "medium" within which this "wholly other" – that the knowing creature itself is not and over which it is not the master – can be encountered' (Heidegger 1990: 79).

In order for there to be an intuited world for an understanding, there must be the opening of a horizon, a transcendence that will allow a world to appear. In the Kant book Heidegger extends the critique of transcendental logic that he began in *Being and Time*. Despite opening the question of the imagination that *precedes* the two paths of receptivity (the given) and spontaneity (the subject), Kant also forecloses the question of metaphysics by halting his inquiry at the pure concepts of the understanding. Kant accepts the transcendental logic of the pure concepts and does not question how such a logic is given, nor how such a logic can be contained within a subject. Kant accepts the distinction between the logical subject and its intuited world. According to Heidegger the 'common source' of understanding and intuition – the original disclosure of the imagination as transcendence – is only alluded to or hinted at. Kant 'shrinks back' from the originary 'springing forth' (the imagination) that enables presence (Heidegger 1990: 115). By taking logic as something *present*, Kant retreats from questioning the specific transcendence of the imagination, a faculty that allows presence to appear *as present*:

> This [*Critique of Pure Reason*] itself thus rattles the mastery of reason and the understanding. 'Logic' is deprived of its pre-eminence in metaphysics which was built up from ancient times. Its idea has become questionable.
>
> If the essence of transcendence is grounded in the pure power of the imagination, or more originally in temporality, then precisely the idea of the 'Transcendental Logic' is something inconceivable, especially if, contrary to Kant's original intention, it is autonomous and is taken absolutely. (Heidegger 1990: 166)

One of the main implications of *Kant and the Problem of Metaphysics* is that the imagination is Kant's own way of thinking the original opening of a horizon for the subsequent determination of the given by concepts. The problem of Kant's *Critique* is, for Heidegger, the problem of schematism: the relation of the concepts of the understanding to the givenness of intuition. The fundamental role of the *imagination* as the unifying power becomes Heidegger's focus of attention. It is the imagination, as a *unity* from which the world *as experienced* will 'spring forth', that indicates for Heidegger the primacy of transcendence. Before any transcendental logic or pure concepts applied to an intuited

world, there must be a going-out-towards. It is this 'springing forth' of
the imagination, as a directedness towards what is not yet determined
conceptually (a 'nothing'), that *then* enables the relation between the
receptivity of sensibility and the spontaneity of the understanding:

> The imagination forms the look of the horizon of the objectivity as
> such in advance, before the experience of being. This look-forming
> [*Anblickbilden*] in the pure image [*Bilde*] of time, however, is not
> just prior to this or that experience of the being, but rather always
> is in advance, prior to any possible [experience]. Hence from the
> beginning, in this offering of the look, the power of imagination is
> never simply dependent upon the presence [*Anwesenheit*] of a
> being. It is dependent in this way to such a small degree that pre-
> cisely its pre-forming [*Vor-bilden*] of the pure schema Substance,
> i.e., persistence over time, for example, first brings into view in
> general something like constant presence [*ständige Anwesenheit*] . . .
> The productive power of the imagination, with which Anthro-
> pology is concerned, never has to do with anything but the forming
> of the looks of empirically possible, or rather impossible objects.
>   On the other hand, the productive power of the imagination in
> the *Critique of Pure Reason* never refers to the forming of objects,
> but refers instead to the pure look of objectivity in general.
> (Heidegger 1990: 90–1)

The fundamental task of metaphysics, the question of how it is
possible to think being, is therefore brought before the human capacity
of imagination. Before any transcendental logic there is the opening of
a look, or a going-out-towards.

   Does Heidegger's emphasis on the originary power of the imagination
which *then* allows the world to appear over against a subject indicate
that the metaphysical question has been returned to an anthropology?
That Kant locates the imagination's power of schematism in the
'depths of the human soul' (Kant [1787] 1933: 183) certainly seems to
indicate that the question of being can only be determined according
to a study of the imagination and that Kant's supposed 'step back' from
the imagination's power is a refusal to consider the specific being of
'man'. But, Heidegger insists, there are two points of view for considering the imagination. Anthropologically, we can see the imagination

as a power of producing images within the world, empirical creations derived from what is not directly present. Here, the imagination would be a self-present thing within the world that then re-presented the world. Considered *critically*, however, the imagination is not an image or representation of this or that particular thing but a *pure* directedness-towards (Heidegger 1990: 91). It is the power of an image of no particular thing, an object in general, an opening out towards what has not *already* been determined *as* some specific entity. Considered critically, the imagination is neither a faculty divorced from the world – the interiority of pure reason – nor a creation of images within the world: *it is the opening of the world as such.* The imagination is the possibility of both anthropology and ontology, a 'springing forth' that then allows a world and subject to appear.

Like Kant, then, Heidegger sets himself against a history of metaphysics that has accepted the world as so much present and systematic order, with its meaning determined as something present, in advance, given to a subject. If Kant had targeted metaphysical speculation for separating itself from the world and departing to a realm of ungrounded ideas and absolutes, he did so with the aim of returning philosophy to its own point of view. Kant's transcendental or critical position is, therefore, an act of self-recognition. The transcendental point of view is not a position outside the world, but a consideration of how the world is given as a world. In Kant's investigation the *contribution* of reason's own point of view is itself uncovered. But Kant's act of philosophical homecoming, according to Heidegger, still remains a stranger to the original source or unity of the imagination. And so Heidegger in his extension of Kant again raises the question of philosophy's place, the point of view of the question of being:

> From whence in general do we lay hold of the point of view from which to determine Being as such and thus to win a concept of Being from out of which the possibility and the necessity of the essential articulation of Being becomes understandable? Hence the question of 'First Philosophy,' namely, 'What is Being as such?' must drive us back beyond the question 'What is Being as such?' to the still more original question: *from whence in general are we to comprehend the like of Being, with the entire wealth of articulations and references which are included in it?* (Heidegger 1990:153)

By *not* asking the question of the imagination Kant avoids anthropologism – defining being according to man as a being within the world
– but he sustains a certain anthropomorphism. The 'will to system' in
Kant's philosophy takes transcendental logic as the ground of being.
Kant's critique defines the *logos* as a logic of judgement, a system of
judgement that is *present*. It is in this determination of logic as a present
order that Kant steps back from the question of the generation, presencing or existence that discloses such a system. He avoids locating
this system within man (anthropologism), but he never questions the
opening of the system. Either logic is generated from 'the depths of the
human soul' (thereby risking anthropologism), or logic itself is that real
ground of which the subject is merely one more effect. But if this
second possibility is the case, and logic just is the ground of the real,
then there is no way of questioning the event or contribution of thought.
And if thought does not acknowledge its representational separation
then it has fallen back into pre-critical anthropomorphism.

GROUND, GROUNDING AND THE
FREEDOM OF THE QUESTION

Heidegger's reading of Kant therefore seeks to retrieve a path not
taken by Kant and occluded by the later system philosophy of German
idealism. Kant alludes to the imagination as a unity that precedes the
two stems of understanding and sensibility. The later German idealists
pursued this unity not in relation to the subject but according to a
theory of system or the Absolute. In so doing, German idealism asked
the question of being as a whole; system was not the form of knowledge imposed on the world but being's own order and organisation.
German idealism was also therefore a striving for the unity of system.
Not surprisingly, therefore – as Heidegger demonstrates in his book
on Schelling – *the* problem of system philosophy was the idea of
freedom. Once being is thought as a whole, as a unified system, with
its own absolute order, then freedom cannot be defined as thought's
difference from the world – for there would be nothing other than the
world and its *own* differentiation, and certainly not the difference of
the representing subject. The will to system, and the attention to the
unity of the absolute, precludes any such difference. Evil and freedom
must be comprehended by the system, for there is nothing beyond

system once system is defined as the absolute's own act of self-grounding. Heidegger's reading of Schelling culminates with a demonstration that a theory of evil and freedom in a philosophy of system cannot be located within human being, but must be defined according to the structure of the system:

> Because evil comes from the ground, the ground, however, belongs to the essence of beings, evil is posited in principle with the Being of beings. Where beings as a whole are projected in the jointure of Being, where system is thought, evil is included and implicated. (Heidegger 1985: 160)

For Heidegger, the problem of philosophy after Kant lies in the location of *logos*. If *logos* is nothing other than being's own self-representation, if *logos* is the coming forth of an already given ground, then both freedom and evil will be within the system. The decision – either of freedom or evil – will not be radically separated from the ground, but the ground's own coming forth. Hence the striving for the unity of *logos*, or an ultimate grounding of being, becomes in the German idealist tradition, a complete unity of system, ground and idea. Thus, according to Heidegger, we can see Hegel's passage from 'phenomenology' to 'logic' as exemplary of the German idealist striving for the Absolute (Heidegger 1988: 12). Man is a moment in an absolute 'logic': this logic is not the subject's ordering of being but being's own appearance to itself.

In opposition to German idealism, Heidegger's avowedly 'different path' from Kant's allusion to a prior unity takes the imagination *not* as an intimation of a pre-subjective, pre-human absolute, but as the factical opening of an originary differentiation. We might, then, follow Heidegger and read the German idealist will to system as a drive to anthropomorphic disownment. The will to system might then be seen as the culmination of a metaphysics of presence. The tendency to hypostatise the structures of *logos* as present, 'forgets' the always located existence from which any 'logic' or judgement springs forth. If there was already in Greek philosophy a tendency to take the world 'mathematically' as ordered in advance according to a present logic, this tendency reaches its zenith in the mathematical character of system philosophy. Here being is thought as a whole, as a present system, or an absolute order: the presencing or revealing of this order *through existence* is subordinated to an Absolute. To a certain extent, then, Heidegger's criticism of German idealism's will to system takes the form of an anthropology set against anthropomorphism. Rather than take the structures of system, logic or categories as present and determined in advance, Heidegger returns *logos* to the specific 'there' or comportment of existence. Kant's original unity is not, he argues, a pre-personal absolute – an absolute that might then be thought as a systematic jointure of Being. By referring to the 'common root' or unity of subject and object, Heidegger's Kant takes the experience of being back to the locatedness of imagination's finite, factical and non-present going-forth. Freedom is, therefore, not a faculty within the world but the condition for the possibility of any world. One 'has' a world because of an original transcendence or determination of what *is*. But this transcendence is not a calculation reckoned by a subject; it is not a decision determined by worldly facts but a decisive becoming of a world (Heidegger 1991: 94). Prior to the presence of any world, *logos* or system is a pre-ontological presencing: always revealed in a determined 'there':

> The verbal meaning [of transcendence] comes from *transcendere* [Latin]: to surpass, step over, to cross over to. Thus *transcendence* means the surpassing, the going beyond. And the transcendent means that toward which the surpassing takes place, that which requires surpassing in order to be accessible and attainable, the beyond, that which is over against. (Heidegger 1992: 160)

Order, system and logic are not structures to be found in being as a whole, but events of the givenness of the world. There is not a given-ness *in general*, and therefore not an ever-present transcendental logic. The 'giving' of the given always bears the character and responsibility of its 'there'. *Logos* is first a *disclosure* from which the world emerges; as such, then, *logos* is originally existence: there, determined, factical. Any transcendental 'logic' is subsequent to the event of existence. And this existence is an event that cannot be taken as present, precisely because it is the condition for the possibility of presence. Judgement and logic are not the transcendental structures for any possible being but are grounded in the specificity or *ownness* of existence. There is not a given world in general, the truth of which might be 'read off' in the form of logical assertions. Rather, truth is always *a way* in which the world is given. Any positing of a transcendental logic – a condition of the given – must itself be given. As such, any logic or *logos* is neither 'in' a subject (anthropologism), nor present in some pre-personal absolute or system (anthropomorphism).

Seen as an extension of Kant's critique of anthropomorphism, we could read Heidegger's 'existential categories' upon which any 'logic' is founded as an intensification of philosophical responsibility in opposition to a representationalism. Logic is not given in advance as a set of representational conditions; logic is the effect of a way of being in the world. Neither the subject nor logic must be accepted as simply present but must be interrogated according to their disclosure, their grounding and their historical/existential mode of dwelling.

Heidegger's anti-anthropologism dislocates transcendental logic from its site within the subject, and in so doing intensifies the responsibility of human ownness. If transcendental logic is not some present-at-hand structure to be uncovered by philosophical inquiry but is the event of a non-present *logos* of existence, then the philosophical point of view is thrown back from the pure formality of logic and system to the facticity of existence. As Heidegger argues in *Being and Time*, factical existence is, *ontologically*, a relatedness of care, a thrownness, a mood, a being-ahead-of-itself. Heidegger is insistent that there is no *logos* in general that could be given as present and in advance of existence. There is no transcendental logic that is not originally an existence. The character of this originality *as existence* already shatters any idea that such an origin might be known or presented as a ground. This is why Heidegger's ontological inquiry begins as an existential inquiry. We can only understand the capacity to question being by beginning from specific ways in which being is given, from events of existence. Certain ways in which the world is given – such as the homeless or abyssal experience of *Angst* – take us beyond existence and open the possibility of questioning the world (the possibility of ontology). The possibility of metaphysics is an existential possibility: the question of the world can only be asked because the world is lived in a certain way. This also means that the question of the world cannot be extricated from the particular world which is in question.

Further, and more importantly, the ground of being does not precede the grounding question. The question is possible only because thought already dwells in a world, but this dwelling is not some ground prior to existence; it is just existence. Once the origin or ground of metaphysics is revealed as existence (rather than a pre-human absolute) it can be neither presented, nor posited. (Indeed the terms of 'origin' and 'ground' hardly seem appropriate any more.) Rather, the return of philosophy to existence is, as *Being and Time* insists, ineluctably *Unheimlich*. Metaphysics is only fully grounded when its ground is neither present nor given, when thought is recognised as *proximate* to its world, rather than present, as near but not fully at home. To disclose being *as* this or that is to dwell in truth, to relate to being. But it is also, because it reveals being in a specific way, a concealing of being (Heidegger 1996: 205). In the metaphysical question this concealing is recognised. We ask not about this or that being, but being in general. The question exceeds any given being, attempting to think the ground of being. The possibility of ground is opened in the question, but the question always begins from a grounded being. And this is why the question of being is both circular and responsible (Heidegger 1996: 143). To question being we must already have anticipated some understanding of being; the question is therefore always our question. And while the question does seek to go beyond our present world, the passage beyond of the question nevertheless bears the hallmark of that world. The question of being is at once homely and unhomely.

The possibility raised by Heidegger is whether we can rearticulate the question of being, such that what we seek is not some present ground or higher being (Heidegger 1990: 168). How might we think metaphysics, not as the grounding of being, but as the question of how any grounding is possible? If the ground is given through the question, or if the question opens the ground, then it follows that the question is decisive or determinative (Heidegger 1959: 39). Thought does not exist and *then* ask questions. Thought is a mode of questioning. If we rearticulate the metaphysical question properly then we may do so, not in order to uncover some ground, but in such a way that we remain proximate to being's continual ungrounding. For Heidegger we can only rethink the question through a re-invigoration of *logos* (Heidegger 1992: 5). The Greek *logos* is the event that has both opened and closed thought. By asking about being, the *logos* opens a world. It is a 'saying-gathering' that 'gives' a world by dwelling, thinking or existing in a certain way. Heidegger's *logos*, redefined in this way, is returned to a way of life; but this dwelling or existence that enables the question is not a culturally determined world-view, perspective or way of seeing within which certain forms of question are articulated. The wonder of the Greek *logos* is that it is a form of question or existence that goes beyond itself, and that can ask about existence in general. The question of being as articulated in Greek thought is the very event of meta-physics, the idea not of this or that being but of being in general. However, this opening is also a closing or forgetting. In the articulation of the question, being is interrogated in terms of the being of being, or the ground of being.

THE HUMANITY OF THE QUESTION

Rather than retreat to the Greeks from the fall into Cartesian moder-nity, Heidegger interprets philosophy's history as one of necessary and positive loss. Cartesian representationalism and mathematicism are already possibilities of the Western *logos*. Technology and the manipu-lation of the world as so much objective presence are not accidents that befall a once fully present being; for it is the very being of being to disclose itself, to disperse itself through time, or to 'set adrift in errancy' (Heidegger 1984: 26). Further, as soon as existence moves beyond itself to question itself it is at risk of an inauthentic mode of questioning. Indeed the fact that the question of being takes an inauthentic form at the beginning is not an accident; it tells us about the character of being and existence. In its inauthentic form the question of being is representational, as though there were some underlying logic or repre-sentational scheme that thought needs only to re-present. The answer to the question of being is sought (initially and inauthentically) as a form of presence, or as an already given ground – a presence that the questioner need only discover or find. In its authentic form, however, the question is recognised as constitutive of its answer. The ground of being is given through the question, and is not something discovered or simply re-presented by a contingent question. The question is no longer an empty form but a responsible engagement with the disclosure of being: responsible because the determinative mode of the question is not passed over or forgotten.

Heidegger's 'existential' categories, that set out to return *logos* to existence, do nevertheless attempt to disclose the 'basic structure' of human finitude in general. The existential categories are not concepts or rules; they are ways in which *Dasein* exists. In the notion of care, for example, we are not given a substantive feature of *Dasein*, not a quality or attribute. Rather, we are given the ways in which attributes are disclosed. Care is an intentional relation; what is disclosed through care is *Dasein*'s world, connected to a totality of located projects. The existential categories are not features of human nature; they are the different modes through which *Dasein* becomes, or moves beyond itself. As such then these *existential* categories are not reducible to the specific facticity of a particular *ethos* but describe the conditions for any possible ethos:

> But if one takes the expression 'Care' – contrary to and in spite of the still explicit, previously given directive that it has nothing to do with an ontic characterization of man – in the sense of an esti- mation of 'human life' which reflects its world-view and ethics, instead of as an indication of the *structural unity* of the transcen- dence of Dasein which is finite in itself, then everything becomes confused. (Heidegger 1990: 161)

These categories are not a theory of man but they do explain that 'man' is one of the modes in which *Dasein* might exist. It is a positive possibility that *Dasein* might understand itself anthropologically, as a being among beings. Anthropologism is not an error that befalls a more properly considered transcendental subject: *Dasein* takes itself *as man* because *Dasein* is the possibility of self-representation. It is this possibility that is occluded in any unthinking anthropologism. The theory of man is yet one more representationalism where the ground of being (the ontological) is given as a particular being (the ontic). What is forgotten is the ontological or questioning capacity that would allow any such ontic or anthropological interpretation to arise. Any humanism has as its prior possibility or condition a being capable of understanding itself: an ontological rather than ontic being. Indeed, in the Kant book Heidegger still insists that a philosophical anthropology must not be reduced to any anthropological question, but must rather pose anthropology *as a problem* (Heidegger 1990: 151).

For Heidegger, then, the *problem* of anthropology is precisely the persistence of anthropological questions in metaphysics. What is human being such that questions of being lead back to human finitude? What is it about existence that leads us back to the question of this particular human entity, or the question of who 'we' are? In this regard anthropology is not an error or lack within philosophy. Regarded *positively* the problem of anthropology is nothing other than the problem of transcendence. To ask about being, or what *is*, is to already ask about the disclosure of being. Metaphysics is, therefore, thrown back to that being who questions and discloses: 'If man is only man on the grounds of the Dasein in him, then in principle the question as to what is more original than man cannot be anthropological. All anthropology, even Philosophical anthropology, has already assumed that man is man' (Heidegger 1990: 156). Metaphysics is primordially a step back from philosophical anthropology. In this stepping back anthropology is not given as a ground but is seen as the *possibility* of ground-laying. The very idea of the human – as one who represents being – is the very possibility of thinking being, and also going beyond the human.

On the one hand, then, anthropology is a requirement or ground of metaphysics. Only with the anthropological illusion – the idea that the world is presented to some representational animal – can metaphysics ask the question of how this anthropological centre is possible. Only then can metaphysics disclose the more primordial ground. In the language of *Being and Time* we might say that the fall into inauthenticity is both positive and original. Initially and for the most part, *Dasein* understands itself anthropologically as a present being within the world. Only from this fallen understanding of *Dasein* is an authentic understanding possible. For it is from this 'fall' that we can ask the positive question of being: what is being such that it is understood (inauthentically) as present for a self-present subject? Anthropology is not an accident for thought but tells us about the very nature of thought and being. Being is never given as a general or absolute ground but is always disclosed through existence. As such, then, *Dasein tends* to interpret being in terms of beings already present, or its own lived world. It is because existence is always concerned, worldly and projective that the primordial revealing of being is passed over, and being is interpreted as already there for a self-present subject. In the beginning, then, is the 'fallenness' of representational inauthenticity; the lived world is given as already present and objective, with its own meaning and order. Only with the question of how this world is possible is the beginning of everyday existence seen as an effect of a prior and pre-ontological revealing (Heidegger 1996: 167). (But this 'priority' comes after, or is recognised after, the effect; it is an ontological and not a temporal priority.)

In the beginning existence has already fallen into 'having' a world. Only with the authentic question of how this world is possible is it disclosed that the world is not a given ground, but is the effect of a ground-laying. The fact that thought *can* ground itself inauthentically – by interpreting itself as a subject – indicates that thought is an act of grounding. Like Kant, Heidegger will argue that the history of meta-physics and its continued attempts to think the system of being indicates that thought is essentially a capacity to exceed itself and think being in general. The very possibility of the question of being – the metaphysical question – is positive evidence that *Dasein* is not a thing within the world but a way of understanding the world. The world, accordingly, is nothing other than this understanding.

In *Being and Time* and the Kant book Heidegger still seeks the basic structure of the inner possibility of the question of being and in so doing discloses what he refers to as *existential* categories. The anti-anthropo-morphism of this gesture is clear: a refusal to accept the pure concepts of logic as simply present. Rather, the transcendental – the possibility of existence – is not a structure to be found as present, but is the consequence of *our own* human and specific relation to a world. But Heidegger's return of the *logos* to *existential categories* might also be likened to Kant's *step back* from the abyss of the imagination towards an anthropologism. How is it that Heidegger is able to refer, if not to a ground, to a series of equi-primordial categories that disclose being? If there is not a ground to be found as present but only the possibility of a ground-laying then *neither* Kant's imagination *nor* the structures of existence can offer themselves as the final 'result' of the metaphysical question (or as the *proper* locus of the metaphysical question).

When Heidegger criticises philosophy for being a representationalism he does so on the basis that the idea of the world as a presence that is then re-presented does not carry the transcendental question back far enough. Kantian transcendentalism is diagnosed by Heidegger as an extension, as well as an overcoming, of representationalism. Descartes assumes that there is a subject who then represents an object world. In

Kant's transcendental objection to Descartes the subject is seen as the effect of the synthesising power of the faculties, and not as an already synthesised or experienceable thing. In both Kant and Descartes, however, there is an explanation through representational conditions. It is assumed that what is given is a representation, and then some certain ground or condition is sought for. (For Descartes this is *res cogitans*; for Kant it is the transcendental subject.) The risk of this critical manoeuvre is that the site of this condition takes the form of a particular being, such as man. Whereas Kant locates his system or logic in the subject (Kant [1787] 1933: 104), Heidegger will insist that this subject is an effect of a more primordial logic of *existence, or being-in-the-world*. For Heidegger this will be neither a humanism nor a representationalism, for the question of being is not brought back to some grounding substance but is brought before the *dispersion* of existence: that is, not a present subject but a movement of presencing. The question that needs to be asked, though, is what prevents this existentialism from being an anthropologism? Heidegger does not call *Dasein* 'man' because *Dasein* is not a thing in the world but a way in which the world becomes a world. But Heidegger does assert certain existential categories that describe the structure of presencing. Heidegger may have resisted the positing of a single and unified ground, in favour of the dispersion of equi-primordial 'existentials', but he is still able to describe the general structure of existence through modes of ground-laying. However, if the ground of thought is only possible because of a directed ground-laying (a certain *way* of living or questioning the world), then any general structure of grounding can only be given after the event. The ground of existence may not be graspable as a *categorial* structure of existence in general. Modes of existence will be determined by the 'ethos', 'there' or 'from which' of the world.

Heidegger's later thought, concerning itself with dwelling, suggests that the step beyond anthropologism might not lead to a general structure (where *Dasein* is defined as the structure of any possible ground or question). There might just be the irreducible locatedness of a dwelling, a dwelling that is never at home or grounded but that nevertheless can only question its *own* homelessness or ungrounding. The question is never a *pure* event or opening but is always the departure *from* or an opening *from*. As such, then, the movement of the question will be determined as both a going-forth but also as a going-back, and a coming-from. The question then arises as to whether this movement of the question, if not its origin, can be given in general terms. Can there be a transcendental logic of the question? Certainly much of Heidegger's work suggests that there can: the fact that we understand ourselves anthropologically, for example, indicates that we are beings who already interpret our own being. And there is a structure to this interpretation. Inauthentically we question man as a being there to be found and represented. Authentically, we ask how it is possible that the question of man – or who we are – occurs. It is in authenticity, the *question* of ownness, that the *general* possibility of ontology is disclosed. This possibility may take many actual forms – including anthropologism and representationalism – but this only indicates the inescapable and primordial possibility of the question.

Heidegger's anti-anthropologism, which asks the question of the possibility of anthropology, however, might still retain an inevitable anthropomorphism: can the *structures* of existence, the 'existential' categories, be granted the primordiality of the pre-ontological, or is their very disclosure not one more determined mode of factical existence, one more way of being in the world? The idea of dwelling in Heidegger's later thought might suggest that Heidegger abandoned the categorial logic of *Being and Time* in order to think an irreducible locatedness. Dwelling is certainly not some grounding substance, for dwelling is a relation and not a thing. Dwelling is not a point of view or perspective but the *way* any viewpoint is brought into existence. But why describe this movement or relation of disclosure as *dwelling*? Can dwelling describe the form of questioning in general? For dwelling is yet one more determined way in which existence understands itself in relation to a world. Other articulations of the possibility of the question might lead us away from metaphors of grounding, foundation, or '*Da*'. For surely 'dwelling' harbours a risk both of anthropologism and representationalism. To think the opening of the question as a mode of dwelling determines thought through metaphors of place, locatedness and grounding (if not ground). Representationalism had been criticised by Heidegger for referring thought back to some present ground, and then for locating that ground within the subject or man. But both the early idea of *Dasein* and the later emphasis on dwelling carry a risk of human parochialism. Even if thought is homeless, for Heidegger, it is still a *relation to home*. And even if *logos* is a question, rather than a logic, it is always a question for which *'we'* are responsible. This risk of the human raises the question of other relations, whether thought might be other than *Dasein*, other than a disclosure of a 'there'. Can thought tear itself from its anthropological home?

AN ETHICS OF THE QUESTION

The metaphysical question – as a question of being – cannot be asked without considering the character of the being who questions. And this question is not added on to existence. In order for there to be existence, transcendence or something other than ourselves there must already be a comportment or relation to this otherness. The early Heidegger refers the question back, therefore, to the being who questions, to the *possibility* of anthropology. Heidegger's later emphasis on dwelling suggests, however, that the possibility of anthropology cannot be extricated from its located articulation. It suggests, that if *logos* is not just judgement but is also existence, then it is also *ethos*: not just the opening of the question but the specific and located point of view of the question. The 'there' of existence is never a pure disclosure directed towards an object in general but a *particular comportment*, which establishes a *medium* of existence – a general locale within which the question moves. Heidegger determines this medium as being; and being remains, therefore, as the proper form or site of the question.

What will later be raised by Michel Foucault is the idea of a *historical* a priori: that the medium or ground of the question cannot be interpreted, once and for all, as *being*. Rather, it is the various media within which questions take place that will constitute 'us' as what 'we' are. For Heidegger, against the parochialism of anthropologism we have to think the events that enable us to think of man or, indeed enable us to think. But any thought of this inhuman 'wholly other' will still be *our* thought; to not recognise this would be to fall into anthropomorphism. It follows, then, that metaphysics is not anthropomorphism's pure other; it is, rather, also the *question* of anthropomorphism as a *problem*. Thought begins anthropomorphically by living its world as already present and as bearing its own objectivity, truth and meaning. Metaphysics is only possible by asking how thought is able to find its world as already given, or as already grounded. What makes our world so homely, so human? It is only from the anthropomorphic illusion of an already ordered or meaningful world that we can step back to recognise thought as an ordering power. The continual risk of anthropomorphism is neither to be dismissed nor explained away but confronted as the very possibility of philosophy:

> But what is insidious about anthropomorphism is not that it gauges according to the form of man, but that it thinks this criterion is self-evident and believes its closer determination and formulation to be superfluous. However, the objection to anthropomorphism does this, too, with the sole difference that it rejects this criterion. But neither the proponents of regular anthropomorphism nor its opponents ask the decisive question of whether this criterion is not necessary and why it is so. If the consideration ever gets this far, then one sees that essential questions lie behind the argument, whether anthropomorphism or not, and they belong to a quite different level. (Heidegger 1985: 163)

Heidegger's 'different path' from Kant sets itself against the direction taken by German idealism; and does so by addressing the anthropomorphic illusion. Whereas German idealism seeks the unity that lies beyond Kantian representation in an existing absolute, Heidegger insists that existence is always given through being-in-the-world. In so doing he provides a number of salutary reminders for negotiating the contemporary critical terrain. The value of thinking ethics through (and beyond) Heidegger can perhaps best be seen in the post-Heideggerian engagement with the Kantian legacy. Kant's critical separation of the world in itself from the world *as given* raises the question of the unity from which any such separation takes place. Any such 'ground' that might be uncovered, as Heidegger insists, will always be an event of uncovering. Any theory of being, or positing of the ground, cannot be separated from existence, cannot be taken as an in itself. On the contrary, the 'in itself' of presence derives from revealing. Revealing, furthermore, always *takes place*. *Dasein* is not a thing but is always a located directedness towards, or horizon, for a thing to appear as a thing. No ground of existence can be established as some present, absolute being; for being *is* only in its existence (Heidegger 1992: 158). A gesture to a pre-personal absolute is (as both Kant and Heidegger insisted) a pre-critical anthropomorphism: a forgetting that thought *takes place*. While the position of thought for Kant is the point of view of reason in general, thought's dwelling for Heidegger is a determined and factical 'there', a site that is never given as present, precisely because it is the ground of presencing.

To locate the structures or conditions of thought as a 'logic' outside existence (as transcendentally real) is to forget thought's own contribution. For Kant, therefore, the system philosophy to which he was opposed was the epitome of anthropomorphism. The projection of reason's own strivings onto some external, transcendentally real absolute suffers from the illusion of ascribing thought's own position to being in itself (which is thought of as an absolute beyond all position or viewpoint). For Heidegger, similarly, the drive of system philosophy to think being as a whole beyond its disclosure is to establish a *ratio* as the present ground of being. System philosophy is the culmination of a history of forgetting the disclosure of any *logos*; the will to system is the forgetting of the originary 'there' from which any world (or Being-as-a-whole) takes place. As Heidegger makes clear in his work on Schelling, the thinking of Being-as-a-whole – the anthropomorphic assumption that an absolute answers directly to thought's own endeavours – has moral implications. In system philosophy's thinking of the totality of being, the specific directedness of existence is referred back to some absolute or system. It is in terms of this present system (rather than finite and located existence) that questions of freedom and evil are defined.

Through his reading of Schelling, Heidegger will identify this substitution or 'reversal' of subject and ground as the very possibility of evil. For Heidegger, Descartes's definition of the subject – or ground of thought – as *thought itself* opens the modern history of idealism. (For Descartes, what 'is' is determined by how it is known, looked at or represented; being is brought within the purview of the look, image or idea.) By the time German idealism has responded to Kant, all being will be defined according to the ideal of the subject and this will be an irreducibly anthropomorphic ideal. In this anthropomorphism it is the character of all being to represent itself to itself, to become itself, and to ground itself; thus the free autonomy that Kant attributed to human thought will define being in general. For Schelling all being is a becoming of the ground into existence, and nature is therefore (unlike

Kant) not radically separate from thought. Rather, free and decisive thought is a heightened mode of the becoming of all being: from the divine ground to the blind will of nature. All being is a self-becoming and self-representing. Man is a difference in degree of this general movement of being. What distinguishes man from this general self-representing is the faculty of speech. For it is through speaking that man can take himself as the ground of all becoming; rather than being a moment within a general movement of the absolute *logos*, man can represent himself to himself and thereby take himself as the subject. It is for this reason that man will be located in Schelling's system of becoming as the faculty of good *and* evil. Because man speaks, his self-representation or becoming can take itself as the ground. And it is this reversal, whereby a mode of becoming takes *itself* as the ground, that constitutes evil. For this turns the general and free becoming of being against itself. The position of man is located as the possibility of a decision: either to attend to the absolute ground of divine becoming, or to will itself as evil. Evil is an ontological rather than an ethical problem. It has nothing to do with this or that way of life and morals; it has to do with a formal structure of being in general. Evil is just that human (and anthropological) capacity to take itself as the ground.

From his reading of Schelling as the culmination of modern subjectivism, several implications in Heidegger's thought can be discerned. First is his criticism of Schelling's *question* of anthropomorphism. Heidegger argues that the interpretation of all being as dynamic and willed becoming is anthropomorphic; it takes a feature of man for the understanding of being in general. The real problem lies, however, with the question of anthropomorphism not having been carried far enough. Schelling interprets all being as system: the striving for grounding and self-understanding. And it is from this that Heidegger approvingly echoes the idea that system is not a logic or set of ideas, but the becoming of a historical decision. System is the way in which being discloses itself, and the systems of philosophy are the sites of this general disclosure. Thus the history of philosophical decisions and systems is the history of a ground coming to existence. Man is not an *anthropos* who invents systems; he is the medium through which being *as system* comes to understand itself.

Heidegger's relation to German idealism is, therefore, more than a question of influence or philosophical disagreement. It concerns the status and locus of man and thought. For the German idealist tradition, as Heidegger makes clear, the character of thought – active and decisive becoming – is attributed to all beings. But this active and decisive becoming is located within an absolute and can thus be grounded, or, as in Schelling, be described as good or evil, proper or improper. Against the German idealist will to system and grounding, Heidegger extends system beyond the limit of man, and this is done by questioning what man *is*.

In his description of German idealism, Heidegger brings the difficult status of anthropomorphism to light. What is significant is not that being is determined anthropomorphically, such that being is modelled on the representing nature of man. Rather, the problem of idealism lies in deciding that the human is representational, so that when the world is determined anthropomorphically it is through notions of idea, representation and concept. Heidegger suggests, then, that it is not just a question of deciding between an anthropologism, in which the subject is the site of logic, and an anthropomorphism, in which there is a more general logic of which the subject is an effect. What needs to be done is to rethink logic (*and therefore the human*) – not as a process of representation, knowing or adequate relation of ideas, but as the gathering, dwelling or shining of being.

The *question* of man therefore takes thought beyond both anthropomorphism and anthropologism. Man is not a relation to a ground, such that the ground might be determined independently of the human relation (as in anthropomorphism). Nor is man his own ground, such that we might locate the general site or representational origin of the world in man (as in anthropologism). Both the anthropological and the anthropomorphic, the grounding and the ground, are effected from the givenness of being. Before there is a being to whom the world is given (man) and before there is an absolute that then is given, 'there is' the giving of the given or the grounding of the ground. Any question *of being* begins from the already given, but this question can also take us beyond the already given to the thought of how the given is given. When Heidegger insists that thought is 'initially and for the most part' inauthentic, he recognises that we cannot begin with a 'proper' notion of man or thought (Heidegger 1996: 113). For the notion of man, as such, is both 'thrown' and improper. The idea of a being who represents presupposes a presence to be represented; being has already fallen into representation and subjectivism. But it is only through this anthropo-logical presupposition that the question begins. The beginning or proper is essentially impropriety. This is why Heidegger's ostensibly moral rhetoric of 'authenticity' problematises the possibility of morality. The fall of *logos* into 'logic' is not an unfortunate event of modern system philosophy. The very act of thinking a world takes that world as other than us, as present or as already ordered. If there were not this inauthentic 'having' of a world it would not be possible to ask the (authentic) question that also goes beyond our world. Only after anthropologism can we see the anthropological as the effect of a prior decision. Alongside the possibility that we take our own being not as a power of deciding being but as a being within the world (anthropol-ogism) it is also possible that we project the power of deciding and questioning onto the world itself (anthropomorphism). Because meta-physical questions are possible (because it is possible to ask about the status of *logos* or revealing), it is also possible that a 'logic' might be reified and projected anthropomorphically onto the world in itself. Only by asking the question of man – how is *logos* possible? – can thought be freed of some subjection to a system that is taken as a logic, reified as a ground, or determined as a representational condition.

There are two ways in which the Heideggerian critique of represen-tation might be interpreted and extended. The idea that metaphysics is inaugurated with the forgetting of the question of being seems to demand an act of recall or remembering. Western metaphysics is defined by an increasingly 'mathematical' comportment towards being. It is through the history of thought as representation that being is defined in terms of a logic, ground or system given in advance. This idea of history as an increasing forgetfulness of being seems to suggest both the possibility of a return, and a point or origin to which such a return might orient itself. We could understand the task of Heidegger's *Destruktion* in just such a way: a re-reading of all the definitions of being in order to disclose a more authentic being that has been occluded. And we could also understand Heidegger's critique of modernity and Cartesian rationalism in terms of some more authentic Greek origin. On such a reading Heidegger would be a predominantly nostalgic philosopher. Opposed to all language and thought that is not grounded in the world and the self-aware purposiveness of existence, Heidegger's philosophy might be used as a way of restoring modernity from its fall into representationalism. Just as Husserl had berated modern science and logic for merely repeating symbols in a purely formal manner without any sense of their truth or essential grounding in the revelation of the world (Husserl [1954] 1970: 301–2), so Heidegger might also be aligned with a phenomenological attempt to return to a sphere of 'ownness'. Whatever ground is supposed to underlie thought – whether that be logic, being or consciousness – it is always possible to ask how any such ground is given, and restore that ground to an original grounding. This phenomenological and hermeneutic attempt to return all forms of life to the horizon of consciousness or the life-world has often been used to criticise structuralism and the post-structuralist emphasis on the separation, autonomy and anteriority of system.

The idea of returning language and thought to the horizon of sense and the 'sphere of ownness' marked phenomenology from the outset with an intense commitment to responsibility and an extension of the Kantian critique of anthropologism. 'We' must not understand ourselves as given beings within the world who have ideas or representations in some subjective or mental space. Rather, 'we' are nothing other than the very givenness of the world. This requires us to recognise our being as being-in-the-world; only through such a recognition does thought become responsible. To see thought as grounded in some notion of 'man' is to give up the task of thinking and to forget that any idea of man or being is always an idea, always thought, always ours. It is this emphasis on ownness that characterises the Heideggerian ethics of authenticity and the criticism both of *Gerede* ('idle chatter') and representation (Heidegger 1996: 157). Language is not a repeated and empty system, nor is it an immutable logic or system. Language is nothing other than a comportment, projectedness or dwelling that gives the world.

Heidegger's criticism of representationalist metaphysics does, however, harbour another possibility for interpretation. Upon examination any pre-representational or 'owned' understanding of language is, as Heidegger makes clear, always positively marked by the possibility of its loss. The clearest example of this logic is the relationship between authenticity and inauthenticity as described in *Being and Time*. How is it that *Dasein* exists inauthentically? That is, how is it that *Dasein* understands itself as a thing alongside other things? For Heidegger this inauthentic way of understanding, which might be understood as a form of anthropologism, is no contingent accident. On the contrary, *Dasein* exists inauthentically 'initially and for the most part' *because it can be authentic*. Authenticity lies in a recognition that our world is *our* world; it is only as a totality of projects, purposes, meaning and self-becoming that I have a world. Whatever *is* is given *as* this or that thing according to the projection of my future and the 'having-been' or 'throwness', of my past. My world is always *my* world. To recognise this is to understand oneself, not as a thing within the world who is determined and carried along by history or others, but as one responsible for the world. But how do I recognise this capacity for authentic ownness and responsibility? Only through having been inauthentic. Originally, I live not as a separate subject who then comes to question or know the world but in a *pre-ontological* being-in-the-world. Existence is initially inauthentic because to exist is to be in one's world; and it is in having a world that I think of myself as one being within the world among others (Heidegger 1996: 164). I come to an authentic understanding only by recognising the very structure of inauthenticity (Heidegger 1996: 250). If I ask how it is that I have a world, a world that is so evidently *there*, I recognise the very meaning of the world. Before the world is grasped ontologically – through the question of being in general – it is *lived* as a world.

Thus, authenticity is recognised not just by asking the question of being. Rather, the question must be asked from the recognition that, for the most part, we do *not* ask the question. Before the world is questioned as an object it is lived as a world. The proper question of being recognises the *essential inauthenticity* of being-in-the-world. For the most part we do not ask the question of being in general. When we do come to ask that question we tend to do so in terms of the beings that – like our world – are experienced as simply given things. Thus the 'opening' of the Greek question had already fallen into an element of representationalism and inauthenticity. Being was questioned as though it were some higher being, as though it were a modified version of the beings with which we are pre-ontologically involved. What needs to be understood is the partial grasp of this opening. To ask the question of being in general suggests that we might think the world not just as so many given things, but as the very possibility of givenness. But we foreclose the question by asking it from *within the world*. We have to first recognise our inauthenticity to ask the proper question of being:

what is being such that the question of being is always asked according to some particular being? This then suggests that being is not something to which we can return. It suggests that the question of being is *essentially* ungrounded. To ask the question of being *in general* forgets that the question will always be asked in a certain way. We have to ask the question in an awareness that it is *our* question, from *our* world (Heidegger 1959: 6). To think that being might be questioned in general – as some ground or origin that precedes the world – is to forget the very *event* of the question. The question of being opens the dimension of being, a dimension that might explain not this or that life-world or epoch but the possibility of any possible world. But to grasp that possibility *in general* would be a delusion: an anthropomorphic dream of a point of comprehension beyond the ownness of one's world.

Against a Heideggerianism that would emphasise a ground, dwelling or homeliness that precedes the fall into representation, and against a Heideggerianism that would seek a return to a Greek homeliness with being, it is possible to pursue Heidegger's critique of representationalism as a *felix culpa*. Thus we can only come to understanding who we are by recognising the possibility of misrecognition. We understand language as a logic, system or representational scheme because we do not only *live* language; language is also that to which we 'fall' prey; language can become a logic or system of representation precisely because language is *more* than representation and *more* than mental content. Language has its own being or 'shining'. We can also ask the question of how we speak our world. This is at once the possibility of representationalism and of poetry. Against Kantian formalism and ideas of general structure, Heidegger interprets language as primordially *poetic*. For Heidegger, in poetic language we *see* language again. Language originally discloses the world; it is not a transparent medium but has to do with a directedness to the world, being-in-the-world or comportment (Heidegger 1971: 73). But this event of disclosure, presenc*ing* or 'worlding' is typically forgotten and we accept the world as present, as already there to be re-presented. In poetry, however, language once again becomes responsible. We see language not as an already given representational system imposed on a world, but as an event that enables a world to be:

> What poetry, as illuminating projection, unfolds of unconcealedness
> and projects ahead into the design of the figure, is the Open

which poetry lets happen, and indeed in such a way that only now, in the midst of beings, the Open brings beings to shine and ring out. (Heidegger 1971: 72)

This is not a crude account of language as original naming (for this would imply that there are things that language then labels). In poetry the world is not named or ordered but disclosed: given *as* being in a certain way. In this disclosure both the world and the comportment towards the world are effected or brought about. Poetry brings us back from representational forgetting. It does so by drawing attention to its own status as event. To see language as nothing more than a representation of a present world would be to disown the event or decision of language. At the same time, speech or 'saying' are not located within human minds, for the human is nothing other than an event that emerges from saying:

> *The essential being of language is Saying as Showing.* Its showing character is not based on signs of any kind; rather, all signs arise from a showing within whose realm and for whose purposes they can be signs.
> In view of the structure of Saying, however, we may not consider showing as exclusively, or even decisively, the property of human activity. Self-showing appearance is the mark of the presence and absence of everything that is present, of every kind and rank. Even when Showing is accomplished by our human saying, even then this showing, this pointer, is preceded by an indication that it will let itself be shown. (Heidegger 1982: 123)

What poetry restores, then, is the very possibility of metaphysics and the question. In poetry one sees the world, not as an already given and determined presence; the world is given *as* a world, *as this specifically disclosed world* (Heidegger 1971: 75). What an authentic metaphysics 'adds' to this *originally* poetic disclosure is the recognition that poetics is originary. Metaphysics and poetics are entwined in this production and disclosure of the origin. There is no origin or presence without a poetic act of origination or presentation. A 'fallen' metaphysics takes this presentation as a re-presentation, a mere mimesis of an already given presence. It is only after this fall from *poeisis* into 'logic', however, that *poeisis* and *logos* can be recognised as one. The poetic disclosure of the world is not added on to a world that might be knowable in itself. The world is originated through its disclosure (Heidegger 1971: 39). The *logos* is just this poetic disclosure, returned to itself and dwelling in language.

Heidegger does not just assert the primacy of poetic language over representation. He argues that in order to have representation – a world and its 'picture' – there must have been some *poeisis*, some forming, gathering or unfolding of a world. This makes poetic language appear in some ways as more proper or originary. But the problem is that the very categories of the proper and the originary have been disrupted. If the origin is *poetic* this is to say that at the origin there is a differentiation:

> What is it that the poet reaches? Not mere knowledge. He obtains entrance into the relation of word to thing. This relation is not, however, a connection between the thing that is on one side and the word that is on the other. The word itself is the relation which in each instance retains the thing within itself in such a manner that it 'is' a thing. (Heidegger 1982: 66)

On the one hand, then, Heidegger marks a *return* to *poeisis*, to a point prior to the representational relation between subject and world. (And this would mark Heidegger's politics, where what is asserted is not this or that value but the assertion of the very origination of value: an assertion aware of its world disclosure and grounding rather than its subjective autonomy or representative power.) On the other hand, the displacement of 'logic' by a *logos* at one with *poeisis*, opens the possibility of thinking beyond all judgement, propriety, grounding and origination. For if *logos* is not a logic that relates properly to some world, and if *logos* is a pre-logical relatedness, differentiation or 'gathering' then this means that rather than a return to the origin, *poeisis* will have disrupted the very structure of the origin. It is this second possibility that is pursued and intensified by Jacques Derrida.

3

DERRIDA: RESPONSIBILITY
WITHOUT AUTONOMY

—————

The idea according to which man is the only speaking being, in its traditional form or in its Heideggerian form, seems to me at once undisplaceable and highly problematic. Of course, if one defines language in such a way that it is reserved for what we call man, what is there to say? But if one re-inscribes language in a network of possibilities that do not merely encompass it but mark it irreducible from the inside, everything changes. I am thinking in particular of the mark in general, of the trace, of iterability, of différance. These possibilites or necessities, without which there would be no language, are themselves not only human. (Derrida 1995a: 284–5)

THE PROXIMITY OF OUR WORLD

The recognition of our representational condition, by its own logic, precludes a recognition of our ownness. We know the human can never exhaust who 'we' are, precisely because we are that which defines and gives what it means to be human. The way out of this anthropological limit, for Heidegger, is to think neither in terms of some ground that precedes the human, nor in terms of some human point of view, but to think that clearing, revealing or dwelling which gives the human as human (Heidegger 1998: 244). Heidegger's redefinition of *logos*, as a 'saying-gathering' rather than a 'logic', is a way of rethinking the Kantian representational limit. *Dasein* is not a subject who possesses and commands a transcendental logic, as though logic were some *techne* applied to the world. Nor is *Dasein* a delimited object of logic or *logos*, such that thought might grasp the nature of its own being. The challenge Heidegger presents to system philosophy – against German idealism – lies in the intimate connection between ownness and unhomeliness. There is no pre-human absolute or ground that might be intimated at the limit point of representation, for any ground will always have to be given through 'our' specific comportment, questioning or ground-laying. But the *question* of ground or being, nevertheless, precludes us from fully recognising or owning our already given, present or grounded world.

Thus it is the question of the possibility of presence, or of that which is near to us, that also discloses what resists presentation and ownness. Presence is only given through a presencing, and this presencing must necessarily preclude full self-presence. To be taken as present an object must be set over against us, separate and other. There must be an essential *relation* to presence that is also in part a separation. To think presence representationally is to miss the very character of what it means to have a world. It is not as though there is a presence that is then represented, as though the *relation* to presence were a contingent feature added on to an already formed world. It is the necessary relation to presence that gives the world. Presence is not some external object to be re-presented, but is always given through a totality of comportments and involvements, a relation to a world. But this totality of involvements cannot be objectified as some representational condition that determines beings in advance, for this totality or 'clearing' is not a present origin, system or ground. Thus Heidegger seeks to restore the idea of *logos* to its original meaning of a 'saying-gathering'. *Logos* is not a logic, ratio or system that precedes the specificity of given beings; *logos* is the very event of givenness. Like Hegel before him and post-structuralism after him, Heidegger is determined to resist a reification of *logos* into 'logic,' and he will do this by returning *logos* from its inhuman status as general system to the intentional, lived and meaningful domain of existence. It is in this critique of *logos* as 'logic' that Heidegger resists the idea of representation, the idea that the world is given through some scheme, subjective condition or system. Any representational scheme has its prior grounding in being-in-the-world, comportment or dwelling.

Like Heidegger, Derrida argues that the concept of representation is linked to the Western *logos* and has persistently determined the very character of thought and experience (Derrida 1987a: 366–7). But Derrida is careful with regard to positing a simple 'other' to representation (Derrida 1982b). For there would be several problems with any such outside to the Western *logos*. Indeed, returning *logos* to the proximity of the world or a grounding intention (as does phenomenology) is the 'logocentric' gesture par excellence; it is yet one more attempt to return all thought to a proper origin. Against the *logos* – as being's own becoming – Derrida will assert the radical errancy of the *gramme*, trace, play, or writing. What Western philosophy has not been able to think is not the *question* of being, for the question is still an act or decision of an intending and meaningful relation to the world. Philosophy's unthought is *play*: a movement of syntax or inscription beyond sense, world, the purposive or being.

REPRESENTATION, METAPHYSICS AND NECESSITY

Philosophy, according to Derrida, has always set itself the task of thinking what lies outside thought and has constituted itself through an ideal of including, grasping and comprehending its other (Derrida 1982a: ix). Indeed, this is why Derrida regards the dream of empiricism as crucial to the entire philosophical tradition.[1] On the one hand logocentrism aims at a thorough representationalism; for the *logos* has been defined as the pure self-presence of being to itself, an adequate re-presentation of a presence that can be brought within thought. This *logos* must think what is other than itself – some presence or being – in order to define the *logos* as *grounded* or fully determined by presence. *Logos* cannot be an undetermined play. It must be the comprehension *of* some proper or original ground, a ground that decides in advance the path and coming forth of being to itself. Any appeal to a being or presence beyond thought is both the representational and metaphysical gesture *par excellence*, as well as being a striving to overcome representation. Thought must be a faithful *re*-presentation; at the same time, the separation of representation must be fully returned to, owned by and decided by the origin. Representation must not be seen as the arbitrary, contingent or playful indeterminacy of an ungrounded syntax or writing. For Derrida, the very concept of representation is tied to the project of ontology. For it is the idea of a being that is *then* re-presented that enables the question of being:

> What is it that is decided and maintained in ontology or dialectics throughout all the mutations or revolutions that are entailed? It is precisely the *ontological*: the presumed possibility of a discourse about what is, the deciding and decidable *logos* of or about the *on* (being-present). That which is, the being-present (the matrix-form of substance, of reality, of the oppositions between matter and form, essence and existence, objectivity and subjectivity, etc.) is distinguished from the appearance, the image, the phenomenon, etc., that is, from anything that, presenting it *as* being present, doubles it, represents it, and can therefore replace and de-present it. . . . And obviously, according to a profound synonymy, what is imitated is more real, more essential, more true, etc., than what imitates. (Derrida 1981a: 191)

Derrida's critique of philosophy as logocentrism argues that the project of ontology has always determined thought according to some given presence that thereby grounds a logic. Rather than returning the *logos* from logic to some more proximate site of dwelling or clearing, Derrida will insist on the radically displaced character of what can no longer be thought of as *logos*. For 'it' is no longer some thing, nor some grasping of the thing, but a differential tracing prior to all ideas of being and priority. This is why Derrida gestures to a radical anteriority that *'is not'*. Further, this anteriority is not an origin but an effect of syntax; the anterior is given *as anterior* in a movement of syntax. This syntax is not the expression of being, nor is it the synthesising gathering of a subject (Derrida 1981a: 220). Syntax is that movement that gives space and time; it is *temporalising*, rather than being the unified medium of time. Whereas Heidegger locates this historicising movement in *Dasein*, dwelling, the giving of being or existence, Derrida attempts to think temporalisation through the future anterior as a syntax, as a multiple differential movement that can be neither presented nor conceptualised. This is why the process of describing this movement that is 'not a concept' and 'is not' (Derrida 1982a: 3, 6) cannot take the temporal form of an origin, ground or simple anteriority, but must work with the movement, spacing or tracing that enables temporal logic. *Différance* is neither temporal nor spatial but the differentiating inauguration of the order of time and space. So, to escape the logic of an originary presence that is then represented, it is not adequate to say that this present remains ungraspable or that this present will always elude representation. It is not that being is always concealed in its disclosure; it is not that there is an originary Same that essentially exceeds determination. Rather, the origin and the Same are effected through a non-originary *différance*, tracing, syntax, sending or 'giving'. The task is not to return to a being that effaces itself in presencing, but to think towards a non-presence that disrupts all thought of the origin.

Accordingly, Derrida deploys a host of tactics that trouble the Western *logos*. The first is to use the structures of language to demonstrate that presence is always effected after an event that never *takes place*. The 'there will have been' of the future anterior tense, when used explicitly, exposes the production of presence to be an effect of rhetorical dispersion. What the tradition of ontology and representation has not been able to think has been the event of syntax. And this is because all play, differentiation, becoming or difference has always been understood as being the play or becoming *of* some ground, order or structure. Difference has always been understood as difference-between, or difference-from. The idea of *logos* has been crucial to this taming of difference or becoming; for it is the idea of *logos* that promises some ground, origin, order or system that enables difference to be comprehended.

This idea of *logos* structures all the concepts of metaphysics, including the concept of the concept (Derrida 1995a: 100). Indeed, Derrida argues that concepts are always forms of metaphysical promise. The concept is an idea or promise of meaning. In order for a concept to *mean*, it must function as an ideal content above and beyond its particular instances and its different uses. Indeed, for Derrida, it is the very idea of meaning that inaugurates metaphysics. One can only have a concept or meaning if, above and beyond the specific signifier, trace or token, a sense is sustained and re-presented through time (Derrida 1982a: 51). The idea that difference can be comprehended is the very idea of meaning. Meaning is nothing other than the intention, sense or conceptuality that allows different instances to be recognised as different instances *of*. The very idea of being as that which exists or remains present depends upon the idea of representation. Representation – the idea of a presence or sense that is there to be re-presented – is precisely the idea of meaning – the idea that above and beyond different tokens or signifiers there is a sense or ideal content. In representational logic writing is the vehicle *of* sense, and textuality is the representation *of* meaning. In order to takes signs *as meaningful* – as the sign *of* something beyond the sign – we have already fallen into a representationalism and a metaphysics of presence. The very idea of a concept is metaphysical and representational, for concepts only function in aiming at or intending some ideal and graspable sense that exceeds any particular inscription (Derrida 1988: 116–17).

For Derrida, then, there is a certain *necessity* to the logic of presence and representation (Derrida 1981a: 109). Philosophy's striving for a presence above and beyond the singularity of existence, the striving for a presence that is then re-presented, is not an unfortunate error of Platonism but inaugurates meaning in general. This also means that it can be no simple question of representing or conceptualising the non-meaningful opening of representation or presence. Any attempt to think philosophy's other or the other of representation will, if it is to be meaningful, already partake in the logic of sense that is being delimited.

VIOLENCE AND *LOGOS*

Nevertheless, while Derrida offers a critique of the metaphysics of presence and logocentrism, he is not necessarily offering a criticism. Indeed, at times Derrida argues for the peculiarly ethical function of concepts, the *logos* and the idea of representation. It can be acknowledged that meaning and representation cannot but do violence to otherness or alterity. To represent an other, or to render the other meaningful, is to subordinate the singularity of the other to an ideal of presence. Derrida identifies philosophy as a violent inauguration of meaning, whereby what is presented is always recognised in terms of a reason or *logos* that can comprehend all otherness. The other that is subordinated to the *logos* of sense and recognition can be the other person but it can also be an otherness that exceeds all humanity, sense and consciousness.

According to Derrida there is a connection between 'structuralist' forms of totalitarianism and 'political' forms (Derrida 1978: 57). The subordination of difference to some *logos*, system or ground can be seen as violence in so far as it also closes off the philosophical opening. To include all difference within a structure – whether that be reason, logic, signification or representation – is to forgo the possibility of asking how such structures take place. Thus Derrida defines philosophy, on the one hand, as a form of violence. To subordinate becoming to some grounding concept is to decide in advance and without question what the order of truth will be. Logocentrism is a violence in so far as it sees a ground as present, without asking how this ground is itself presented or grounded. All forms of structuralism that preclude asking the question of the genesis of structure therefore repeat the violence of logocentrism. Similarly, all naive representationalisms that enclose what *is* within what can be represented, close off the question of truth or justification. This is why Derrida so often uses the word 'juridical' to describe the concealed or disavowed decision that grounds any structure. To take a term like context, structure, representation or logic as the final limit of thought is to impose a law on thought.

At the same time, however, that we might identify concepts such as truth, reason, logic or ground as violent forms of closure, Derrida also insists on their ethical function. As *questions* these terms also facilitate an opening of structure. This is what constitutes the very 'ethicity' of the metaphysics of concepts according to Derrida (Derrida 1988: 122). As Derrida had argued in his early essay on the notion of genesis in Husserl, 'Pure truth or the pretension to pure truth is missed in its meaning as soon as one attempts . . . to account for it from within a determined historical totality' (Derrida 1978: 160). Concepts such as truth are incoherent if explained as merely effects of a particular struc- ture. It is the *concept* of truth that aims at a sense that is independent of all structure. Concepts such as truth, reason and logic may always be effected within a particular structure but, once effected, they open the possibility of questioning (or promising) what lies beyond all structure. While these concepts can be seen as violent subordinations of singu- larity and syntactical becoming, they nevertheless avoid a *worse* violence: the violence of remaining within a structure or system *without question*.

It is this essential ambivalence of concepts that Derrida analyses through a radicalisation of the Kantian argument for representational conditions. If something is to be taken *as present* or as empirically real, then it must have been determined, differentiated and given in some

way. The condition for the possibility of presence is, therefore, some
'logic' of differentiation or some 'trace' (Derrida 1982a: 13). However,
the logic that makes any presence *possible*, also renders full presence
impossible. If something *is* only though some process of being given,
then there will always be some excess that is not present. Presence
both relies upon, and is impeded by, its condition of possibility. The
process that gives presence *as presence* is, for Derrida, just that syntax,
movement or tracing which is itself not present. In the case of concepts,
for example, what makes a concept meaningful and possible – its
repeatability and independence from any single speaker – also makes
full meaning and presence impossible; for a concept is just this possibility of further sense and of a presence that exceeds any particular
instance. Through this necessary link between conditions of possibility
and impossibility, Derrida also demonstrates the essential violence
and non-violence of philosophy. Philosophy is the striving for pure
presence. And in this regard philosophy is a form of violence that
represses what lies beyond its own *logos*. But what makes this striving
possible – the concepts of truth, reason and being – also renders philosophy impossible and non-violent. It is because concepts, such as truth,
exceed the closure of any system of logic that philosophy will always
be opened beyond itself. Derrida demonstrates this peculiar violent
anti-violence of philosophy in a number of ways. The most significant,
perhaps, is his critique of structuralism.

POST-STRUCTURALISM

In 'Structure Sign and Play in the Discourse of the Human Sciences'
Derrida describes Lévi-Strauss's idea of the *bricoleur*: one who recognises the groundless nature of concepts but proceeds to use one's conceptual scheme in full recognition of its lack of validity (Derrida 1978:
286). In so doing one refuses to ask the question of the origin of the
structure – the question of genesis – and remains within a structure
with its attendant movement of play, indeterminacy and groundless-
ness. Such a structuralist manoeuvre presents itself as the possibility of
moving beyond metaphysics and beyond representation. Here, one
would accept the play of signifiers without asking the question of the
ground of signification. Rather than seeing signs as representations of
some presence one would recognise signs as effects of a differential

play of signification. From such a position the very ideal of philosophy – the ideal of a truth beyond structure – would be an unfortunate illusion, and one that would be overcome by remaining at the level of structure alone (Derrida 1978: 287). But this idea of remaining within structure, as Derrida points out, would lead to the problem of how one might decide among discourses or competing structures. Further, it would also enclose difference or play *within* structure. It would not ask the question of the origin of this or that structure. It is because of this unquestioned assertion of structure that Lévi-Strauss, according to Derrida, remains thoroughly within the determinations of metaphysics. And this for two reasons. Firstly, by *not* asking the metaphysical question of the origin or genesis of structure, Lévi-Strauss leaves structure as the system that effects play or difference; he *cannot* think a play that is not the play *of* some system, and he cannot think a difference that remains beyond all sense and comprehension. Further, the very idea of the structuralist or *bricoleur* produces a point of view that recognises, and stands in a point of observation to, the limit of structural totalities.

The idea of a decision or point of legitimation that observes structure, that negotiates between structures, and that recognises structure from without is, as Derrida goes on to argue, what underpins the task of the human sciences, and ethnography in particular (Derrida 1978: 282). In order to function as a purely structural discourse and one that would set itself outside the grand claims of the Western *logos*, ethnography must locate itself in the position of one who observes cultural totalities. Not only does the ethnographer, like all human scientists, have to commit himself to the idea of structure as some arbitrary representational overlay (and thereby also commit himself to some pre-cultural nature or pre-structural presence), the ethnographer does not question the position of structure or culture *in general*. For terms like 'structure' and 'culture' that supposedly function to de-centre all notions of ground or presence do so through the idea of some closed totality. What such closed totalities necessarily imply but refuse to thematise is what Derrida refers to as 'the structurality of structure': the origin or genesis of structure (Derrida 1978: 278). It is not enough, then, to remain within a structure without ground; this is only to reverse, but not undermine, the logocentric idea of ground. For concepts like 'culture', Derrida argues, presuppose some pre-cultural nature. It is not sufficient, in challenging metaphysics, to simply assert the lesser or subordinated term, to argue that all nature is effected through culture, representation or structure. One needs to re-figure the very logic of these concepts.

According to this logic of concepts, what is known, understood or meant precedes and grounds the structure of knowing. For Derrida this is what unites the idea of *episteme* and structure (Derrida 1978: 286). Philosophy, Derrida insists, has always tended to a form of structuralism: the attempt to think what is in terms of a logic, system or order (Derrida 1978: 159). Structuralism of the Lévi-Strauss variety differs in its attempt to think a structure that is neither grounded nor centred, a structure that would abandon the metaphysical concepts of presence and ground. But the concept of structure still works to contain play and difference. What is not thought in structuralism is the very becoming of structure, not from some pre-structural presence or ground but as *'genetic* indetermination' (292). This 'genetic indetermination' or 'untamed genesis' would be a becoming, play or differentiation that would not be determined beforehand as the play *of* some logic or structure (Derrida 1978: 292, 156). According to Derrida it is *this* sense of play that remains unthinkable for structuralism. And this is because of structuralism's naive anti-empiricism. On the one hand, structuralism presents itself as the overcoming of empiricism; what is, or presence, is deemed to be effected by structure (Derrida 1978: 288). But this anti-empiricism conceals an unquestioned empiricism, and like all empiricisms this returns structuralism to logocentrism. For what is taken to be present or experienceable is the totality of structure itself. Structuralism commits itself to remaining at the level of structure alone, without positing some origin or ground. In so doing it abandons the metaphysical question of the origin, but does so only by accepting the simple givenness of structured elements – the instances of a language, the occurrences of a myth or the positivity of discourse. And this commitment to the given structure, Derrida insists, also harbours a violence. In staying at the level of structure alone, structuralism must mask, silence or leave implicit what exceeds the structural totality. This violence can only be overcome through the philosophical question of the origin. But Derrida also suggests that the traditionally violent question of the origin that has served to subordinate structure and difference might be asked in a way that is neither structuralist nor genetic, neither a silencing of what exceeds the totality nor a simple assertion of its presence. One might ask what exceeds structure in a properly philosophical manner, but this would also open philosophy to the non-present: a genesis or play that can be neither conceptualised nor represented, but only thought at the limit of structure or logic. Against Lévi-Strauss, Derrida wants to insist that philosophy cannot, and ought not, be dismissed as an illusion. At the same time, a certain interrogation of both philosophy and structure might lead to a new ethics beyond representation. In this case structure would not be, as in Lévi-Strauss, that which precludes us from arriving at a centre or presence, as though structure were a way of knowing or differentiating some pre-structural and *lost* origin. Structuration, 'thought radically', would be that which actively and affirmatively *produces* all forms of origin, centre or presence. For Derrida, '*This affirmation then determines the noncenter otherwise than as loss of the center*':

> There are thus two interpretations of interpretation, of structure, of sign, of play. The one seeks to decipher, dreams of deciphering a truth or an origin which escapes play and the order of the sign, and which lives the necessity of interpretation as an exile. The other, which is no longer turned toward the origin, affirms play and tries to pass beyond man and humanism, the name of man being the name of that being who, throughout the history of metaphysics or of ontotheology – in other words, throughout his entire history – has dreamed of full presence, the reassuring foundation, the origin and the end of play. (Derrida 1978: 292)

At the same time as Derrida aims to think a sense of play that lies beyond structuralism, he also insists that there is a certain *necessity* to the metaphysical question. The idea of an outside to metaphysics is the most metaphysical of notions, for metaphysics has been nothing other than the dream of a pure presence grasped in its independence from all determination, decision and articulation. Further than this, though, metaphysics is also essential to the very logic of meaning and existence. In order to speak or write to an other, what is said must be taken as the sign *of* some sense, intent or meaning; and thus one must presuppose an idea or sense that goes beyond the specificity of the signifier. But this also applies to existence (and this is where Derrida unites the phenomenological notion of 'intentionality' with the intention of meaning [Derrida 1988: 121]). To have the consciousness of an object or existing thing is to be directed towards, or to intend, its presence. Like concepts, objects only *are* if they promise some eventual fulfilment or presence. The question of metaphysics, the question of what *is* and what remains present, is not imposed on speech and experience. *All* meaning is the promise of some intention; all existence is the anticipation of presence. To take the structure of meaning *as nothing more than a structure* is to deny the already-metaphysical nature of meaning and existence. Further, the very functioning of structure relies on the law of a supplement – some point of promised presence that would render any instance of the structure meaningful. This promised presence is given through structuration – it is always expressed or articulated – but it is also a term that seeks to ground structuration. The idea of truth, for example, is at once a term within a language or structure; at the same time, the very *concept* of truth promises what lies beyond the contingency and effects of structure. The supplement is therefore both inside and outside the structure, *and necessarily so.* This logic of the supplement has, unavoidably, always been both raised and tamed by metaphysics.

For Derrida, then, it is not an avoidance of logocentrism but its radical extension that is demanded. A structure has always been centred through some notion of a supplement. In Lévi-Strauss the supplement – the explanatory point of all structure – lies in the argument of incest prohibition (Derrida 1978: 290). Structures of exchange emerge in the passage from the brute immediacy of nature to the meaningful organisation of culture. And this passage is effected through incest prohibition: nature is organised, objectified and structured through lines of kinship exchange that prohibit the free and unbounded fulfilment of desire. The originary division between nature and culture – the birth of structure – is inaugurated by incest prohibition, but incest prohibition can be reduced to neither nature nor culture. It is an idea that explains their division and structure; it is a *concept* that divides nature from culture. Thus the origin of structure is explained through a distinction or structuration: the divide between nature and culture. One term – that of incest prohibition – explains the very birth of all possible terminology. The concept of incest prohibition functions as a supplement: a term that explains the key binary of a system while remaining ambivalently poised on either side of that binary. Neither fully natural nor cultural, incest is that supplement that explains the originary division between nature and culture. Whatever supplement opens a structure (such as the notion of culture, representation, or exchange) is not itself fully reducible to a term within the structure.

From the problematisation of structure, then, Derrida demonstrates the thought of a new mode of question. What one might think is not the genesis *of* structure but 'genetic indetermination' or an 'untamed genesis'. This demands doing something other than ontology and other than epistemology. Rather than seek a being that precedes structure, and rather than define knowledge as the grasping or representation of a presence that is there to be known, the question of the supplement or excess might be thought beyond being and beyond knowledge. It is this possibility that is both opened and closed by the idea of philosophy, but will be pursued by Derrida's deconstruction. Philosophy has always opened any determined structure to the question of its grounding decision or founding event. In this regard metaphysics has an ethical function. At the same time, however, this decision or event has always been defined in terms that are all too human and representationalist. It has always been as though the opening of structure might be understood as a self-present decision that could be located within thought and represented. The subordination of all being to a totality or structure *of reason* disavows the becoming or genesis of reason itself. Only a question of the supplement can open thought to what exceeds structure and logic. This is the non-violent promise of philosophy, albeit one that has always been violently recuperated into a series of groundings.

THE METAPHYSICAL IMPERATIVE

What Derrida criticises in structuralism is a certain violent closure of the question of metaphysics. In the case of Levi-Strauss it is the provisional acceptance of structure, alongside a recognition of the structure's lack of validity, that enables Lévi-Strauss to avoid confronting the *decision* that has opened structure. Now Derrida does not want to question this decision as a present and human intention. On the contrary, he refers to the structural opening as essentially irreducible to the autonomy of human thought, or as 'undecidable'. The division between nature and culture, for example, cannot itself be comprehended by the

explanatory rubric of culture. In any structure there is always a supplement, a term that marks the limit of structure but which is itself
irreducible to structural explanation. In many ways, then, a structure
functions as the effect of a decision; but this decision is the condition
for thought and not an outcome of thought. It is an untamed genesis,
not the efflorescence of consciousness from itself but a division or
differentiation that then enables thought to turn back to itself. We might
think this supplement or decision as radically anterior, pre-human and
non-semantic.

If thought is necessarily thought-*of*, then it must be differentiated
from some thing. In Heideggerian terms we would describe this difference that opens the subject–object distinction as ec-stasis, existence,
transcendence or the 'giving' of being. Derrida, however, uses an
entirely different terminology in order to render this originating difference *multiple*. It is not a difference *of* being, nor a difference *of* the
subject from itself. Rather, Derrida's focus on the supplement, the
trace, *différance* and *gramme* suggests that there is no single modality of
difference, nor a single medium or locus of difference. Textuality, for
example, is a way of thinking differentiation as both prior to thought –
for it takes the form of material tracings such as phonemes, texts, and
marks – as well as being multiple: what 'gives' thought is not a single
being or Same but 'sendings' or syntax. Against the coherence of structure or *logos* Derrida's project of grammatology is the attempt to address
the singularity of events – events of tracing, marking, difference or
writing that are not tracings *of* some presence. The singular event
would be a becoming neither governed by being nor comprehended by
structure.

Thus grammatology indicates the utopian (or impossible) possibility
of a movement beyond ontology, a play not subordinated to logic, a
differential movement beyond point of view, recognition and the
predicament of autonomy. Whereas the thought of *being* provides a
prior ground for the effects of writing, grammatology thinks only the
difference of writing itself. No presence can ground this writing. In the
absence of any such grounding presence, writing itself must be
affirmed and no longer seen as the effect, supplement or representation
of presence:

> There may be a difference still more unthought than the difference
> between Being and beings. We certainly can go further toward

naming it in our language. Beyond Being and beings, this difference, ceaselessly differing from and deferring (itself), would trace
(itself) (by itself) – this *différance* would be the first or last trace if
one could still speak, here, or origin and end.

Such a *différance* would at once, again, give us to think a writing
without presence and without absence, without history, without
cause, without *archia*, without *telos*, a writing that absolutely upsets
all dialectics, all theology, all teleology, all ontology. (Derrida
1982a: 67)

For Derrida, philosophy has not just subordinated or devalued writing
within its conceptual scheme, as though this lesser value attributed to
writing were a bias or prejudice within philosophy. Only with the idea
of writing as representation does the very possibility of philosophy
emerge.[2] The idea that writing is the writing *of* some presence, or that
signification is effected *from* some ground, is not one idea among
others, but the very opening of all ideas and meaning. One needs to
think representation as 'representation *of*' in order to have the very
possibility of sense, presence, meaning and intent. Derrida is often
insistent that such a possibility of meaning and philosophy is neither
lamentable nor avoidable. The possibility of metaphysics – as an idea
of truth, meaning, law or right that precedes representation – does
open thought to what lies beyond any of its present representations.
But this critical dimension of Derrida's thought, a dimension that
acknowledges the limits of representational logic, is set alongside a
more utopian challenge to think beyond representation and concepts.
The affirmative possibility of a grammatology – of a thought beyond
presence and representation – is an extension, rather than a disavowal
of what Derrida refers to as the messianic promise of ideas or concepts.
In this imagined transformation of philosophy beyond ontology, the
promise of concepts – their intention toward a future presence – will
be affirmed, affirmed by thinking the 'perhaps', the 'to-come', the
non-present or 'a spectral messianicity'. If the *gramme*, trace or *écriture*
is not subordinated to being or to an autonomous subject; if contexts,
the proper or presence no longer provide writing with some pre-given
foundation, then the perpetual *possibility* of philosophy will be
heightened.

What Derrida sets against structuralism, then, is the properly
philosophical question of the opening or origin of structure. This is,

then, *more* than structuralism's recognition of the arbitrariness of structure, for it is a question of the specific, singular and decisive opening of this or that structure. It is an attention to the juridical force of any structure. To accept that a structure cannot coherently be centred or grounded – to remain within structure with a full sense of its arbitrariness – is to avoid the question of the *decision* of structure. To speak within a structure is to repeat the decision of a structure. One may not be the author of that structure and so, for Derrida, there is no autonomy. But in so far as one deploys the concepts of a structure one is responsible. Derrida's idea of a 'responsibility without autonomy' is located thoroughly within the antinomy of representation (Derrida 1995a: 261). If thought takes place through representational conditions then it is not at home with itself; its law comes from elsewhere and is non-autonomous. But thought does, nevertheless, repeat the determinate effects of its structural or representational condition. Thought may not decide or govern the decisive force of its structure, but it does have such a force – the force of a law. It is through this force of a structure that is not its own that thought is nevertheless responsible. This responsibility is disclaimed by any structuralism that refuses to question the *decision* of structure. And this is why responsibility, thought through deconstruction, is always *excessive*; it cannot be contained within the present, the known, the subject or the human (Derrida 1995a: 286).

The refusal of responsibility has been, since Hegel, identified as the hallmark of 'mathematical' or representationalist thought. It makes no sense to accept language, logic or representation as a simple medium or organon through which thought arrives at presence. This would be the anthropologistic illusion: that thought is a thing to be known and accepted as given. For thought is not an inert and given thing but the decisive force that renders any thing possible. It makes no sense, then, to accept the structural conditions of any thought as simple givens, for structurality is a specific event.

This is where Derrida's thought also breaks from phenomenological accounts of the genesis of structure. Once again, the issue is one of responsibility. Phenomenology opens as the very project of responsibility; logic must not be accepted as a given system but must be grounded in the activity of consciousness. Even the late phenomenology of Merleau-Ponty and Heidegger sustains this emphasis on responsibility. All being, existence, space and world depend, for Merleau-Ponty, on the comportment of the body. While Merleau-Ponty sees existence or the givenness of the world as extending beyond the domain of consciousness, his phenomenology is one of a world disclosed from a point of view. Point of view, now, is not reducible to the mind of the subject but entails her entire physicality, movement, imaginary and desire.[3] Heidegger will also criticise the language of consciousness but will nevertheless be critical of any mathematical or representationalist idea that there simply 'are' systems of meaning or conditions through which the world is given. In this regard we can see the phenomenological tradition as the very antithesis of structuralism; and this antithetical attitude is intensified with phenomenology's own criticism of Husserl's notion of consciousness. Against the idea of a transcendental logic, Husserl argued that all logic was originally grounded in an experiencing subject, a subject who constitutes the essences that are then formalised in logic (Husserl 1929). Against Husserl, both Heidegger and Merleau-Ponty criticised the extent to which Husserl did not ask about how consciousness itself came into being. Merleau-Ponty explains the genesis of consciousness through the comportment of the body. Heidegger's notion of comportment or *Verhalten* places the opening of being or the world in the temporal movement of ec-stasis, while his later thought is less human in its attempt to think the sending of being. In all cases, though, what Husserl, Merleau-Ponty and Heidegger will criticise in the notion of logic, structure or representation is *a passive acceptance of system*. The question of genesis is the opening of responsibility. It is the question of how any logic, system, or ground of logic is itself decided upon, given or determined. Phenomenology thereby sustains the enlightenment opening of representation; no representation ought to be accepted as a given law, for it is always possible to ask the question of *who* or *what* represents. It is the idea of representational conditions, or the question of the genesis of representation, that opens any given representation.

However, as Derrida's critiques continue to demonstrate, this opening is belied the minute any genesis is explained as a grounding presence. Terms like perception, consciousness and being *locate* and determine the opening of thought. To this problem there are two responses. The first is to sustain a continual critique; any question of how a logic or system is grounded or opened will take place from some higher order ground. This is the continual vigilance against anthropologism. Thus

Husserl criticises Kant for assuming that transcendental logic (and the subject) simply *are*. Husserl will respond with the question of the genesis of logic in the consciousness of a temporal subject: how does the transcendentally judging subject come to be formed? Husserl will thereby step back from the transcendental subject of logic and locate this logic within the experience and acts of consciousness and its self-production through time. Heidegger will respond to Husserl by arguing that time cannot be located within consciousness; rather the coming into being of consciousness presupposes time. Consciousness is already a temporal and spatial notion. Merleau-Ponty will then locate temporal becoming within the lived existence of bodily comportment. In all cases – from Kant to Husserl, Husserl to Heidegger, and Heidegger to Merleau-Ponty – what is taken as the ground of the world is subsequently criticised as being one more thing within the world, already grounded by a more radical origin. This form and tradition of critique is radically anti-anthropologistic. Whatever is first offered as the ground of thought is subsequently seen as too reified or too intra-worldly. Rather than think the subject we need to think the consciousness that constitutes any subjectivity; rather than think consciousness we need to think the existence that opens consciousness. And we could see Derrida in this line of critique. Against Heidegger's sending of being, Derrida will offer the sendings of the *gramme* or trace. Derrida also, however, seems to be attempting a more radical response. Rather than moving the act of transcendental grounding back ever further to some ever receding point of responsibility, Derrida will use this logocentric procedure to think beyond logocentrism.

THE AVOIDANCE OF *LOGOS*

In *Of Spirit* Derrida discusses Heidegger's attempt to overcome a history of metaphysics, a metaphysics that has always been determined by some fundamental or grounding concept of subjectivity or spirit. Initially, Derrida argues, Heidegger *avoids* using the word 'spirit' in *Being and Time*, for two reasons. Firstly, as used in German philosophy (particularly Hegel), the idea of spirit has always grounded or located being as presence *within thought*. Spirit itself is not questioned, but organises a philosophical system. So, for Heidegger, spirit would be one more *ontic* determination of the *ontological* question. (A particular being, such as spirit, answers the question of being in general.) Secondly, according to Heidegger, spirit is connected with a 'vulgar' or fallen concept of time. According to this vulgar or fallen account, there are two forms of presence – spirit and being – that are then related or come to know each other through time. It is as though being already exists and only passes through time to become known by spirit. For Hegel, this history or temporal passage of spirit's encounter with being is a necessary fall, whereby being appears as opposed to spirit. But this fall is overcome when spirit realises that this separation between spirit and being is an effect of spirit *positing* some separate being, an effect of separating itself *through time*. So, for Hegel, the end of philosophy is the end of history. It is the point at which spirit realises that being is spirit's own temporal becoming; and so time is subordinated to being the mere vehicle for the recognition of being and spirit (Heidegger 1988: 145). In Hegel's absolute idealism, spirit realises that what *appeared as* another presence was nothing other than the self-presentation of spirit. Heidegger argues that this theory of spirit accepts too readily the *presence* of spirit (and locates time as secondary). For Heidegger, however, there could be no spirit (no presentation) without time: time is not something *within which* presences come to appear. Presence is nothing other than the coming-to-presence of time. Heidegger will therefore avoid terms like spirit precisely because they have been understood as forms of presence that ground time. Instead, Heidegger will aim at terms like *Dasein*, for *Dasein* is nothing other than its temporal becoming.

Derrida, however, argues that Heidegger cannot simply *avoid* or overcome the metaphysics of presence: and this impossibility of avoidance is revealed in Heidegger's use of the word spirit in his later work. Heidegger tries to free the word from its fallen (or subjectivist) connotations by relating spirit back to the original thinking of the Greeks. The Greeks, Heidegger argues, thought of being as presence, as revealing, as the truth of unveiling, as something to be thought, and *not* as a representation, idea or substance. From this, Heidegger argues that spirit, *thought properly*, should not be a self-present substance, but a historical projection, an authentic possibility. Rather than positing a separate human substance that then encounters being, spirit should be thought as the temporal being-in-the-world of *Dasein*.

But, Derrida argues, despite Heidegger's attempts *not* to determine

Dasein as a type of substance, and despite his attempts to see *Dasein* as pure possibility, Heidegger cannot but determine *Dasein* as a form of human spirit. This is revealed, Derrida argues, in Heidegger's claim that only *Dasein* 'has a world' and that the animal has no world. Here, according to Derrida, Heidegger reveals a certain determination of *Dasein as human*. In so doing Heidegger delimits *Dasein* as a type of being, a being who has history. Further, Derrida argues that this anthropologism is not an error on Heidegger's part. Any metaphysical or ontological question cannot *avoid* the 'doubling' of spirit. It cannot avoid *determining* the ground of determination as this or that determined thing. Heidegger's *question* of being manifestly refuses any *ontic* determination; but in so doing it has to constitute some *non*-ontic 'double', 'ghost', spirit or spectre which *can only ever be defined against any specific ontic determination*. (That is, metaphysics must at once *not* be reducible to any particular being; it must be ideal, pure, above being, or 'spectral'. At the same time this pure and ideal metaphysics is haunted by all those determined or ontic figures it must employ to represent this spectrality. Philosophy is haunted by that which refuses to be *purely* ideal. Philosophy is never quite ghostly enough.) It is this 'haunting' or 'doubling' in metaphysics by various notions of spirit, mind, subject or consciousness that Heidegger's anti-anthropologism sought to *avoid*. But for Derrida these 'specters' are constituted through such avoidance. In an attempt to think being *without* reducing it to the ontic, metaphysics inaugurates a certain spectrality or haunting. For Derrida, the history of metaphysics has been nothing other than an attempt to free the presencing of being from any specific, particular, worldly, determined or ontic being. Heidegger's project of *Destruktion*, which attempts to suspend the language of metaphysical subjectivism, seeks a 'proper' determination of being. This proper way of thinking will retrieve the *logos* from subjectivism, logic and representationalism and return it to the original saying-gathering of the *logos* as dwelling, proximity or comportment.

Derrida, on the other hand, argues that metaphysics is always a logocentrism. Metaphysics is essentially juridical, effected through a decision or division as to what counts as the proper. There can be no pure origin or being prior to all representation, and in this regard we might see Derrida's critique of Hegel and Heidegger as a Kantian and critical reminder: whatever is offered as a being beyond all ontic determination will always be contaminated or haunted by its ontic articulation.[4] Further, metaphysics is a *double* haunting. Any gesture to a grounding presence or essence requires the *seemingly* inessential vehicle or supplement of representation. Not only is any presence or origin haunted by the difference that renders the thought of the origin possible, any concept of difference, tracing or the *gramme* has also been haunted by the *concept* of difference: the reduction of difference to an origin. There will always be a certain metaphysical *haunting* whereby what *is* is doubled by the thought of its ground or origin. There can be no post-metaphysical overcoming of all thought of presence, the proper, ground or origin. There can be no purely empirical grasp of being, for the empirical is always haunted by the *concept* of the empirical. There is an essential conceptual determination in any thought of the non-conceptual. This suggests, in the manner of Kant, a *necessary* separation of thought from being. One cannot be at one with being itself, but must always determine being in some way. Any *thought* of being will be a concept or determination; and it this separation, or representation, of the non-conceptual that renders us responsible. This separation cannot be overcome through a more authentic dwelling or proximity. Rather, what needs to be affirmed, according to Derrida, is that trait, trace or syntax that renders the separation possible (Derrida 1995a: 274).

We have already seen that Derrida offers a somewhat phenomenological response to structuralism. It is not enough to accept a system of signs, or any totality, as simply given. Reason cannot be located within structures but enables the thought of the validity or decision of structure. Indeed, structuralism would be one more anthropologism – the location of the condition of the world within the world. In response to this, however, Derrida does not offer a prior ground or presence from which structure is derived. Neither consciousness, nor time, nor being can be coherently located in a point of responsibility beyond all structuration: 'For what is put into question is precisely the quest for a rightful beginning, an absolute point of departure, a principal responsibility' (Derrida 1982a: 6). But Derrida is also aware of Heidegger's sensitivity to this problem. Indeed Heidegger seems to offer a manoeuvre that is the antithesis of structuralism, while also recognising the difficulty of offering some pre-representational presence or origin. For any such term – including 'being' – would always run the risk of functioning as yet one more unquestioned presence. Heidegger's strategy is therefore neither critique nor unquestioning inhabitation. Rather, Heidegger will attempt to return certain concepts and terms to their original moment of decision. ('*Logos*', for example, is originally a saying-gathering that will later be misrecognised as 'logic'.) According to Derrida this Heideggerian 'etymologism' is yet one more instance of the avoidance of the *gramme* or trace. For Heidegger will attempt to *return* disowned concepts to their point of decision and responsibility, their emergence in the time of a philosophical event or an event of being. What Heidegger will not consider is that perhaps any medium to which thought might be returned will be the effect of a random, accidental, pre-human and undecidable textual accident.

Heidegger's *Destruktion* will be guided by thought's origin and proper home (its Greek home), for Heidegger will avoid the possibility of a language that runs awry and that cannot be housed within the Greek origin. For Derrida this can be seen most clearly in Heidegger's engagement with the language of the metaphysical tradition. Whereas Lévi-Strauss will deploy a structure of concepts with a suspension of the question of validity, Heidegger will be thoroughly aware of the *decision* of concepts. Indeed this is the rationale behind Heidegger's acute attention to etymology. To speak the language of metaphysics is to already determine being in a certain way; it is to partake in a decision. At the same time, for Heidegger, this tradition is also thought's only home. Rather than accept this tradition uncritically, and rather than objectify the tradition as though one might step outside it, Heidegger's *Destruktion* involves a certain *avoidance*. On the one hand certain terms – such as consciousness, spirit or mind – are too representationalist and ought to be avoided. Such terms serve to close off the question of being, a question that is only possible if one returns to a proper sense of *logos*. On the other hand, even the original articulation of being has already been contaminated by a certain subjectivism and representationalism. It is the very character of being, as presencing, to be determined as presence, and thereby to conceal or veil its coming to presence. Indeed if being is always revealed *as* being in a certain way, then it will always be threatened by an ossification into representation. This is why Heidegger will ultimately place the word 'being' under erasure. For any determination of being will already have forgotten the *being* of being. Once taken *as present*, the sending, presencing or giving of being is already belied. In a move that directly opposes the representationalist or structuralist acceptance of a system of terms,

Heidegger will place the language of metaphysics under erasure, aware of its contamination, decision and essential forgetting.

For Derrida this Heideggerian strategy of erasure and avoidance raises a problem of responsibility, and the location of responsibility. Heidegger's thought offers itself as a path or journey which returns language to the opening of the *question*. In so doing it leaves other paths untraversed (paths that Derrida argues 'lead to another strategy and another stratigraphy' [1989: 132]). To open this new 'stratigraphy' – that is, a strategy no longer returned to a human decision but thought in terms that are *'purely graphic'* (Derrida 1982a: 3) or textual[5] – Derrida focuses on Heidegger's attempt to avoid, or lead thought beyond, the corrupted language of metaphysics. As an example, Derrida cites Heidegger's remark that an animal 'has' no world. In order for Heidegger to make this claim he has to already speak from the position of *Dasein*, the position of having a world. And this raises the problem of the limits of speaking. If our way of understanding is worldly, and if to speak is to have a world, how do we speak about a being who has no world? The only recourse is to speak with a proviso, parenthesis or caveat around our concepts. We have to talk about the animal's 'world' in order to argue for the animal not 'having' a world. Heidegger's claim that only *Dasein has* a world relies upon an understanding of the non-worldly being of the animal, but it can only do so from its own position of worldliness. Aware of this problem, which is the problem of our metaphysical concepts in general, Heidegger attempts to mark a distance, bracketing or avoidance of certain concepts.

Heidegger's suspension or erasure of metaphysical concepts such as 'being' or 'spirit' is an attempt to arrive at a point uncontaminated by representationalism, at the *proper* path of thinking. It is this proper path that Heidegger identifies as the path of the question: a path that is characterised by an active and authentic saying and by a refusal to accept any given conceptual scheme that is not grounded in the self-becoming of *Dasein*. According to Derrida, this intense focus on the 'piety of the question' in Heidegger is what drives Heidegger to move beyond the given concepts of a language to seek the proper saying of the question. For Derrida, this distinction between a given language and an active saying marks 'the remnant of *Aufklärung* which still slumber[s] in the privilege of the question' (Derrida 1989: 131).

For Heidegger an authentic approach to the question must 'erase' subjectivist concepts and return to the proper path of thinking. One

would need to avoid certain concepts in so far as they corrupt, conta-
minate, or depart from the nearness of being. Such a suspension or
avoidance might, Derrida suggests – perhaps no less than structuralism
– be thought of as *evil*. And this evil would take place in the name of
being, for Heidegger's *question* that enables a point beyond logic, representation and 'spirit' would perhaps, like the animal, *have no world*. It
would be the passive, near, immediate and unseparated 'letting itself
be said'. It is as though, for Heidegger, being might properly speak
itself without the corruption or contamination of representation. Derrida
contemplates this possibility of a nearness to being that would avoid
the corruption and separation of representation:

> Pause for a moment: to dream of what the Heideggerian corpus
> would look like the day when, with all the application and con-
> sistency required, the operations prescribed by him at one moment
> or another would indeed have been carried out: 'avoid' the word
> 'spirit,' at the very least place it in quotation marks, then cross
> through all the names referring to the world whenever one is
> speaking of something which, like the animal, has no *Dasein*, and
> therefore no or only a little world, then place the word 'Being'
> everywhere under a cross, and finally cross through without a
> cross all the question marks when it's a question of language, i.e.,
> indirectly, of everything, etc. One can imagine the surface of a text
> given over to the gnawing, ruminant, and silent voracity of such
> an animal-machine and its implacable 'logic.' This would not only
> be simply 'without spirit,' but a figure of evil. (Derrida 1989: 134)

What does Derrida mean when he refers to evil here? A machine with
no intent, no decision: not the separation of a judging and responsible
subject but an 'implacable "logic"'. Derrida takes Heidegger's own
definition of evil from the lecture course on Schelling (Heidegger 1985),
where evil is defined as the one of the system's effects – the human
– taking over or grounding the system in general. But Derrida turns
this definition of evil against Heidegger's notion of the *proper* path of
thought. Heidegger's logic of erasure, avoidance and 'crossing through'
is a 'figure of evil' precisely because it is the figure of a language that
could speak itself without the responsibility or limitation of concepts, a
language of an 'animal-machine'. Derrida's use of 'evil', like his use of

'violence', is insistently anti-dichotomous. Words like 'violence' and 'evil' describe the *necessary* contamination of all thought, and cannot be isolated as moral events that befall an otherwise 'proper' thinking. The use of a concept for Derrida is always improper; it cannot be returned to its faithful home. To conceptualise or speak is to already depart from any presence; it is a movement of infidelity, contamination and corruption. There can be no good representation, no pure and proper concept, no non-violent saying that would be at home with its ground. Evil and violence cannot be located on one side or other of the representational antinomy, and this explains Derrida's critique of both representationalism and anti-representationalism.

The questions and anxieties surrounding representation constitute a powerful moral axiology. In enlightenment terms, human reason can only delude itself through representation. It is when representations become disembodied, dehumanised, reified or institutionalised that human freedom becomes subordinated to an imposed form. (This is also how Derrida understands the 'Platonic' denigration of writing; for it is in the separation of text that meaning can be divided from its home, proper context or expressing subject.) At the same time as Western logocentrism has harboured an anxiety regarding the separation of representation, ethics has also been consistently identified with representation: the capacity for moral agents to express themselves faithfully or authentically. Heidegger's reading of Schelling had already problematised this association between the separation of a *logos* from its ground and moral evil. For Heidegger (reading through Schelling) the very possibility of human freedom *is* the separation of *logos*. Difference is not an accident or corruption that befalls identity and sameness, the same is given *as same* only through differentiation. For Heidegger, the limitation of German idealism lay in its moral and anthropomorphic rhetoric for expressing this logic. Perhaps it is not the human or the 'ego-logical' that differentiates *from* some presence; perhaps presencing is just this differentiation of being in general. Derrida extends this critique of anthropomorphism against Heidegger's own thought of the *logos*. Wouldn't the idea of being's *own* rhetoric – a rhetoric that did not *own* its separation from the ground but attempted to be at one with the ground – be the very 'figure of evil'? Rather than seek, as Heidegger seems to do, a way of speaking that is proximate to being's own presencing, Derrida recognises a certain necessity to the

violence and evil of concepts. In so doing 'violence' and 'evil' are dislocated from the moral axiology of representation and anti-representation.
All concepts are violent – precisely because they must exclude and
limit the singularity of any event. The very structure of meaning is evil:
to represent is *of necessity* to partake in a system beyond the purity of
intent or the singularity of a self-present sense. Rather than seek a pure
representation – a representation at home with its ground – Derrida
will demonstrate that the very possibility of representation is *misrepresentation*. The very possibility of ethics is a certain infidelity. Only by
being differentiated, separated and divided can an utterance be taken as
a representation *of* some presence. The condition of a grounding
presence is the separation from presence. And this also means that any
act of ethical responsibility is also, and necessarily, an act of irresponsibility. To respond to an other involves a decision, a decision that can
never be at home with, or adequate to, all alterity (Derrida 1995b: 77).
There cannot be a good decision on the one hand set over against the
possibility of evil; all speaking, deciding and existing is radically
involved in an economy of loss, difference and decision which cannot
be contained within the good intent of a moral subject. Evil is not an
accident that befalls a proper and ordered world of presence; the
very possibility of existence and of subjectivity is just this 'gnawing,
ruminant, and silent voracity' of a pre-human 'machine'.

Evil is figured by Derrida in a thoroughly ambivalent manner, as an
animal that chews away at a system or world – without any *sense* of
that system. (For, as we recall, an animal has no world.) So, against the
violence of structural totalitarianism and against the violence of a pure
point beyond structure, Derrida describes an evil that is *neither* inside
nor outside *logos*. This evil would possess another logic, a logic beyond
the boundary between good and evil. It would be an evil that gnaws
with a 'silent voracity'. At the limit of the Heideggerian text Derrida
discerns the possibility of his own project – a writing or 'stratigraphy'
not subordinated to the moralism of the proper. To consider texts for
their *positive effects* – what they *do* rather than what they *represent* –
would *open* the grammatological question of the determination or
inscription of values. The idea of an 'animal-machine', writing or
'stratigraphy' would free thought from the ground of the good and
the proper and open the question of textuality – all those effects that
produce the good and the proper.

Despite Heidegger's overwhelming insistence on 'the proper of man' and man's *own* responsibility, Derrida argues that Heidegger's later turn to the piety of a *listening* over saying opens the question of 'the very origin of responsibility' (Derrida 1989: 132). Having put the *question* forward as thinking's proper path, Heidegger will later 'cross through' the question marks that he had earlier used to suspend the traditional concepts of being. For Derrida this opens an entirely new possibility for metaphysics. Heidegger's first strategy – to think beyond the signs of metaphysics by placing question marks after certain concepts – depends upon locating the event of a question prior to all representation. But Heidegger later questions these question marks. This suggests that there might *not* be a point of autonomous responsibility or saying beyond language. This suggests that ethics might not just be the enlightenment manoeuvre of the knowledgeable decision, and that we might consider that which effects thought beyond all thought. This suggests that ethics might be the affirmation of the 'always anterior concern of this appeal addressed to us' (Derrida 1989: 135). In contradistinction to Heidegger's *proper* path and call to man (135) Derrida isolates the possibility of 'another stratigraphy'. In this thought of an appeal that cannot be reduced to an active saying or 'zero point' of a recommencement, Derrida will argue, following Heidegger, that the *being* of language is such that it displaces the very logic of being:

> The 'letting itself be said' which urges the crossing through of the question mark is not a passive docility, much less an uncritical compliance. But no more is it a negative activity busy submitting everything to a denial that crosses through [*une dénegation raturante*]. It subscribes. Before us, before everything, it inscribes the question, negation or denial, it en-gages them without limits in the correspondence with *langue* or *parole* (*Sprache*). *Parole* must *first* pray, address itself to us: put in us its trust, its confidence, depend on us, and even have *already* done it (*muss sich die Sprache zuvor uns zusagen oder gar schon zugesagt haben*). The *already* is essential here, saying something of the essence of this *parole* and of what en-gages in it. At the moment when, in the present, it entrusts or addresses itself to us, it has *already* done so, and this past never returns, never again becomes present, it always goes back to an

older event which will already have engaged us in this subscribing to the en-gage. (Derrida 1989: 135)

In his reading of Heidegger and the critique of phenomenology's return to a sphere of ownness, givenness and responsibility, Derrida formulates a new question of the ethics of metaphysics. If thinking does not have a proper path, then representation cannot be seen as a sepa-ration *from* some prior presence. Indeed, the idea of re-presentation would have to be challenged in Derrida's 'other logic'. Rather than an origin and its subsequent dissemination, Derrida asks that we think a writing, *gramme*, text, tracing or trait that does not *take place* from a proper point and does not *precede* a representation. Rather than a *Dasein* that discloses the world to itself or a spirit that returns to its origin of self-understanding, Derrida suggests etymologies that cannot be reduced to the intention or self-revelation of the subject. Rather than offer a more proper word for spirit (such as *Dasein*) Derrida explores all those words that exceed Heidegger's tracing of *logos* back to its Greek home. In fact, it is on the issue of 'logic' that Derrida challenges Heidegger's privileging of the German language as the ety-mological site of thinking and being. Can a logic – truth in general – be housed in a delimited language, such as the tradition that runs from Greek to Latin to German? (Derrida 1989: 68). How is it *decided* that being is housed in the human? Who decides on the border or limit of the human? And can these decisions be grounded in a logic?

REPRESENTATION

There can, for Derrida, be no simple overcoming of the language of representation. Heidegger's *Destruktion* attempts to think being and metaphysics through a different way of speaking – through the near-ness of poetic thought or saying. Derrida's deconstruction argues that any act of meaning or language will necessarily be separated from what it intends. Rather than find a new way of speaking or *logos* that is *closer* to being, Derrida's deconstruction is an attempt to think the necessary gap, difference or distance that enables the project of meta-physics to emerge. There is not, he argues, a presence that falls into representation. Rather, representation is the necessary effect of a number of sendings, departures, differentiations or traces. If it is possible for representation to befall presence, then presence must already bear the mark of this possibility. If being comes to be represented, then representation cannot be a secondary accident. The Greek world may not have had a word for representation, but its *possibility* was already within Greek philosophy:

[A] criticism or a deconstruction of representation would remain feeble, vain, and irrelevant if it were to lead to some rehabilitation of immediacy, of original simplicity, of presence without repetition or delegation, if it were to induce a criticism of calculable objectivity, of criticism, of science, of technique, or of political representation. . . . The advent of representation must have been prepared, prescribed, announced from far off, emitted, I will say signalled at a distance in a world, the Greek world, where, however, representation, the *Vorstellung* or the *Vorgestelltheit des Seienden* had no dominion. (Derrida 1982b: 311)

This illustrates the 'double bind' of Derrida's philosophy. In arguing that the Greeks did not conceive the world in terms of representation, we have already determined their world as *a different representation* of being or presence. This is an instance of the general double bind of all attempts to consider thought in general: one can only gesture to another way of thinking by way of one's own way of thinking. To describe a world as pre-representational is to already determine it in terms of representation. Unlike Heidegger, Derrida does not see representation as a delimitable accident within a specific epoch. Whereas Heidegger argues that being is primordially a 'sending' of presence into history and not a presence that is then re-presented, Derrida argues that any thought of a pre-representational 'origin' – or an origin at all – itself partakes in the logic of representation. To determine an origin *as an origin* requires that the original term be set against its subsequent translations, departures and derivatives. The origin is already within representation, already the origin *of* its later determinants. There could be no *faithful translation* of the Greek origin. All translation necessarily falls into representation: 'Neither *Vorstellung* nor *repraesentatio* would be able to translate a Greek thought without diverting it elsewhere, which, moreover, all translation does' (Derrida 1982b: 315).

Derrida's project of seeing the origin as already divided by representation is a further radicalisation of Husserl's theory of intentionality and the disruption of presence. If consciousness is always 'consciousness of', or if consciousness is always an intention or a going beyond itself, then consciousness will never be self-present and will never be able to coincide with or comprehend what it intends. It is from this Husserlian insight that Heidegger concludes that any posited being will at once be a concealing and a revealing. But Derrida extends this even further, beyond a rhetoric of concealing, revealing and presencing. Rather than Heidegger's origin of a sending that then falls into the separation of representation, Derrida argues for a *multiplicity* of 'sendings' (or differentiations). It is this multiplicity of 'envoi' that then constitutes the origin through division, separation and re-presentation. These sendings or 'envois' are necessarily divided from themselves and cannot be comprehended or gathered together:

> Beyond a closure of representation whose form could no longer be linear, indivisible, circular, encyclopedic, or totalizing, I have tried to retrace a path opened on a thought of the *envoi* which, while (like the *Geschick des Seins* of which Heidegger speaks) of a structure as yet innocent of representation, did not as yet gather itself to itself as an *envoi* of being through *Anwesenheit*, presence and then representation. This *envoi* is as it were pre-ontological, because it does not gather itself together or because it gathers itself only in dividing itself, in differentiating itself, because it is not original or originally a sending-from (*envoi-de*) (the *envoi* of something-that-is or of a present which would precede it, still less of a subject, or of an object by and for a subject), because it is not single and does not begin with itself although nothing present precedes it; and it issues forth only in already sending back: it issues forth only on the basis of the other, the other in itself without itself. Everything begins by referring back (*par le renvoi*), that is to say, does not begin; and once this breaking open or this partition divides, from the very start, every *renvoi*, there is not a single *renvoi* but from then on, always, a multiplicity of *renvois*, so many different traces referring back to other traces and to traces of others. (Derrida 1982b: 324)

LITERARY EXCESS

All this would seem to suggest that Derrida is a primarily *critical* philosopher. There could be no point beyond or outside of the metaphysics of representation, for the very predicament of meaning demands that one accede to some representational system, some separation from presence. However, while Derrida does argue for a certain metaphysical complicity in any simple critique of representation, there is also an apocalyptic, messianic and reformist aspect of his work that suggests that philosophy might be otherwise. This would not be a metaphysics thought *more properly*, but would be a future-oriented metaphysics of the 'perhaps'. While much of Derrida's work on philosophical texts is *critical* – demonstrating the production of the pre-rhetorical origin through rhetoric, or presence through representation – there is also an appeal in his work to another logic and a philosophy to come. In addition to the idea of a non-presence or non-origin that can only be thought after the event, Derrida also suggests that we can do more than think the effect of presence from our current grammatical and rhetorical structures. His work on Mallarmé is exemplary on this point as it renders explicit the idea of *gramme* or trace.

For Derrida, the concept of representation is inextricably intertwined with the logocentric idea of meaning and ideality: the idea that writing is a detour or vehicle for a sense that can be rendered present. Writing has always been defined through a representational logic of mimesis: as a mirror, repetition or double of some present origin or founding sense. However, to counter this logocentrism it is not sufficient to celebrate literature over philosophy. If one were to say, à la Richard Rorty (1982), that philosophy is really a form of literature, a forceful utterance that has forgotten its textual, rhetorical and fictive nature, then one has still left the structure of truth in place. One has merely celebrated the other side of the binary. Derrida, on the other hand, suggests that literature be rethought beyond the binary of presence and representation. One must see the text not as subordinate to some meaning or sense, and not as the vehicle of ideality. Further, one would not locate the differential, unfounded, dispersed and multiple features of textuality in writing alone – as though textuality were some inescapable condition imposed on a pre-textual being or world. One might think the textual and the differential as more than effects or supplements. This would demand attention to the non-semantic dimension of writing, where writing works as affect, as force and as production rather than replication. A certain form of literature presents us with this 'lustre' of the text (Derrida 1981a: 194). Here, writing does not unveil or disclose meaning but 'is'. But if it is writing that *is*, then this troubles the very word 'is'. For writing 'is not'; it is perpetual difference and non-presence. It does not ground itself on some being. In *not* being representational, writing would disrupt the very project of ontology:

> The operation, which no longer belongs to the system of truth, does not manifest, produce, or unveil any presence; nor does it constitute any conformity, resemblance, or adequation between a presence and a representation. And yet this operation is not a unified entity but the manifold play of a scene that, illustrating nothing – neither word nor deed – beyond itself, illustrates nothing. Nothing but the many-faceted multiplicity of a lustre which itself is nothing beyond its own fragmented light. Nothing but the idea which is nothing. The ideality of the idea is here for Mallarmé the still metaphysical name that is still necessary in order to mark non-being, the nonreal, the nonpresent. The mark points, alludes without breaking the glass, to the beyond of being-ness, toward the *epekeina tes ousias*: a hymen (a closeness and a veil) between Plato's sun and Mallarmé's lustre. This 'materialism of the idea' is nothing other than the staging, the theater, the visibility of nothing or of the self. It is a dramatization which *illustrates nothing*, which illustrates *the nothing*, lights up a space, re-marks a spacing as a nothing, a blank: white as yet unwritten page, blank as a difference between two lines. (Derrida 1981a: 208)

It is this notion of a writing that is not the sign of some being but a writing that upsets the very understanding of what 'is' that Derrida elsewhere refers to through grammatology. Rather than think what *is*, grammatology attends to the differential movements or tracings that effect presence. In literature, however, this effecting of presence is resisted; for literary texts emphasise textual dispersion, non-semantic connections (such as alliteration, rhyme, puns and spurious etymologies). Literature, as offered by writers like Mallarmé and Joyce, displays the power of the text itself. Literature makes explicit the *silence* of literature: before literature says or means, it is the effect of textual pro- duction. Literature presents texts as text, as the movement of a trace. It is not the expression *of* presence, sense or point of view, but the inauguration or pre-human movement that produces effects of sense and presence. Derrida's reference to a primal *scene of writing* directs any theory of being or presence back to its textual conditions of possibility, conditions that cannot be *owned* by a subject precisely because they create all those points of identity and ownness (Derrida 1987b: 340). It is in his references to Mallarmé that Derrida also refers to the 'shining' of language (Derrida 1981a: 211). Language is not the contingent vehicle of some otherwise pure sense but has its own positive lumi- nosity, a force that exceeds the decision or autonomy of a self-present subject. Literature, then, would be at the limit, or beyond, *logos*. It would not be the writing *of* some ground or presence; it would not be subordinate to anything other than itself. It would be the anarchy, untamed genesis or play of a *gramme* not determined in advance by some reified logic, and not reducible to some ultimate telos of sense.

Through a new understanding of language as non-representational, then, Derrida aims to move beyond ontology. It is the very character of what *is* to be already pervaded by all those features usually confined to writing: what *is* is already differentiated, other than itself, never fully present to itself. The ideas of presence and being are effects of a prior grammatological multiplicity. The problem in *theorising* this prior or originating *gramme* is that one already relies on concepts that belie the multiplicity of a radical grammatology. Concepts such as the 'prior', 'origin', 'being' and *the very concept of the concept* have already gathered the multiplicity of the *gramme* into an order, identity and existence. Within philosophy, then, one can only realise this grammatology as a necessary impossibility. Any reference to, or representation of, that which exceeds representation will always already be in the thrall of representation. What literature offers, then, is not a freedom from philosophy – a liberation from the burden of meaning – but an inter- rogation into the limit of philosophy. For Derrida is not arguing that all philosophical texts are just metaphors, figures or literary effects. For it is this very opposition – between the literal/figural or philosophical/ literary – that has sustained a notion of truth as presence. Literature itself needs to be rethought: not as the rhetorical flourish or ornament that precludes pure truth, but as the very production of philosophical truth. Literature could not, then, be celebrated as a realm of pure form and affect, against the meaning and concept of philosophy. For no such purely affective realm is graspable; the aesthetic will always have been taken or framed *as aesthetic* – that is, *judged* or *determined* as other than meaning (Derrida 1987a: 41). That which offers or gives meaning (the *gramme*, the trace, *écriture*) is never given in itself. This means that Derrida would be critical of a certain naive Nietzscheanism where literature would be identified with a force or rhetorical effect opposed to the truth claims of philosophy, and where philosophy would be parasitic upon literary metaphor (Derrida 1982a: 217). On the contrary, the very idea of metaphor and literature defined in this way is what has enabled and inaugurated a metaphysics of presence. Derrida will insist on thinking beyond metaphor and beyond the literary as defined through metaphor. This will also lead to thinking beyond representation and its specific metaphorics of exchange, equivalence and system.

In *Given Time* Derrida's use of the gift, as that which disrupts economies of exchange, questions the representability of any truly counter-economic notion. If the gift is to be a gift, it must exceed any notion of return, debt, exchange or equivalence. The gift, which is always radically outside an economy of exchange and return must also, then, never be represented *as gift* (Derrida 1992: 13). To represent the gift is to locate the gift within a network of obligation; in doing so the gift as such would be annulled. In its difference from re-presentation, the gift would form something like an event. But the radical alterity of the gift, if it is to remain other, must also disrupt the self-presence of a subject. In his attempt to think the radical anteriority of the gift, Derrida, like Heidegger, locates representational closure at the heart of subjectivity:

> But whereas only a problematic of the trace or dissemination can pose the question of the gift, and forgiveness, this does not imply that writing is *generous* or that the writing subject is a *giving subject*. As an identifiable, bordered, posed subject, the one who writes and his or her writing never give anything without calculating, consciously or unconsciously, its reappropriation, its exchange, or its circular return – and by definition this means reappropriation with surplus value, a certain capitalization. We will venture to say that this is the very definition of the *subject as such*. (Derrida 1992: 101)

Any counter-economic notion (such as the gift) must also challenge the idea of the representational system that enables the subject's self-presence. If a certain idea of economy underpins a metaphysics of representation, calculation, equivalence and exchange, Derrida's work also shows that any counter-economic idea (the gift, justice, the other) has to be thought alongside and against tropes of economy. Derrida's use of the gift to represent the limit of economy and representation, posits the gift as an excess – an excess which, to remain as excess, must be 'forgotten' – beyond the realm of a self-present consciousness (Derrida 1992: 101). The very idea of subject is, then, bound up with a metaphorics of calculation and representation. But what is the 'surplus value' or 'capitalization' that Derrida (above) sees as definitive of subjectivity? This raises the question of the investment or value that has inaugurated Western metaphysics as a discourse on value. The idea of an originary 'capitalization' suggests a grounding interest that opens the epoch of subjectivist metaphysics. We might ask, then, who or what benefits or profits by establishing this system of terms? For Derrida the subject is not someone who autonomously *owns* the opening of such a system, and so the decision or juridical force that opens philosophy creates positions of interest – subject positions. Is it possible that we might refer the decisive opening of metaphysics back to a point of view? To do so would open a position of autonomy; it would suggest that subjects are more than effects within a field of distribution. It would suggest that one might ask of a system: who speaks? To propose an answer to this question I want to turn to the work of Luce Irigaray.

NOTES

1. 'The breakthrough toward radical otherness (with respect to the philosophical concept – of the concept) always takes, *within philosophy*, the *form* of an a posteriority or an empiricism' (Derrida 1981a: 33).
2. 'In determining Being as presence (presence in the form of the object, or self-presence under the rubric of consciousness), metaphysics could treat the *sign* only as a *transition*. Metaphysics is even indistinguishable from such a treatment of the sign. And neither has such a treatment somehow overtaken the concept of the sign: it has constituted it' (Derrida 1982a: 71).
3. For Merleau-Ponty, 'the permanence of my body is entirely different in kind. . . . It defies exploration and is always presented to me from the

same angle. Its permanence is not the permanence in the world, but a permanence from my point of view (Merleau-Ponty 1962: 91).

4. 'The relation which unsticks being from the existent without making something else of it, another existent, but merely a nothingness, a nonexistent which is there without being there as being present, this relation has some connivance with haunting. *Unheimlichkeit* is the condition – take this word however you will – of the question of being, of its being-on-the-way, inasmuch as it (does not) pass(es) via nothing' (Derrida 1987a: 378–9).

5. Elsewhere, Derrida has tied the notion of strategy to writing, where neither writing nor strategy are governed by conscious intent or human purpose. On the contrary, strategy signals an empiricism of responsibility, for empiricism thought in a subtle manner would not be the reference to some pure ground or foundation, but an attendance to what leaves us ungrounded: 'In the delineation of *différance* everything is strategic and adventurous. Strategic because no transcendent truth present outside the field of writing can govern theologically the totality of the field. Adventurous because this strategy is not a simple strategy in the sense that strategy orients tactics according to a final goal, a *telos* or theme of domination, a mastery and ultimate reappropriation of the development of the field. Finally, a strategy without finality, what might be called blind tactics or empirical wandering if the value of empiricism did not itself acquire its entire meaning in its opposition to philosophical responsibility' (Derrida 1982a: 7).

4

IRIGARAY:
THE SPECULA(RA)TIVE EC(H)ONOMY

———✑———

The Copernican revolution has yet to have its final effects in the male imaginary. And by centering man outside himself, it has occasioned above all man's ex-stasis within the transcendental (subject). . . . As things now go, man moves away in order to preserve his stake in the value of his representation, while woman counterbalances with the permanence of a (self)recollection which is unaware of itself as such. (Irigaray 1985a: 133–4)

MODALITIES OF TRANSCENDENCE

Like Heidegger, Irigaray's critique of Western metaphysics seems poised between an attempt to think the ground of thought – a ground that has always been figured as feminine – and a refusal to posit that ground as a presence, being or essence to which thought might simply return. Irigaray's thought concerns the modality of transcendence: the *way* in which thought directs itself towards what is other than itself. If Heidegger's *Destruktion* of metaphysics can be understood as neither a simple return to thought's ground, nor a location of thought within a representational scheme, Irigaray's uptake of the question of transcendence can be seen to harbour a similar double strategy. The feminine ought not to be thought of as an essence to which thought might return; for it is the very logic of essence that has figured the feminine. Only with the idea of a being that precedes the act of representation by a separate subject can there be a notion of essence. And it is through this logic of essence that the feminine has been thought of as an inert matter to be rendered intelligible by thought. Irigaray undermines this logic of essence, but not by appealing to another way of thinking that is *already given,* such as a feminine logic or viewpoint (for the very ideas of logic or viewpoint are still determined by a subject/object relation). Irigaray's strategy is neither a return to an already given viewpoint, nor a step outside point of view to a general essence.

Irigaray opens the closed logic of essence by repeating, mimicking or miming the way in which thought has always *produced essence* in terms of its own activity of grounding. Her writing in her classic study of philosophy's tropology, *Speculum of the Other Woman,* focuses on all the metaphors of repetition, reflection, return and reproduction that enable an act or event of thought to understand itself as a subject: as a mirror or representation of a sensible presence. In many ways Irigaray's work can be considered as a critique of a metaphysics of point of view: a metaphysics that asks the question of being from the point of its apprehension or representation. Rather than think of thought as a critical or speculative relation between the limit of thought and its ground, Irigaray poses the possibility of an entirely different mode, path or quality of transcendence. This is the audacious possibility of an ethics of sexual difference. Is it possible that thought might do more than recognise the limit of its own position and the way in which it thinks its world? The perpetual metaphysical oscillation between criticism and speculation – between accepting the limit of point of view and thinking the origin of point of view – always determines thought as a relation between logic and ground. What Irigaray's thought questions is how *this* question has been articulated, and what such a question entails. For where the question has effect is not just as a *theory* but as a comportment, existence or – to use Irigaray's way of speaking – an ethics. Why has the good always been thought through a logic of the subject and the grounds of thought?

Luce Irigaray's *Speculum of the Other Woman* relies heavily upon Heidegger's notion of the metaphysics of presence. Irigaray's work also extends Heidegger's critique of representation in terms of what she refers to as a specular/speculative economy. On the one hand, then, we might see Irigaray's notion of the 'sensible transcendental' (Irigaray 1993: 115) as an extension or radicalisation of Heidegger: any ground or transcendental is already the effect of a certain comportment or, in

Irigaray's case, a sensibility. (Thus Irigaray would be critical of any system, structure or representational scheme that might explain subjectivity *in general*.) On the other hand we could read Irigaray's project of sexual difference, and an *ethics* of sexual difference, as effected through a post-structuralist reversal of Heidegger. Here, Irigaray would insist on the impossibility of 'attending' to being, for there is no being in general whose call we hear, no being that might be rendered proximate through a relation of *attending*. Rather, being or the given, is always given through a relation *from* a specific sensibility. Thus, transcendence is not a neutral anticipation or going-out-towards; it is not the pure punctuality of a point of view. The relation to the given is emphasised as a *relation*, and therefore involves two terms: not two terms that are simply given, but two terms that *in their differentiation* enable the given, or the possibility of transcendence.

To *attend* to a ground is to already have a relation to the ground; rather than assert this relation as *transcendence in general*, Irigaray asks if there might be *modalities* of transcendence: different ways in which the given appears. One modality would be that of the subject, for whom the given is the object, or that which transcends. Another modality might be that of the sexually different feminine – neither subject nor object (Irigaray 1994: 19). This feminine would have to be articulated according to an entirely different economy. This would certainly not be an economy of representation, of a subject who re-presents a present world. But it is also questionable whether a mode of transcendence as sexual difference would be an *economy* at all, where economy is understood as the differentiation of a uniform field, the becoming of a single medium, or the forming of a silent materiality. Thus, Irigaray at once uses metaphors of economy to disrupt any Heideggerian appeal to origin. Any being or Same, she argues, is always given through a differential relation or an economy of differences. But Irigaray also undermines the idea of a *single* economy, the reduction of difference to a single value or unit of exchange. At times Irigaray suggests that the feminine is nothing other than a certain figure within a standard metaphysical economy of representation. The feminine has always been figured as the ground against which the subject functions as self-representing. But Irigaray also suggests that the feminine offers something *more* than the idea of thought as an economy, or system of relations within a single medium. And so a project of sexual difference would offer the idea of a transcendence that is not just the pure function of relation or differentiation but a sensible becoming, a specific mode of differentiation. Irigaray would be critical *both* of the phenomenological attention to genesis whereby any system or logic is the effect of the activity of consciousness, *and* the structuralist attention to system whereby any genesis is the effect of a determining structure or system. Thus, typically, we might have two Irigarays: an anti-structuralist Irigaray who insists on that which exceeds any representational system (such that the feminine for Irigaray functions in the same position as being for Heidegger, as that which is forgotten in any thought of the object as present); and another Irigaray who is critical of any grounding or Same. This second Irigaray, rather than returning to some pre-systemic sensible, would remain within metaphysical rhetoric only to disclose, through parody, the impossibility of exceeding the representational economy. On the one hand, then, we could see Irigaray's project as a post-Heideggerian appeal to the proximity of a sensible and originary site of differentiation (the maternal, the feminine, the body). On the other hand, *Speculum* could be read as a playful inhabitation of philosophy's rhetorical structure where the feminine has been produced as ground or origin.

HOW TO READ IRIGARAY READING METAPHYSICS

The history of Irigaray's reception in feminist thought has demonstrated the impossibility of deciding between these two readings. Indeed, the division between the essentialist and tactical Irigarays emphasises a difficulty opened by the Heideggerian critique of Western metaphysics. It is possible to read Heidegger as a nostalgic metaphysician of presence, advocating a return to a Being or Same which sends itself through language. (Here we would emphasise the status of proximity and authenticity in Heidegger.) But it is also possible to recognise a positivity granted to fallenness, errancy and difference in Heidegger's thought. (Here one would emphasise ideas of comportment, historicity, the equi-primordial and the *question* of being.) What is telling, however, is the impossibility of strictly separating Heidegger clearly into one or the other possibility. Similarly, the challenge of Irigaray's thought lies in the recognition of the risk and complicity of any critique of Western representationalism. Against notions of origin, Sameness and ground,

Irigaray deploys a primarily economic tropology to emphasise the differential structure of thought (and its concomitant values). Her work
would therefore set itself against any notion of an outside to metaphysics or a pre-representational ground. But Irigaray also shows the
connections between economic tropes, a metaphysics of presence and
the masculine imaginary by gesturing to that which must be left out of
account in the representational economy. Central to Irigaray's critique is
the *question* of the profit and debt which inheres in the representational
economy. And it is this excess of any economy that raises her speculative question: who or what profits by thinking in terms of profit?

THE TIME AND PLACE OF THE FEMININE
IN METAPHYSICS

Irigaray's critique of metaphysics as representation, proceeds by
showing the investment or interest which produces the tropology of
representation – an interest which cannot be accounted for within, or
as, the representational economy. Attempting to think the other of
representation would involve thinking the remainder or non-equivalence
of the phallic economy. If what *is* has been determined, valued or
presented in terms of what can be represented, then it is only a
thinking which tries to think beyond representation and its tropics of
equivalence and exchange that can challenge metaphysics. Heidegger's
notions of comportment, dwelling and thrownness attempted to think
a relation to the world which would be non-representational. Irigaray's
use of the caress and proximity try, in other ways, to approach experience in non-representational terms. However, it is in her thinking
through of the relation between transcendence and temporality that
Irigaray's most effective challenge to representational logic takes place.

   If something as fundamental or transcendental as time were shown
to be sexed then the very generality of metaphysics itself would need
to be questioned. Accordingly, feminist philosophy would not be a
practice of examining gender from *within* philosophy but would demand
a rethinking of the most fundamental motifs of metaphysics and a
redefinition of philosophy. The connection between time, metaphysics
and sexual difference is central to Irigaray's work and provides a way
of thinking the connection between her critical approach in *Speculum*
and her affirmation of feminist transcendence in the later work. The

importance of Irigaray's work lies, in fact, in the complex intertwining of time and sex; and it is only if we accept this connection that the task of a feminist metaphysics, as a challenge to phallogocentrism, is not only possible *but necessary*. That is, the reformulation of metaphysics through sexual difference is not just an issue for feminism. On the contrary, the very project of metaphysics as the thought of the system or re-presentation of being, demands the thought of a ground. Irigaray demonstrates that the metaphysical idea of ground and grounding has continually had to *figure* a present ground, and has done so through the negation of the feminine. Rather than think the representation of ground more radically, Irigaray will raise the possibility of a non-representational mode of metaphysics. Here, thought will not be a re-presentation or a relation to presence, but a temporal going-out-towards, and this going-out-towards will also extend beyond the domain of thought to include the tactile, the visceral and the proximate. Indeed, this will challenge the very boundary of thought such that metaphysics might be a *sexual relation* rather than a cognitive judgement. The idea of time and transcendence will be crucial in extending the domain of the metaphysical question beyond the bounds of the representing subject.

As Derrida has argued, the philosophical drive to pure truth must always take place according to a certain temporality whereby the origin is posited as radically prior to any contingent determination of the origin. To argue that the temporal self-affectation of logocentrism is a *phallo*gocentrism is to already suggest that philosophy in general might have a sex. Derrida's discussion of philosophy in *Dissemination* connects a metaphorics of self-fathering, legitimation, origination and insemination with the very meaning of the metaphysical *logos* (Derrida 1981a: 76–7). Pure truth must, by its very meaning, remain above and beyond any factical, contingent or historically determined instance; as such, then, pure truth remains present prior to any of its determinations, disseminations or textual offspring. Truth is that which fathers the sign and which must always remain anterior to, and govern, any subsequent act of signification. Presence, as that which precedes re-presentation, can only sustain its originary status through a certain determination of time and a certain legitimacy granted to an origin.

Such a reading of metaphysics suggests that the meaning of the *logos* is articulated according to a patrilineal tropology, and that sexual difference is not a difference within logic but a difference that effects logic. Sexual difference occurs as the *necessary* positing of an origin. That is, the very idea of the necessary or essential – the idea of that which is true *as such* independent of all subsequent presentation – is only possible through a division between thought and ground. But this division must be *figured* as a relation between the necessary or proper character of the ground, and its subsequent figuration. The idea of the *logos*, or of a necessity that then enables thought to appear to itself, is determined through the figure of a thought that fathers itself (Derrida 1981a: 77). If thought were the relation between two separate and non-equivalent terms then there would always be the possibility of a misprision, non-contiguity, dissemination or errancy. Only if thought is the *necessary* return and recognition of itself, and at one with its origin, can truth be assured *as truth*: as the necessary coincidence of the *logos*. Thus, for Derrida, thought opens or is inaugurated with the idea of the *logos as necessity* and this demands a metaphysics of a single and patrilineal economy (Derrida 1981a: 81). Thought is determined as *logos* only with the idea of *meaning*, with the idea of a sense that presents itself prior to all signification or representation (Derrida 1981a: 184). Thus the trace or mark must be seen as secondary or representational. And so a single term saturates the economy: sense and presence determine the secondariness of the sign and mark. Only an economy governed by a single term can present itself to itself; its birth and inauguration must be deemed as immanent, self-present and autonomous. The idea of the secondariness of the sign – the idea of *re*presentation – is what enables this logic of self-fathering:

> The father is always father to a speaking/living being. In other words, it is precisely *logos* that enables us to perceive and investigate something like paternity. If there were a simple metaphor in the expression 'father of logos,' the first word, which seemed the more *familiar*, would nevertheless receive more meaning *from* the second than it would transmit *to* it. The first familiarity is always involved in a relation of cohabitation with *logos*. Living-beings, father and son, are announced to us and related to each other within the household of *logos*. (Derrida 1981a: 80–1)

Where Irigaray differs significantly from Derrida is through an understanding of the character of this necessity and the limits of logo-centrism. For Derrida, the idea of necessity – of that truth that precedes all writing and difference – is the very opening of philosophy (Derrida 1981a: 85). It is the idea of representation as *re*presentation (as second to some truth or *logos*) that enables thought to take place. For Irigaray, however, there is a possibility of a non-representational metaphysics, a metaphysics not tied to the logic of a *logos*, and not subordinated to the thought of a grounding difference or differentiation. This is possible through Irigaray's *delimitation* of the logic of representation. Because this logic has worked by positing some ground or presence which it will then re-present, it can be short-circuited if this presence ungrounds itself. This is what will happen in an articulation of the feminine. Thought would no longer be the relation to some ground or presence, for that which has been figured as ground (the feminine) will itself become through transcendence.

The history of logocentrism, for both Derrida and Irigaray, has been a phallogocentrism precisely because the inauguration of meaning occurs as the differentiation of the origin, as the marking out of a ground which will then be re-presented through the activity of the *logos*. Logocentrism is the very ideal of meaning *as idea,* as a looking at, representation of, or pure seeing of presence. But, as Irigaray insists, this relation to presence has always been effected through the figuration of some pre-representational feminine passivity. Thus, sexual difference is not an event *within meaning* but is the primary figure that enables meaning. The idea of sexual difference – the idea of a feminine or maternal origin from which thought liberates itself in recognising and positing that origin – is also the idea of meaning, the idea of the ideal re-presentation of a non-ideal content. The figuration of a sexual binary is what enables the idea of the origin. Irigaray's critique does not therefore place sexual difference *at the origin*. Rather, the idea of the origin and the (conventional) idea of sexual difference are co-determining or equi-primordial. Only with the idea of a ground or presence that is *then* comprehended can one think the sexual opposition between a passive female matter and an active male idealisation. At the same time, only with such a sexual figuration or differentiation between maternal ground and masculine self-representation could the very logic of origins be articulated. As a result, sexual difference cannot be used to *explain* the origin. Nor does sexual difference emerge from some origin (as though there were an original neutral ground divided by sexual difference). Rather, both ideas – of sexual difference and the origin – *produce each other*, support each other and constitute the very logic through which origin and sex are thought. Sexual difference has been effected in a logic of the origin, in the very thought of the necessity of a ground that is then grounded. And this is also a manifestly temporal logic: an origin is original in its firstness, and a ground is only a ground if it precedes any grounding. Sexual difference, for Irigaray, does not precede meaning; it is what enables the very ideas of precedence and meaning. Accordingly it would make no *sense* to posit an origin prior to sexual difference; for the origin is nothing outside of its (sexed) determination as origin. The question that presents itself for Irigaray is whether the marking out of this logic as a logic of sexual difference will then open the way to thinking another logic, or beyond logic. Is it possible for another way of thinking, another mode of relation, to establish itself? Is there only one (logical) way of relating to being as presence? That is, can the thought of the *logos* be seen as the effect of a *particular* mode of transcendence, transcendence as representation? And would another mode of transcendence be possible?

FEMININE METAPHYSICS

How does one make the transition here from physics to metaphysics? (Irigaray 1993: 55)

If the commitment to being as presence is not just a metaphysical proposition but is the very mode of our being, the way we live the world, and if presence is also constituted according to a sexual and corporeal dynamic, then a rethinking of presence and temporality would be crucial for a feminist philosophy and philosophy in general. According to this argument, identity and metaphysics are not contingently related – through metaphor or historical association – but are essentially intertwined: metaphysics is identity. As Heidegger argued the *way* we question the world gives us our world, and gives us who we are. As subjects we dwell metaphysically. But is it possible to think this problem *beyond the question and beyond the idea of world*? Is it the *world* to which thought relates, or is there some other modality of otherness? In this case metaphysics might be something other than the thought of the possibility of the world. If the subject/world relation has been determined though a sexual metaphorics, then an *other* mode of otherness would have to enter at this point. What is *other than* the feminine as the inert, representable matter that grounds metaphysics? An autonomous feminine, or a feminist metaphysics.

Irigaray's work presents itself as the strongest case both for the link between metaphysics and sexual difference, and for the metaphysical imperative (whereby existence relies upon an implicit metaphysical positing or comportment). Irigaray's work also suggests that if the idea of presence is coterminous with a particular (masculine) way of being, presence is more than just a logical condition. The Irigarayan focus on comportment, corporeality and the *logos* as a form of dwelling or relating situates her work (critically) within the tradition of Heideggerian *Destruktion*. For Heidegger, metaphysics is not just a question for philosophers and academics; metaphysics is also a particular relation or comportment [*Verhalten*] to the world. The *logos* is a 'saying–gathering', a dwelling with being, a mode of revealing. As such, then, metaphysics is a relatedness to being. The emphasis on relatedness in Irigaray's work is, in contrast to Heidegger, not between being and the site of its revealing, but between two different sexes.

Like Heidegger, Irigaray undertakes a critique of the logic of the *a priori* through the question of time and transcendence. As Heidegger's critique of Kant's transcendental logic had argued, the very idea of an a priori (or *prior*) logic already deploys the notion of temporality (Heidegger 1996). Temporality cannot, then, be explained as a subjective intuition. Time is not a concept within the world, nor is it explicable as a condition. For the idea of grounding condition is again already spatio-temporal. Rather, time *is* transcendence, the coming to being of being, existence itself, or the very givenness of the given (Heidegger 1996: 384). The meaning of being is time. And it is here that the Heideggerian project opens the possibility of its own *Destruktion*. It is quite clear that Heidegger is right in determining the *meaning* of being as time. The very idea of being – as what *is*, as that which presents, or remains present – is already a temporal notion. Through this argument Heidegger can demonstrate an implicit metaphysics, or positing of being as presence, in the very possibility of existence. To 'have' a world is to already have gone-out-towards some existence, an existence taken *as present*, as synthesised or gathered in time. The very possibility of an experiencing subject rests upon this temporal going-forth and an anticipation of *being*. But what if this structure of transcendence as temporal self-constitution – and going-out-towards being – could not be investigated 'in general'? What if the self-constitution through relatedness to the object were both characterised by the nature of the object and the quite particular mode of relating to the object? Heidegger is insistent that the temporality in which the present thing comes to be present is a question of comportment or existence. It is within this connection between temporality, comportment and being that Irigaray launches her critique of phallogocentrism. If it is the case that the subject is produced through transcendence – a passing beyond or a projection towards an object – then this passage, path or projection *may have a character*. (And so Irigaray will focus on metaphors of axis, turning, returning and reflection to emphasise that transcendence is not a pure and featureless projection, but bears the character of its point of departure and the way that point is reflected upon as a point.) If there are *modalities* of transcendence, then the horizon of temporality would not be a general universal ground. Rather, temporality would be the projection of a particular medium. The *logos* would not be pure self-affectation without remainder, nor the production of the empirical in general, but a specific comportment.

THE QUESTION OF SEXUAL DIFFERENCE

If it is possible to think other modalities of transcendence then this possibility cannot simply be located outside the metaphysics of presence. Precisely because the *meaning* of being has been determined as present – and therefore as transcendent to the subject – Irigaray must do more than offer another theory of being or another ontology. Rather, the very project of ontology must be brought into question in so far as the question of ontology, as Heidegger insisted, presupposes a fore-understanding of some transcendent existence. And the idea of the subject has always been effected from this fore-understanding. This is why *any* theory of the subject has already determined some notion of being, existence or transcendence from which the subject determines himself. In Irigarayan terms, there has always already been some ground, matter or support that acts to provide the medium of the subject's recognition and reflection. Rather than posing another ontology Irigaray asks whether the question of philosophy might be articulated in a different modality: not towards being but towards the transcendence of the other. But in order for a question to be articulated in a different modality one must not only find another object to question, but must think the question as other than a grasping of the object. In order to arrive at an ethics of sexual difference, then, one must go over the ground of the traditional question in order that this ground be disrupted. This is Irigaray's project of reading metaphysics in *Speculum*. How has the ground been grounded and what does such a grounding presence disavow?

The traditional metaphysical determination of truth as presence is, for Irigaray, the effect of a 'sexual scenography' in which the 'path' of the subject's transcendence is produced in a 'theater of representation' (Irigaray 1985a: 266). That is, the idea of a representational relation to being – one in which a subject repeats an already given presence – is an idea forged around the figure of the sexual binary. An active self-comprehending consciousness projects itself towards a pre-given ground, and successfully comprehends and repeats this ground in the meaning of the *logos*. For Irigaray, this path away from the subject to the object, and the reflective 'return' which constitutes the subject as such, takes place in a sensible milieu. Indeed, she argues, the sensible must be rethought, not as ground, but as milieu. The idea of the sensible transcendental is just such a thought. Irigaray therefore rejects both an empirical idealism – the explanation of being as a subjective representation – and transcendental realism – the idea of some matter, ground or existence that also includes thought. The *sensible* transcendental is a way of thinking 'what is' *neither* in terms of a grounding subject *nor* in terms of a pre-subjective ground or real. For 'sensibility' at once describes 'what is' in terms of affect, relation and comportment but does not reduce that affect to a conscious or ideal representation. Further, sensibility is felt *between* at least two terms; it goes beyond philosophy's usual metaphorics of a distanced looking or point of view; sensibility encompasses the visual, tactile, aural and non-ideal engagements with existence. The sensible is transcendental, not because it is prior or that which logically grounds all that is. If the transcendental is *sensible* then it undercuts all questions of priority, grounding and conditions. Thus, Irigaray puts the 'path' of transcendence – the relation towards – in the medium or milieu of the sensible. This is also why she will extend transcendence beyond thought and the visual to the caress, the tactile and the erotic.

The traditional *logos* is, according to Irigaray, nothing other than the retracing of the path of transcendence, a retracing that incorporates and sublates the path as the subject's own condition. It renders the sensible ideal, but then disavows this process of rendering. In response to a history of traditional logic that has disavowed transcendence (or the becoming towards being) Irigaray will demonstrate that the path or passage of transcendence must *take place*. The transcendental – the passage to the object in general – is always located, and occurs as a mode of sensible becoming or as a peculiarly sensible 'path' (Irigaray 1985a: 252).

In erasing its coming to presence, the traditional *logos* therefore relies on a debt; the subject presents itself as self-originating but nevertheless uses the feminine as a figure or metaphor for its own condition. A classic example is, of course, Plato's cave in *The Republic*: a figure that enables a story of how the subject can turn towards and discover his own *logos*. This metaphor that disavows the feminine also *re*-figures the subject's emergence from its maternal/material home; the cave is the negation of the maternal as well as being the trace or remnant of the maternal. It is that figure which effaces the movement of figuration, imagining knowledge as able to turn away from all shadow, materiality or duplicity. (Derrida will refer to this movement as an 'ontospeleology' – a metaphor that produces a myth of the possible pure ideality of the *logos* [Derrida 1981a: 40].) For Irigaray, the sexed nature of the Western *logos* is generated through the *specificity* of its disavowal. Like Hegel and Lacan, Irigaray will argue for a certain positivity of negation; what is negated by the subject is not simply lost but remains as that which has been negated. The subject is an effect of idealising or representing its other as meaningful. But if the other that is rendered meaningful has always been the sensible/corporeal origin, and if masculinity is nothing other than this path of idealisation, then it follows that sexual difference is not an idea introduced into metaphysics. (It is not simply a feminist question.) On the contrary, only with sexual differentiation – with the idealisation of the sensible as a subjective ground – is the question of *being in general* possible. It is through the metaphysical idea of presence that the origin is reproduced as ideal, eternally present and representable. It is through representation that the specific maternal ground is negated as maternal and repeated as the general condition of the intelligible.

The Heideggerian rhetoric of ec-stasis, projection, anticipation and fore-having are not, then, neutral descriptions of the conditions for any possible being or being in general; for the very idea of a single horizon or general condition is already a particular way of relating to the world. In passing beyond itself the subject effects transcendence in a particular way. By taking up and re-presenting the thing, the subject understands or comprehends the thing as already present. Both Heidegger and Irigaray argue that this notion of being as re-presentation for a self-present subject fails to think the prior transcendence or 'passing beyond' through which the presence of being is revealed. The question of temporality, however, uncovers the *passage* of ec-stasis which produces presence. The temporal directedness to being is, for Heidegger, a comportment, a concern or engagement. Heidegger is at great pains, however, to make sure that this concern is not confused with a particular worldly attitude; it is not an anthropologism. On the contrary, concern is *ontological* and enables any subsequent representation of the world:

> The peculiar *neutrality* of the term 'Dasein' is essential, because the interpretation of this being must be carried out prior to every factual concretion. This neutrality also indicates that Dasein is neither of the two sexes. But here sexlessness is not the indifference of an empty void, the weak negativity of an indifferent ontic nothing. In its neutrality Dasein is not the indifferent nobody and everybody, but the primordial positivity and potency of essence. (Heidegger 1992: 136–7)

Irigaray wants both to sustain the Heideggerian problematic of the subject as an effecting of transcendence, at the same time as she regards the philosophical motifs of projection, reflection, comprehension, affectation and return as phallogocentric. For while the conditions for subjectivity are seen as the relation to transcendence, this relation has traditionally been defined as neutral, *pre-empirical* and self-present. The mode or positivity of this relation is not itself considered. The relation is, in traditional phenomenology, a condition of the world and not a particular event within the world; it is the event *of* difference and not itself different. In response to this, Irigaray will raise the question of different modes of difference, or different ways of having a world: 'Men and women thus occupy different subjective configurations and different worlds' (Irigaray 1995: 16). The denial of different modes of relation is, for Irigaray, the repression which constitutes logocentrism as phallogocentrism. The transcendental grounding of metaphysics for a subject-in-general is nothing other than a forgetting of the difference which marks the subject's passage away from immediacy to mediated subjectivity. For Irigaray, the putative universality of this passage is achieved by seeing the medium or mediation through which the subject achieves the return of reflection as ideal rather than sensible. The subject is seen to become or transcend itself through time, and time is defined as pure and pre-worldly ec-stasis. From this it follows that time, considered as pure self-projection toward the thing, can only be one more way of repressing different possibilities for subjective becoming. On the other hand, it also follows that if transcendence beyond itself is what constitutes the subject as such, then the rethinking of time as *sensible* transcendence would be central to the project of sexual difference.

SENSIBLE TRANSCENDENCE

A birth into a transcendence, that of the other, still in the world of the senses ('sensible'), still physical and carnal, and already spiritual. (Irigaray 1993: 82)

Western metaphysics has only ever thought a singular mode of transcendence, and because this transcendence is one in which the thing is seen as inert, passive, *present* and available for representation, transcendence has necessarily repressed that which resists ideal comprehension. It is in the representational relation to the already-present object that femininity has traditionally been constituted. The feminine is produced as the matter, corporeality and sensibility which are already there for the subject's self-understanding. Sexual difference is, then, not one difference among others, but the difference which constitutes the subject-in-general. Sexual difference is effected in the comportment towards the *object*. For the object-in-general to be determined *as presence*, the subject must have determined the object *in advance*; the

subject must be the origin of the object, self-originating, self-affecting
– in essence, phallogocentric. On this model, femininity, posited as
the inert and sensible origin which can always be comprehended by
the transcendental subject, cannot achieve its own transcendence. The
feminine will always be that through which, or against which, transcendence is achieved. Figured as the corporeal medium or ground of
becoming, femininity itself can never become. In order to achieve
transcendence as disembodied and pure self-projection, the masculine
subject must negate his corporeality; empiricity, in its naivete, must be
repeated as the secondary effect of a more prior ground. This constitutive
negation of the sensible is achieved in the originary act of transcendence which is also sexual difference. Sexual difference and time thought
as pure self-affectation or projection are, for Irigaray, co-originary.

The idea that it is *sexual* difference which characterises the relation
between temporality and transcendence is grounded in Irigaray's
understanding of the importance of the corporeal origin and sexual
difference as the break or distancing which marks that origin *as
meaningful*. For Irigaray, in contrast to both Kant and Heidegger, it is
not being in general or a transcendental object = X that the subject
originally posits. Rather, sexual difference is effected in a moment of
subjective becoming in which the origin is posited as female/maternal/
material for a male, self-representing subject. For Irigaray, any anticipation of being 'in advance' will rely on a figure of a *particular* being
– the feminine – and not a 'no-thing' (Heidegger 1990: 90–1) or
object = X (Kant 1933: 137). In Western metaphysics the subject is
effected as the representation of its own origin; it is this which Irigaray
refers to as the 'patriarchal' transcendence and intentionality which
admit of only one form of temporal becoming set against a world
already present (Irigaray 1996: 122). This is nowhere more clear than
in the Kantian 'discovery' of the a priori. The a priori, according to
Speculum, closes an 'irreconcilable gap between the sensible and
supersensible' (Irigaray 1985a: 209). This closure of the gap between
sensibility or 'what is', and the supersensibility of meaning, is also the
production of sexual difference. By not acknowledging the gap, break,
loss or distance from the sensible, the subject is always able to include
and comprehend the origin as its own: 'Between empirical and transcendental *a suspense will still remain inviolate*, will escape prospection,
then, now, and in the future' (Irigaray 1985a: 145). It is the very idea of

an *ideal* break with, and representation of, the origin that orders a masculinity that negates the feminine. Closure – the forgetting of the gap which separates the subject from the sensible – *is* metaphysics, such that metaphysics is the thought of a symmetry between the ideal and its material other. This idea of representation is also the constitution of the masculine subject. Kantian closure is, then, a form of subjectivism in which sensible being is reconciled, included within, or comprehended by the 'supersensible' (meaning, the concept, ideality).

By pointing out the *gap* between the sensible and supersensible, Irigaray's work draws attention to the process, labour and production of meaning. There can be no seamless continuity between the formation of the subject's world for itself and the 'naivete' of empiricity, nature, the elemental or the sensible. If conventional sexual difference is effected in the closure of this gap, by producing a subject that simply re-presents its world, then it follows that *feminist* philosophy must be a more radical transcendentalism, an opening and questioning of metaphysical representationalism. For Kant, according to Irigaray, the subject's transcendental self-constitution occurs as a negation of empiricity; for what lies outside the subject is always reduced to the domain of representation. The corporeal origin is re-figured as a (subjective) logical condition:

> Thus the function of the transcendental schema will be to negate an intrinsic quality of the sensible, and this irremediably. Nature is foreclosed in her primary empirical naivete. Diversity of feeling is set aside in order to build up the concept of the object, and the immediacy of the relation to the mother is sacrificed. . . . The object cannot be known, therefore, for the simple reason that it allows the conceptual window to be put in place in which nothing is seen per se but whose frame enables all the rest to be intuited. (Irigaray 1985a: 204)

Within the Kantian transcendental project the subject is seen as a mode of self-presence; all being or exteriority is enclosed within the subject's own capacity for representation. Time, as the horizon of inner sense, is, then, a *comprehension* of the medium within which the subject is constituted. Temporality, seen as pure intuition, is central to what Irigaray refers to as the 'Paradox A Priori' of Kantianism: all that the subject 'receives' is already determined, in advance, as an effect of the subject's projection of presence. Defined in this Kantian way, time manages, represses, re-includes and appropriates that which precedes cognition. Time is not a thing but the way in which all things come to be included within the horizon of representation: 'temporality is in fact not the same but that of a transcendental *property/propriety* that alleviates the horror of the inchoate and unpossessable as well as the disgust for the misshapen refuse that will be executed under the form of matter' (Irigaray 1985a: 204–5). The repression and negation which constitute phallogocentrism occur as a certain determination of time. It is through time that the subject gains the capacity of turning back and re-including, as its own, the origin as prior presence:

> Space and time, are to be viewed as forms of the outer sense that organize and thereby subsume a diversity that is ridiculous in its confusion of feeling, whether it comes from an outside world peopled with objects which thereby receive their specific geographical destination, or from an inner world under the control of changes that can henceforth be analyzed in a function of time. But which time? (Irigaray: 1985a: 205)

TRANSCENDENCE AS SEXUAL DIFFERENCE

For Irigaray, then, the Kantian and early Heideggerian focus on time as a transcendental condition would be a final moment in a history of self-fathering, in which the subject is its own origin, and in which the materiality of representation is repressed, effaced and negated as feminine. The same might also be said for later 'quasi-transcendental' motifs of ec-stasis, difference or *différance*, in so far as these terms are generated by the question of the condition for the possibility of existence *in general*. In this *generalisation* of the origin, or the rendering of the origin as a transcendental condition, the subject must repress the particularity of its sensible becoming. The very idea of transcendence-in-general is, therefore, a masculine transcendence – defined as *other than* the empiricity of the maternal body: 'the masculine transcendence is problematic in terms of what it annuls of the reality of engendering' (Irigaray 1996: 67). To see engendering as *real* is to see the subject as effected within existence, and not as the prior condition of existence. A central psychoanalytic premise is involved here: the subject is *nothing other than* its break with a radically anterior and non-meaningful origin: an origin subsequently rendered meaningful in being *posited as maternal*. It is this positing of the origin that constitutes the subject as such and its mode of transcendence. There is still, then, the function of a transcendental object = X, a being in general to which the subject is directed: but this transcendence is now marked by sexual difference. This is what links metaphysics and day-to-day existence. The very idea of the world, which makes existence possible, has been determined in Western culture in the subjectivist and representationalist mode of transcendence: a mode of transcendence that figures the presence towards which it is directed as feminine. Objectivity-in-general depends upon an originary and constitutive negation of the proximity of the maternal body. Sexual difference and transcendence are co-originary. Or, as Irigaray argues in *I Love to You*, 'In sexual difference, the negative as limit is present from the very fact of respecting natural reality as constitutive of the subject' (Irigaray 1996: 51). The subject's emergence from immediacy to self-representation traditionally takes place by a distancing from, and negating of, the maternal origin.

Irigaray also thereby radicalises and extends one of the most startling claims of psychoanalysis. Rather than begin with a subject and a world, psychoanalysis asks about the genesis of the subject. It must explain the very emergence of being. (This is why Lacan insists that he is not offering an ontology, but questioning how ontology is possible [Lacan 1982: 142].) From Kant through to German idealism it had been recognised that the subject is an effect of differentiation or positing. There must be an object or posited otherness for the subject to differentiate itself as an 'I'. Of course what this otherness or object *is* is the question that has divided various philosophical camps and competing ontologies. Psychoanalysis will take a different tack, not by asking what the otherness or object *is*, but by asking how the relation to an otherness is effected and understood. This brings us back to the emergence or genesis of logic. One argument of Freud's is frequently repeated regarding the emergence of thought and judgement. Before any *ideal* or *logical* relations are formed there are certain corporeal arrangements: approval and negation are figured as 'I take this in' or 'I spit this out': 'Judging is a continuation, along lines of expediency, of the original process by which the ego took things into itself or expelled them from itself, according to the pleasure principle' (Freud 1925: 239). Only subsequently are such bodily organisations formalised into ideal terms. Difference, or differentiation, begins through concrete relations. The crucial difference that opens the world is, of course, the presence/ absence distinction. Without the idea or organising form of *presence* the perceiving subject would not have a world. There would be perception – the influx of stimulus – but no *world* – the forming of that stimulus into a present thing. The often-quoted moment when Freud witnesses his grandson throwing and retrieving a cotton reel to the tune of *Fort/Da* (here/there) demonstrates that the idea that opens metaphysics – the idea of presence – is inaugurated in specific bodily movements. As Lacan goes on to insist, all experience of a world is an aiming for presence. One takes what one perceives as the perception *of* a world. Existence is an aiming beyond itself in so far as one takes one's expe- riences as experiences *of* some being or presence that exceeds our own perception. This is why Lacan locates the logic of the signifier at the heart of existence: what is perceived is taken as the sign *of* some thing (Lacan 1977: 175). But this existential aiming for presence is not, as in Heidegger, a projectedness towards no-thing, nor, as in Kant, a 'tran- scendental object = X'. This passage of transcendence is first formed through the imaginary of the body. The opening of transcendence occurs in relations between bodies. In Western culture this first object that will figure presence is the maternal body; and so the body of the mother stands as the figure or ideal of *Das Ding* – not this or that thing but the anticipation of any thing or presence in general (Lacan 1992: 54).

The consequences of this Lacanian argument regarding transcen- dence and existence are crucial for Irigaray's critique of presence and representation. Lacan's diagnosis of the Oedipal character of existence relies upon the assumption that existence is representational, that having a world is the aiming for some presence. In so far as this is true, Lacan is quite accurate in diagnosing this fantasy of precluded presence as figured or imaged by a maternal body. Within the phallic economy of representation, as described by Lacan, the very logic of existence is opened by sexual difference. It is through the idea of a denied maternal presence, barred by the function of the prohibiting paternal law, that the subject is formed. For the *subject* is not a thing within the world but a *signifying function*: one who lives their world *as* a meaningful totality and is thereby located within a logic, system or structure. But this function of *meaning* depends upon what Irigaray refers to as a 'phallic intentionality'. One takes the world as signified lawfully, through a structure accepted by all. And one takes one's place in this differential logic because pure presence is denied. The denial or prohibition of this presence is, furthermore, figured through the fantasy of sexual difference and prohibition. The pure presence of the maternal *Das Ding* lies *outside* the prohibiting and universalising structure that renders that presence *re*-presentable (recognisable, repeatable, and lawful). Only with the fantasy of the maternal as original (but denied) presence is the signifying logic of transcendence able to take hold. The signified – that which the sign intends – is only possible with an anticipation, projection or transcendence that goes beyond the sign and aims for presence. And this movement towards presence is figured, fantasised and desired *as the maternal origin*. It is for this reason that the feminine cannot be a subject for-herself within the phallogocentric structure of intentionality. For the feminine is nothing other than that which is desired, and not the transcendence of desire itself (Lacan 1982: 145).

In contrast with Lacan, Irigaray's response goes beyond a diagnosis of Western culture and beyond the recognition of the fantasy of maternal presence. It is possible, she suggests, that there might be a transcendence that does not go out towards a thing, presence or an object. This transcendence would not be an aiming at presence, but a relation to another transcendence. In order to effect another form of transcendence the recognition or alterity of the sensible other would need to be involved. The origin would have to be *more* than the subject's own limit or logical condition. The originating movement of transcendence would be a relation between bodies. For Irigaray, the break with immediacy is a break with a sensible origin, and a break that occurs sensibly – through bodily comportments or relations.

THE SENSIBLE TRANSCENDENTAL

It is this primarily embodied character of originary transcendence which Irigaray's reading of philosophy brings to light. From Plato's cave to the axis of Kant's 'Copernican turn' philosophy has occurred as a repetition and re-figuring of the turn from the origin. It is this 'break' with the origin, through representation of the origin *as object*, that produces the subject as masculine. The sexual difference of the subject is not an essence but an ex-istence: the way in which it posits presence in general.

This phallogocentric 'ec-stasis', then, constitutes the object or presence *as non-subjective* – as that towards which the subject aims. But if subjectivity is figured as set over against some maternal presence, it must also be *other than* maternal or feminine. According to Irigaray, this means that the maternal or feminine provides the axis or the medium of mediation. Without the idea of a barred or pre-subjective presence, the subject would not be able to take itself *as a subject* – as one who re-presents a world. If the subject, from Kant to Heidegger and Lacan, is not a thing within the world but a function who signifies a world, then there must be some way in which this subject/object difference is *figured*. For Irigaray, this figuring of original difference or transcendence is sexual.

The feminine, as the negative of masculine subjectivity, is produced through a philosophical tropology of reflection, turning and folding. In addition to the dominant specular and visual metaphorics which proliferate throughout *Speculum*, Irigaray's work is also marked by a concern with the 'axis' upon which the turn, fold or constitutive return of the subject takes place. If the subject of presence is a self-reflecting subject, then it must depend upon some medium for reflection, or some axis upon which it can turn. For Irigaray, the 'fold' of being is not purely immanent but always folds *upon some point*, a point that is then re-figured, after the fold, as the subject's own point of view. This suggests that the subject's object which is posited as present is not just 'being in general' or a 'transcendental object = X'. Rather, the original object is part of an embodied relation; presence is effected through sexual difference. To introduce the possibility that the object toward which the subject exceeds itself may not be an object-in-general, is to open the possibility of different horizons, different modes of passing beyond and different relations of transcendence. Rather than seeing time as the very possibility of existence (as did Heidegger), time would be a certain mode of existence. *The way in which differentiation between self and world took place would differ according to the concrete and embodied character of the relation.* A relation between two sexes, for example, would effect a different temporality from that between a subject and world (Irigaray 1994: 19; 25).

If we were to accept Irigaray's critique of the transcendental horizon, time would be a highly ambiguous motif. As an originary condition through which being is revealed, as a subjective ec-stasis, or as a general ground, time would be synonymous with phallogocentrism, the production of a single and pre-determined comportment towards the world (Irigaray 1985a: 150). On the other hand, by understanding the subject as a *relation* to transcendence Irigaray's critique of temporality also suggests different modes of 'passing beyond'. The possibility of other modes of transcendence could only occur, Irigaray argues, not by setting feminine temporality alongside the phallogocentrism of metaphysics but by achieving two different intentionalities. Because transcendence is relational, and because the originary axis around which the subject returns to itself has traditionally been the feminine other, new forms of horizon would require new relations of sexual difference. Both masculinity and femininity would need to relate differently to their origin. At present, the feminine cannot be a subject for-herself precisely because the feminine is constituted as that against which the for-itself of temporal projection is effected. In order to attain another form of transcendence the recognition or alterity of the sensible other would need to be involved. In a relation of *recognition* transcendence would no longer return to itself within an enclosed, singular, transparent and self-reflective horizon. It would recognise the relation of transcendence *as a relation*, not to presence, but to an other: 'And of an other whose body's ontological status would differ from my own' (Irigaray 1993: 157).

For Irigaray, then, transcendence is a mode of embodied comportment, a particular mode of passing beyond towards a particular object. From this it follows that sexual difference is not one form of difference among others. Sexual difference is not an *ontic* difference (between already existing objects). On the contrary, sexual difference characterises the *possibility of the object*, our relation to objects in general, and is, therefore, *ontological difference* (Irigaray 1996:146). The way in which objects in general are given depends upon the character of transcendence, the *way* in which one anticipates, goes beyond or exists. For Western culture to date, transcendence has been figured as an active, representational and masculine grasping of a passive feminine. The question of being traditionally depends upon an idea of grounding presence (a presence fantasised as the maternal origin). Because of the *already sexual* nature of the very project of ontology, re-figuring the relation to being entails re-figuring sexual difference.

For Heidegger, the uncovering of time and the *Destruktion* of metaphysics yielded the possibility of a more authentic dwelling with being. For Irigaray a renewed comportment would take the form of (at least) two modes of transcendence or two temporalities. Only with the proximity of the sexual other would the representationalism of Western metaphysics be overcome. Being would no longer be understood from within a single existence or ec-stasis. For Irigaray, then, it is not *being* that exceeds representation and forms the question of our epoch but sexual difference (Irigaray 1993: 5).

THE TIME OF SEXUAL DIFFERENCE

If, as Irigaray argues, time is not a universal condition but is a particular comportment – a comportment with a corporeal morphology and ethical implications – then why, we might ask, is temporal projection not characterised by other forms of difference? Why sexual difference? This is where Irigaray's acceptance of time as an *ontological possibility* remains important. By accepting that prior to any ontic distinction (between beings) there is a general relatedness-towards, Irigaray can posit a transcendental horizon. This transcendental horizon is nothing other than the *possibility* of the object or presence. Re-figuring this horizon would entail that transcendence not be towards the present object but towards another subject. But another *subject*, to be truly other, could not be a reflection of the subject (for this would sustain the self-presence of the subject–object relation). Another *subject* would have its own mode of comportment or transcendence. Another subject would not be a presence, but a temporal passing-beyond, a becoming, or a comportment. And, as *ontological*, this comportment must be prior to any *particular* thing. One would recognise in the other, not an other thing, another presence, but another comportment, another becoming. Otherness would need to be ontological rather than ontic. But if this otherness were ontological it would also be non-particular or universal. This is where Irigaray deploys Hegel's idea of the concrete universal. The universal is not a purely formal or empty condition. A concrete universal recognises its necessary relation and concretisation; only through concretion or instantiation is the universal given as universal.

Translated into sexual difference, this means that one can only have a *genre* or mode of transcendence if one includes difference as a condition for the recognition of the same. One can only acknowledge one's self as a specific self if there is another specific self. This relation also generates a new mode of autonomy, where autonomy is not pure *self-relatedness* but the recognition of one's self in relation to an other.[1] Only a feminine autonomy – a feminine as subject not object – would allow the masculine relation of transcendence to be a relation to *another transcendence* (and not to an alien, ungraspable and passive presence).

The combination of claims for the concrete universality *and* sexual specificity of the other depends, then, upon seeing sexual difference as a general/gendered comportment towards being, as a mode of temporality. If the subject were to have a sexual *essence* then it would not be a subject, a for-itself. Its being would be given or anthropologically determined as some thing within the world. What a subject relates to, then, must also not be a sexual *essence* (the feminine presence) for this would reify sexual relations into relations between beings and not between subjects. What characterises the subject to whom transcendence relates, *as an other subject*, must be its *own* mode of existence. The other must therefore be defined *as* other (and so have a sex); but the other must also be a *subject* (sex must be a question of *ex-istence* not essence). Transcendence (or the passing beyond to what the subject is not) would be both transcendental and sensible; for the transcendental occurs as a particular way of becoming-from the corporeal origin:

> Transcendence is thus no longer ecstasy, leaving the self behind toward an inaccessible total-other, beyond sensibility, beyond the earth. It is respect for the other whom I will never be, who is transcendent to me and to whom I am transcendent. Neither simple nature nor common spirit beyond nature, this transcendence exists in the difference of body and culture that continues to nourish our energy, its movement, its generation and its creation. (Irigaray 1996: 104)

Sexual difference is a difference of temporality, a difference of horizons within which transcendence occurs. Thinking sexual difference would be an ontological and metaphysical issue for it would concern our relation to being, the modality of our temporality. Feminism, for Irigaray, ought to concern itself with this constitution of sex both as identity and as a relation or form of transcendence. For feminism there is, then, a philosophical imperative: because one's sex is a relation to what one is not, only a rethinking of transcendence can re-figure sexual difference (Irigaray 1996: 45). At the same time, there is also a sexual imperative for philosophy: if the transcendental horizon has a character, a corporeal morphology, then any thinking of this horizon – any ontology – would already be an inquiry into sexual difference:

> Without such a gesture, philosophy risks its own demise, vanquished along with other things by the use of techniques that, in the construction of the logos, undermine man's subjectivity, an easier and quicker victory if woman no longer maintains the pole of nature standing opposite to masculine *techne*. The existence of two subjects is probably the only thing that can bring the masculine subject back to his being, and this thanks to woman's access to her own being. (Irigaray 1995: 12)

The idea of a *sensible* transcendental (Irigaray 1993: 115; 129) would see the temporal path or passing-to the object as corporeally determined; transcendence or ex-istence would always take place from a body and towards another body. The privileging of *sexual* difference in this embodiment of the temporal horizon depends upon accepting (however critically) the maternal as the posited ground or origin from which transcendence projects itself. And while Irigaray is careful to avoid some pure maternal in-itself, it is nevertheless *this* object and *this* relation that characterises the constitutive distancing or mediation of the subject (Irigaray 1993: 98). Irigaray's location of *sexual* difference as *the* modality of difference depends upon giving the transcendental horizon a meaning, a sex. It depends upon locating sexual difference not within the given, nor within time, but at the level of temporal transcendence itself. Sexual difference is identified with the very production of the origin, the distancing, passage or transcendence that constitutes presence. But if this is the case – if the temporal horizon is never pure spontaneity but determined by the specificity of comportment – then the *meaning* of this horizon might also be *more* than that of sexual difference.

The value of Irigaray's work lies – perhaps – in her refusal to abandon metaphysics: the subject is not a given thing but the way in which the thing is given. Transforming identity, or the ontic, therefore demands an ontological question. But for Irigaray sexual difference also shatters the ground of the ontological question. Sexual difference suggests that there is not *being in general* towards which existence tends. Thus Irigaray's work is oddly poised around the problem of anthropology and ontology. One cannot determine the character of human being in an inner-worldly fashion. Masculinity and femininity are ways in which the world is given. Further, the idea of an autonomous feminine for Irigaray suggests going beyond the very problem of the *world*: perhaps it is not having a *world* that opens the relation of the subject, but having an *other*. But to place the opening to the world *after* the opening of sexual difference is to describe a pre-worldly condition. To what extent does this fall into anthropomorphism? Has one not failed to ask how *this* difference explains the origin of man? From what point of view can one determine *sexual* difference as the opening of difference in general? One answer would be that both Lacan and Irigaray's account is descriptive and diagnostic. The origin has been figured through sexual difference in the tradition of Western metaphysics. Both Lacan and Irigaray's arguments recognise an already determined understanding of the origin, rather than being assertions regarding origination. They are not ontological arguments – regarding some foundation – but arguments about how ontology is possible and how ontology has been figured.

BEYOND THE LOCATION OF
THE SEXUAL TRANSCENDENTAL

The theorisation of time as a general horizon has, as *Speculum* makes clear, continually been articulated within a tropology of projection, ec-stasis, autonomy and singularity, a tropology that has also defined what it means to be a masculine subject. Exposing the sex-constitutive character of this putative universality goes further than locating a philosophical bias. It suggests that the determination of the very meaning of subjectivity and the determination of sexual difference are co-originary. Metaphysics is, on such a reading, a way of being or a mode of comportment. But if transcendence – the relation to being – is a quite specific 'passing beyond' and temporality is always more than an empty or neutral horizon, it is not clear that the determination of the subject's becoming can be located within sexual difference alone. Irigaray's work is, quite avowedly, not an anti-subjectivism. Like Heidegger, she regards the question of the *difference* of the given as the question of philosophy, and sustains the importance of philosophy as the asking of this question. Furthermore, she sees the development of a feminine transcendence and identity as the task of feminism. In so doing, she accepts the definition of the subject *as transcendence*. By her own argument, however, this transcendence is not a neutral passing beyond but is determined by its own (and the other's) embodiment. To define this relation, in advance, as governed by sexual alterity seems to return to the very logic of conditions, presence and representation that *Speculum* had criticised.

Read critically, however, *Speculum* exposes the impossibility of any single horizon. If transcendence is a relational phenomenon it will always be effected by that towards which it directs itself and the way in which this directedness is achieved. There is no question of simply abandoning or stepping outside metaphysics; the very possibility of existence and identity is effected through a metaphysical positing. However, within the very logic of metaphysics itself, temporality – as relatedness – could not be reduced to a single, transparent and absolute spontaneity. Once the transcendental horizon is revealed as always already sensibly determined, its determination cannot be contained within the dichotomy of sexual difference alone. Nevertheless, precisely because of philosophy's history – its production of being in terms of meaning and representation – the feminine serves as the privileged opening towards new modalities of transcendence. If the feminine has been produced through a logic of being as presence, then a feminine transcendence provides the first question for thinking otherwise. Thus the feminine is neither an underlying essential condition nor a representational effect of gender construction; rather, the feminine is that point from which the essence/construction divide can be deconstructed.

Further, and this is also suggested by *Speculum*, it may be the very risk of the *transcendental* problematic that needs to be interrogated (if not abandoned). For it is the idea of a single horizon or being-in-general that has always returned difference to some prior anterior condition. Irigaray's critique *divides* that prior condition but she both sustains the function of the *condition* and halts the division at the level of *sexual* difference. Perhaps the metaphysical imperative – the task of thinking the possibility of being – is what produces the *aporia* of Irigaray's work. For Irigaray, autonomous self-becoming is a fundamental and necessary concern for feminist philosophy. This autonomy is defined, not as a capacity bestowed upon worldly individuals, but as the way in which a subject is given a world. Autonomy is aligned with intentionality: the relation towards what is other than the self. Ethics is therefore defined as the subject's authentic discovery of her own intentionality:

> We need to go through this valorizing of the two pronouns *he and she* in order to uphold the intentionality of the I that operates in the relation between I and you; otherwise it becomes pathological. In order to constitute a free and active temporality, the I-woman needs a she that is valorized as a pole of intentionality between she and she, I-she and she-herself. (Irigaray 1996: 67)

Emancipation is a question of autonomous self-constitution. One's autonomy, or the sense of oneself as different, is achieved through the recognition of the (sexual) other who in revealing my limit also reveals my sex. It is temporality, as the horizon of self-becoming in relation to an other, which constitutes for Irigaray the fundamental ethical horizon. This makes feminist ethics not one ethical demand among others, but a way of rethinking the very possibility of ethics. Subjectivity, as temporal transcendence, is defined by a projection towards what it *is not*. From this understanding of transcendence, ethics is then defined as a question of the *general relation* of the subject to that which it is not. For Irigaray a truly ethical transcendence would be to an other, not an other as thing, nor an other of the same genre of subject, but a truly *different* other. Such difference is opened with the recognition of sexual difference. Thus, autonomy would be a sticking point of difference; autonomy would not be the pure giving of law to oneself but a recognition that the difference through which one becomes is *a specific mode of difference*, and a difference that is never fully one's own but occurs in relation to an other.

AUTONOMY

What I have tried to suggest in my reading of Irigaray is a certain paradox surrounding her anti-representationalism, and it is this paradox that is reflected in the reception of her work and the contentious status of essentialism. On the one hand, we could place Irigaray in the Kantian tradition of anti-anthropologism. Her critique of Kantian 'a priorism' would be an extension of the spirit of enlightenment autonomy. *Speculum* demonstrates that the supposedly transcendental subject is in actual fact a specifically embodied subject; and her response is to see the very notion of a self-representing subject as the elevation of a particular sensibility to a putative supersensible. This aspect of Irigaray's work would align her with the enlightenment striving to see the self not as a represented being but as a power or capacity for representation. The ideal of sexual difference and genuine recognition in Irigaray's work is in accord with not reducing the other to the mirror of one's self-representation. The subject must not be perceived in terms of some given representational condition or logic, but as the transcendence towards an other. For Irigaray autonomy is achieved in relation to an other. In such a relation the other is not a represented thing, but another mode of relating.

On the other hand, Irigaray also recognises the problem of seeing the self as *pure* transcendence defined in opposition to positive or sensible representations. Rather, transcendence is both a 'going towards' and a 'genesis from'. The body from which transcendence takes place marks the character of the passage or path to the other. Thus there are *modes* of transcendence or sexed intentionalities. Consequently, alongside a demand for autonomy as transcendence and becoming, there is also in Irigaray's work the desire for recognition. And recognition is only possible in terms of the specific and particular embodiment of one's sex, for only a *sexed* other is sufficiently other to grant me true recognition (not just as another thing but as another becoming).

Read this way, with an attention to the specificity or non-neutrality of transcendence, Irigaray's work is more than critical. If feminist philosophy is to be more than critique and more than an extension of universal enlightenment demands, then it must demand a representation of the feminine. The feminine must be that which transcends itself through positive becoming (and therefore be more than a represented object for a self-representing male subject). At the same time, the feminine must also be represented and recognised, for only in such an act of recognition will ethics deal with *difference*. This difficult ambivalence regarding representation in Irigaray's work cannot be confined within Irigaray's work alone but typifies the problem of feminist ethics in general. Within popular feminism there is a clear rejection of the feminine *as represented* or *as representation*; and this generates widespread criticism regarding clichéd, stereotypical or tyrannical images and representations of women. Women, it is argued, must not be reduced to mere representations. (This is aligned with criticisms of women being regarded as *merely* embodied or passive objects of the male gaze, and subjected to imposed representations.) Nevertheless, there is an equally widespread demand *for representation* which constitutes the very core, not only of identity politics, but of any positive feminist ethics. Women must be given representation, not only in the sense of representative democracy, but in the inclusion of women's perspectives, knowledges, bodies and experiences. This is also expressed in the demands for *feminist* philosophy, *feminist* epistemology and various other disciplines that do more than consider women from *within* a discipline or method, arguing that the feminine contributes a specific mode of a discipline.

In this regard the issue of feminism can be seen to turn around the antinomy of representation. One must recognise that women are not just representations or images; women are not just objects for a subject. Woman is not a represented thing but is also a representing being. (This mirrors the rejection of anthropologism: woman cannot be defined essentially as an object in the world, for women also constitute and live their world.) But feminism has also been a demand for representation: the subject must not be seen as some general, universal or neutral power. There is no general or transcendental subjectivity; subjects are only given as, or known through, particular modes of embodiment, and it is the specific contribution of women's embodiment that demands a *feminist* understanding of subjectivity. (Like the critique of anthropomorphism this demand for a *positive* feminism refuses to see a general ground, logic or subjectivity that is not *lived* in a certain way. The subject is not a general condition but is always given or known in a determined way.) Irigaray's representational *aporia* might be seen as exemplary, not only of feminist ethics, but of any post-enlightenment demand for a specific or positive ethics. What makes representation crucial to this *aporia* is its location as the very limit of experience and the world. In order to *have* a world there must be a subject to whom the world is given; pure immediacy would preclude the possibility of the very idea of experience. Thus, the world must in some sense be effected through a relation of representation. And the subject can be defined as nothing other than this relation of representation, and not as a represented thing. The reduction of man to a being within the world (anthropologism) or woman to an object for a male subject (phallogocentrism) are analogous in their failure to recognise the representational condition. Neither man nor woman can be exhaustively defined as beings within the world, for the world *is* only in so far as it is given *to* experiencing subjects. But to acknowledge the representational condition, the point of view of the human or the subject, already raises the possibility that there is no such general or transcendental point *to be recognised*. For what is posited as the condition of the represented world is only thought, recognised or given as represented. The demand for various forms of positive ethics – such as feminism – lies in representing the different modalities of representation, the different ways in which the world is given. And this is why the notion of autonomy becomes a site of contention: is ethics the recognition of the point to which the world is given, or is ethics a responsibility or striving for that which lies beyond autonomy? For Irigaray ethics can only begin with autonomy, with the recognition that there is no transcendence in general, but only specific, embodied and different modes of transcendence. And so ethics is tied to transcendental questions; ethics is not an event within the world – it is not an anthropologism. Ethics is the question of the (different) openings to the world.

For Irigaray, an ethics of sexual difference would be beyond representation precisely because the primary relation would not be between a subject who re-presents a world, but between two subjects. But her ethics would still locate itself within the problem of autonomy as transcendence. This autonomy would be defined against anthropologism, against accepting the subject as already differentiated. Rather, for Irigaray the subject is nothing other than a relation of difference. But does Irigaray's emphasis on autonomy go far enough? Does the emphasis on *sexual* difference not risk an anthropologism by describing a site from which difference is given? These questions can be approached by thinking anti-representationalism alongside an anti-transcendental philosophy of immanence. These are, indeed, the terms in which Gilles Deleuze has defined his philosophy of 'transcendental empiricism' and in which Michel Foucault has launched his project of overcoming the 'subjection to transcendence'.

NOTE

1. The importance of autonomy in Irigaray's work is brought out most clearly in Elizabeth Grosz's *Sexual Subversions* (1989: 109). Grosz provides an intelligent response to the early criticisms of Irigaray as an essentialist. Demanding a feminine autonomy does not require an appeal to an already present female essence; on the contrary, if the feminine were autonomous it would not be a represented essence but a movement of its own existence.

5

FOUCAULT:
ANTI-REPRESENTATIONALISM
AND LOGOPHOBIA

———◁▷———

Anthropology constitutes perhaps the fundamental arrangement that has governed and controlled the path of philosophical thought from Kant until our own day. This arrangement is essential, since it forms part of our history; but it is disintegrating before our eyes, since we are beginning to recognize and denounce in it, in a critical mode, both a forgetfulness of the opening that made it possible and a stubborn obstacle standing obstinately in the way of an imminent new form of thought. (Foucault 1970: 342)

THE BEING OF MAN AND THE BEING OF
LANGUAGE

In his archaeology of the human sciences (*The Order of Things*), Michel Foucault defines modernity as representational and also makes the astounding claim that the 'being of man and the being of language have never, at any time, been able to coexist and to articulate themselves one upon the other' (Foucault 1970: 339). There is a certain widespread reading of Foucault that would make sense of this claim in the following way: for Foucault there is nothing outside discourse; and man is nothing other than a discursive construct. But it is just this type of 'discursive' or linguistic reading of Foucault that misses the crucial point of Foucault's archaeology and his critique of representation. We need to remember that the French title of this work was 'Words and Things' (*Les mots et les choses*). This, alongside the English title, raises the question of the *relation* (the 'and' or 'order') between words and things. If the being of man and language have not been thought together this is not because we have naively posited a human spirit free of discursive contamination or representation. On the contrary, the question of the *ordering* of things, or the words added to things, is for Foucault a question concerning the difference between what *is*, and what is said. The being of man is not (necessarily) representational: he is not a mirror of the world. Words are not the expression of already meaningful things. The world itself is not already *ordered*. To think the *being* of man and the *being* of language entails thinking their difference. We can't assume a representational unity whereby words are nothing more than the faithful repetition of things, and where man is nothing more than the articulation of an already meaningful world.

Foucault's history of representation, described from *The Order of Things* to *The History of Sexuality, Volume One*, is a history of man as a representational animal. The transition from the Renaissance to modernity is framed by a pre-representational origin and an imagined post-representational future. At both ends of this history there is no *man* – that being who replicates the already given order of the world in his own logic. Originally, Foucault argues, prior to the fall into representation, language functioned as a *being in its own right*. Truth was not some ideal entity, nor some correspondence with facts, nor some thing in itself, but was the *force of words*. Truth was not what words conveyed or revealed but was the very dynamism of articulation. Language was originally non-representational; it was not subordinated to some being outside itself. The division between a true world and a concomitant representing discourse is, Foucault insists, 'a historically constituted division' and one whose boundaries we can discern:

> For, even with the sixth century Greek poets, true discourse – in the meaningful sense – inspiring respect and terror, to which all were obliged to submit, because it held sway over all and was pronounced by men who spoke as of right, according to ritual, meted out justice and attributed to each his rightful share; it prophesied the future, not merely announcing what was going to occur, but contributing to its actual event, carrying men along

with it and thus weaving itself into the fabric of fate. And yet, a century later, the highest truth no longer resided in what discourse *was*, nor in what it *did*: it lay in what was *said*. The day dawned when truth moved over from the ritualised act – potent and just – of enunciation to settle on what was enunciated itself: its meaning, its form, its object and its relation to what it referred to. A division emerged between Hesiod and Plato, separating true discourse from false; it was a new division for, henceforth, true discourse was no longer considered precious and desirable, since it had ceased to be discourse linked to the exercise of power. And so the sophists were routed.

This historical division has doubtless lent its general form to our will to knowledge. (Foucault 1972a: 218)

Language once had the force of its own being. It was not 'subjected to transcendence' or legitimated by some external ground or presence. It is in thinking of language *this way* – as a being and force in its own right – that we might overcome what Foucault diagnoses as a series of slavish *reactions* – including the 'Western episteme's' 'subjection to transcendence'. Language is *active* when it presents itself as assertion, force or power or when it 'emerges in all its brute being as a thing' (Foucault 1970: 118). Before Plato and the 'routing' of the Sophists, language was force and ritual; its authority derived from its act of enunciation and not what was being said. Language avowed its own being as effective, rather than meaningful or representational. Language becomes *reactive*, however, when seen as the mere replica, mirror or representation of some 'outside' (and when power is seen as something that might corrupt language, rather than enabling the very being of language). The Western 'subjection to transcendence' is, in Foucault's genealogy of humanism, also at one with a persistently reactive representationalism. For Foucault, any transcendence – any outside, presence, ground or being – is not beyond the field of force or power – as though there were being or what is on the one hand, and its representation or givenness on the other. If this were so then we would think of power as that which distorts or precludes the relation between what is and what is known. But power is crucial to the formation of knowledges. It is through power that a transcendence is given. Indeed, power just is the production of 'empiricities'; power is the differentiation, distribution or dispersal within which the events of language and experience take place. To see language or thought as subordinate to transcendence is to forget that transcendence *transcends* (or is rendered external) through power. Transcendence is not some presence which language might double or re-present. Transcendence is always given as transcendence through relations. And these relations are *active, ungrounded* and *multiple*. These relations of distribution produce positions and empiricities (and hence are active). It is precisely this history of relations that Foucault undertakes, for it is in the relation to an outside, or truth, that the self is also established as a modality of relation or reflection (Foucault 1998: 446).

Further, there is no presence that is *then* ordered by power. Power is just what gives order, but not as an ordering *of* some ground that precedes power. More importantly, power itself is not a ground, for it is not a single medium. Rather, power distributes itself in different modalities – through the spatial, linguistic, corporeal, visual and incorporeal modes of difference:

[P]ower must be understood in the first instance as the multiplicity of force relations immanent in the sphere in which they operate and which constitute their own organization; as the process which, through ceaseless struggles and confrontations, transforms, strengthens, or reverses them; as the support which these force relations find in one another, thus forming a chain or a system, or on the contrary, the disjunctions and contradictions which isolate them from one another; and lastly, as the strategies in which they take effect, whose general design or institutional crystallization is embodied in the state apparatus, in the formulation of the law, in the various social hegemonies. Power's condition of possibility, or in any case the view point which permits one to understand its exercise, even in its more 'peripheral' effects, and which also makes it possible to use its mechanisms as a grid of intelligibility of the social order, must not be sought in the primary existence of a central point, in a unique source of sovereignty from which secondary and descendent forms would emanate; it is the moving substrate of force relations which, by virtue of their inequality constantly engender states of power, but the latter are always local and unstable. (Foucault 1981: 92–3)

To see power as the differentiation *of* some pre-powerful presence would be an inherently reactive mode of thinking. It would aim for some presence or ground to which thought might respond; it would locate truth *beyond* force and action, and would subordinate action to some presence. On the other hand, to see power itself as at one with what is (and what is said) would *activate* thinking. Thinking would no longer have to disavow its interests or aim at disinterest. If all that is and all that is said is at one with power, then thinking, language and being will be considered in terms of what they do (and not their fidelity or accuracy). Language will be an event with an effective force, and not the mirroring of some real.

This is why from early on Foucault wanted to think the *being* of language non-representationally. This would demand seeing language *neither* as an ordering scheme or logic *nor* as the expression of some pre-linguistic logic. What needs to be thought, he insisted, is language as one site of ordering or force among others. This separation of language from a notion of a natural order or logic would be achieved in two ways. Firstly, the field of logic or constitutive difference would need to *exceed* language. Foucault locates language in a discursive formation, where discourse is broader than language. Discourse includes the truth functions granted to statements, speaking positions, institutional boundaries, rules of production and other features (Foucault 1972a: 226). This means that language is not some locatable schema or structure but is part of a wider field of difference or distribution. Secondly, not only does logic exceed language – with Foucault granting a logic to bodily practices, spatial relations and fields of the visible – language also exceeds logic. Language is not just an ordering of the world or a communicational medium. Like all the media through which difference takes place – light, bodies, space – language also has a being not reducible to its ordering function.

Foucault's criticism of representation and its concomitant modern motifs differs from other accounts in that it does not just attack the Enlightenment separation between the subject and the world. Whereas representation is often criticised for posing a Cartesian 'ghost' or mirroring subject who then has to meet or find a world, Foucault's anti-representationalism targets the unifying or normalising force of the representational Western episteme in general. The problem with the idea of representation is that it creates a passage or right path between presence and representation, and in so doing *submits* thought to a proper relation to an outside. In contrast, Foucault will assert the break, gap or force that characterises any event of language. The world itself does not speak; things are not meaningful in themselves. Thought is not a proper reaction to the world but an active event. Nevertheless, it is because language is a positive event – with its own force, effect and being – that Foucault will also assert a *logic* of existence. Experience is not the immediate or self-present apprehension of a world; rather there is a *logic* to experience. But this logic is neither at one with the subject – for the subject is always effected through relations – nor at one with the world, for the empirical is given through the differentiation or dispersing force of power. Thus the logic or system of existence is not reducible to subject or object, for both are effected within a logic. This logic or system of existence is just that perceived regularity of a distribution that then effects meaning, subjectivity and decision:

> Behind the visible facade of the system, one posits the rich uncertainty of disorder; and beneath the thin surface of discourse, the whole mass of a largely silent development (*devenir*): a 'presystematic' that is not of the order of the system; a 'prediscursive' that belongs to an essential silence. Discourse and system produce each other – and conjointly – only at the crest of this immense reserve. What are being analysed here are certainly not the terminal states of discourse; they are the *preterminal regularities* in relation to which the ultimate state, far from constituting the birth-place of a system, is defined by its variants. Behind the completed system, what is discovered by the analysis of formations is not the bubbling source of life itself, life in an as yet uncaptured state; it is an immense density of systematicities, a tight group of multiple relations. (Foucault 1972a: 76)

For the most part Foucault describes this dispersal (which can then be recognised in its logical regularity) as *power*. One can't simply assume the existence of a structure, order or logic of existence, for one can always ask about the force or genesis of that logic. To think this force or genesis as ungrounded is the task of Foucault's project, and explains the importance of power in his work. Power is not the power *of* some originating intent, nor is power *over* some pure presence, nor is power itself a medium through which difference takes place. Power is just that positivity, effect or force that produces regularities. Power is the production of certain effects. The reactive illusion then often follows of thinking of power as some preceding cause, as though power had a *nature* or *being* which is expressed through its effects. But the contrary is just the case. Power is effect or activity. It is in the *reaction* to power that we think of these effects as issuing *from* some cause. It is after the event of power that thought can become reactive. We take power as the effect of some ground, or as the limit of some existence. But we have reversed the causal relation. We take the regularities of power – its distributions – as a logic or order to be recognised. But the regularity comes after the event of power. Power as an active event is contingent, irregular, *ad hoc* and pre-logical. But once this event takes place it can be taken as necessary (rather than being the contingent production of what then becomes necessary). The challenge of thought is not to recognise or represent the logic of existence, but to become worthy of the event of power: thinking the groundless character of *our* logic.

Like Heidegger, Foucault insists that any order or system (any logic) is an effect of a dispersion. Heidegger's reference to *equi-primordial* conditions in *Being and Time* had already insisted that any ground of thought is effected through a prior differentiation, and that this differentiation was neither purely spatial nor temporal – for both space and time are differentiated through each other. Space is always determined through the specific historicity of existence; and temporality is always located in a 'there' or *Dasein*. Similarly, Foucault will demonstrate that thought takes place in a *medium* which cannot be reduced to a single condition or system. What is important for both Foucault and Heidegger is not just that thought has an 'other'. The significance of Heidegger's contribution lay in stressing the different modes of this separation; thought's other, or being, is disclosed by the way in which thought questions its world (Heidegger 1959: 6). The significance of Foucault's demonstration of *historical* a priori is not just an argument regarding thought's context or conditions (Foucault 1970: 157); it is not the simple historicist thesis that all thought is located in some world-view. Foucault does not argue for history *as an* a priori; he argues that thought's medium or condition – the a priori itself – differs historically (Foucault 1970: 158). That is, whatever is taken as the ground or medium of thought is not a timeless ground but is determined by the different ways in which thought is distributed. In the nineteenth century, for example, history was understood as an a priori; thought was understood as the development of ideas through time; consciousness was defined as nothing other than an unfolding temporality (Foucault 1970: 370). But thought has also been otherwise. There have been different games of truth. In Ancient Greece thought understood itself as the management of bodies and pleasures (Foucault 1988). In premodern Europe thought was defined through analogy, as the reflection of some infinite divine order. In the classical age thought becomes representational, a repetition of the world's order (Foucault 1970: 208); and then in modernity thought itself becomes the finite medium of order, categorisation or system. It is this idea of *historical* a priori that changes the very problem of *logos and* a priori. Thought is nothing other than the different modalities in which it produces its other. The distinction between what thought is and what is known is not a once and for all subject/object distinction, but varies according to the questions, practices and procedures of truth: practices that effect a medium within which truth, the empirical and transcendence will be constituted. There is not an unthought in general – such as being – that is then articulated. Nor can we think of thought as essentially a single medium differentiating itself – for how thought questions and goes beyond itself will both differ historically and also depend on certain positive conditions. (The questions of the human sciences, for example, were only possible given certain material and contingent events: the construction of prisons, hospitals, and asylums that allowed the human mind to become an object of investigation.) The *fold* of thought – the difference between thought and the unthought – varies historically and itself depends on a logic that exceeds thought.

Through this focus on the modality of questions, Foucault's genealogy of representation presents itself in opposition to transcendental inquiry. Foucault presents his work as a strategy, and not a general theory (Foucault 1998: 451). This, however, is the very problem that Derrida identifies in Foucault's work: the problem of the point from which Foucault's own critique will be based. If Foucault can argue, as he does in *Madness and Civilization*, that Descartes's notion of reason is objectifying and totalising, this is only because Foucault himself must assume some (Cartesian) position of critical judgement. The very possibility of Foucault's own history, Derrida will insist, is a notion of reason that can step outside any particular formation and judge its limits, exclusions and effects (Derrida 1978: 43). Foucault's entire corpus will confront this problem: whether it is possible *not* to think in terms of *justification in general* and whether it is possible to proceed ethically – in terms of what thought can do – rather than transcendentally – in terms of the conditions of thinking. Can thought ask about its specific effects, decisions, force and procedure *without* subordinating itself to some ideal of an overarching reason or *logos*? Could thought avow the difference of its own event, rather than efface itself as the reaction *to* some transcendence?

In setting itself this task – the task of recognising the force of thought and language, rather than seeing thinking as the simple double of things – Foucault's genealogy refuses to locate all that is within human representational conditions. Rather, from our current concerns – regarding representation, structure, genesis and the transcendental – Foucault traces how these questions became possible. This means that his own point of inquiry is contingent and implicated within the field of knowledge. Foucault is *neither* asserting that there is just some system of differences with no ground (discourse) *nor* that there is some general medium (history) within which difference can be located. Foucault's idea of a discursive formation does not describe a system of difference, nor does it refer to a differentiating condition. Discursive formations are *dispersions*: different ways in which difference is effected, the production of various sites and modalities of difference. A discursive formation is the carving out of a domain of knowledge and contestation, with a concomitant production of an exteriority, a substance or medium that provides the ground or unthought (Foucault 1972a: 231).

If there are modes of differentiation or dispersion this means that we will be unable to have a general theory of the subject; rather, the subject is nothing other than the contingent and specific ways in which it differentiates itself from an outside. And this differentiation is not the subject's own, but depends upon technical or juridical procedures. In the first volume of the *History of Sexuality*, for example, Foucault will show how 'life' was produced as a site of knowledge and domain of inquiry. This medium (of 'life') through which thought and knowledge will take place depends on various conditions: the discourse of sexuality, modern medical procedures, the spatial distribution of certain institutions such as hospitals, courts and prisons, and modes of visibility such as the medical gaze, self-inspection and body discipline. For Foucault, then, the focus on life would be one mode of the a priori, one way in which the medium of knowledge and questions was effected across a variety of domains and practices. Further, this particular mode of a priori, he argues, is inherently *normalising*; for the attention to 'life' sees thought as located within a general ground, a ground that is then endlessly interpreted, recognised and re-presented: 'A normalizing society is the historical outcome of a technology of power centred on life' (Foucault 1981: 144).

As described by Foucault, representation is a specifically modern modality of knowledge but it is also a mode of a priori that intensifies the reactivism of the Western episteme. Representation ultimately locates thought within a grounding condition or logic – such as history, structure, culture or the unconscious – and in so doing denies the active event of thought. Thought then turns towards itself, discloses itself and interprets itself, as though thought were a presence to be re-presented, or an origin to be infinitely disclosed and brought before itself:

> [I]n showing that man is determined, it is concerned with show-ing that the foundation of those determinations is man's very being in its radical limitations; it must also show that the contents of experience are already their own conditions, that thought, from the very beginning, haunts the unthought that eludes them, and that it is always striving to recover; it shows how that origin of which man is never the contemporary is at the same time with-drawn and given as an imminence: in short, it is always concerned with showing how the Other, the Distant, is also the Near and the Same. (Foucault 1970: 339)

In opposition to this process of a modern *cogito* that continually recuperates itself, Foucault insists that the logic of existence is not a given ground to be discovered. Any grounding of thought is itself an event within existence and ought to be affirmed as such. The ground of thought is the outcome of certain procedures and practices of truth. It is through discourse and its relations – what discourse does – that modes of the pre-discursive are effected. This is why Foucault sees modernity as the culmination of a 'profound logophobia' (Foucault 1972a: 229). We have always assumed that thought was the faithful representation of a general *logos*, and in so doing we have refused to consider the force, effect and power of thinking. We have seen language as a 'signifier' – a mere copy of the world – rather than an event in its own right (Foucault 1972a: 229). For Foucault, anthropologism is crucial to this logophobia. The production of man as an object of knowledge, or as a finite being within the world, allows us to think logic as an objectified system and not as the very opening of all objectivity. Through various institutions man is produced as an object whose subjectivity would provide the ground of all truth and decision:

> That was the aim of judicial institutions, that was the aim also of medical and psychiatric practices, that was the aim of political and philosophical theory – to constitute the ground of the subjectivity as the root of the positive self, what we could call the permanent anthropologism of Western thought. And I think that this anthropologism is linked to the deep desire to substitute the positive figure of man for the sacrifice which for Christianity was the condition for the opening of the self as a field of indefinite interpretation. (Foucault 1993: 222)

The human sciences are the culmination of this general anthropologism that locates the *logos* within the being of man. Through the study of biology, economics and linguistics human life is studied through an 'analytic of finitude' (Foucault 1970: 316). Whereas pre-modernity had regarded 'man' as a being in an infinite order of beings, now man functions as the limit of a system or logic. As such, then, the being of man functions as the ground of all logic and system. Modern anthropologism is both the culmination of the Western episteme as well as its intensification; for in its modern form anthropologism no longer studies an infinite 'unfolding' of truth of which man is a part. In modernity man himself is the ground of truth. Man's finitude – his location within systems of life, labour and language – not only produces man as an object of knowing, it also established a peculiar modality of the knowledge/power relation. In the anthropologism of the human sciences thought is reduced to a system or logic within the world. By this means modernity produces representational conditions as an object of knowledge (Foucault 1970: 339). Recognition of these representational conditions becomes a normalising procedure and culminates in what

Foucault refers to as the 'anthropological sleep' (Foucault 1970: 340). Thought has taken itself as a being within the world to be known and normalised, rather than as an event or encounter alongside other events.

Thinking ought not to be a matter of recognition, as though the ground of thought could be disclosed. On the contrary, by questioning *where we are* – by examining our own dependence on concepts of representation and man as a thinking animal – Foucault's project attempts to dislocate thought. This will be achieved not by appealing to some radical outside or transcendence but by confronting all those inhuman, unrecognisable and positive features that determine thought from within. Language, for instance, would be neither the seamless expression of man's self-representing being, nor some pre-given representational scheme or structure. Foucault's notion of discourse takes the very medium of human becoming in order to demonstrate its inhuman *being*. Discourse is positive. It marks differences, produces empiricities, effects relations and constitutes decisive limits. Foucault will attempt to theorise this effective power of discourse through the twin notions of 'incorporeal materialism' and 'immanence'. Both these notions will attempt to take thought from its human and representational home to other possibilities.

IMMANENCE AND EVENT

How does the idea of immanence do this? A representational understanding of language is tied to transcendence: language is the representation of some outside (such as meaning, being, sense, context or structure). But if language is thought in terms of immanence, signs will not be the re-presentations *of* some outside. Signs will themselves be events, acts, or instances of force and power. In a philosophy of immanence, it is not as though there is some being, presence or transcendence that is then doubled or mirrored through signs. There is just a domain of immanence that includes discursive events, alongside other events – with neither being the sign of the other. This is why both Foucault and Deleuze make so much of the idea of *series*: language or representation is not the grounding condition of the world, nor is the world some pre-representational ground for language. The two exist alongside each other. Metaphysics has organised language and being into a representational series, whereby signs are grounded upon some pre-linguistic transcendence. The task of both Deleuze and Foucault is the creation of different series.

Foucault's project of immanence is clearly critical of the idea of thought as a representation, but this critique does not issue in an attempt to restore thought to some pre-representational or pre-modern moment of non-separation. Indeed, Foucault is critical of the 'logo-phobia' that reduces language to being the mere mirror of things. Against this, Foucault's own work had articulated an 'incorporeal materialism' – all the ways in which knowledge is a force that acts, effects and constitutes certain beings. This is expressed most clearly in Foucault's 'Theatrum Philosophicum', a review of Deleuze's *Difference and Repetition* and *The Logic of Sense*. What Foucault finds in *The Logic of Sense* (in Foucault 1998: 343–68) is a theory of meaning that liberates thought from the representational paradigm, and does so through the notion of incorporeality. Foucault begins by describing all philosophy since Plato as an attempt to reverse the Platonic series. What is this series? It is the establishment of a certain order or grammar that grounds the copy on the original, a representation on a prior presence, or a phantasm on the essence. Against this, Foucault argues, Deleuze comes up with the concept of the event. This creates a new series. In the Platonic series, sense and meaning are grounded on a model of re-presentation, such that thought has a ground or being upon which it is founded. Just as Foucault's *The Order of Things* attempts to open some room for thought by describing the way in which this represen-tational series is effected (that is, how a ground, table or foundation for thought is effected), so Deleuze's notion of the event tries to point out that thinking and meaning are positive and differential: not the replications of some prior presence but forms of force and difference in themselves. It is not that there is a grounding substance that is then known or thought. Any such division – between what is and what is thought – is the effect of a differential event. The event is more than substance. It is not the replication of being – as a copy or double – it is a force in its own right. There is, therefore, no possibility of reducing 'what is' to brute corporeality, for there are also incorporeal events such as words, images, thoughts and simulations. What Deleuze will do, according to Foucault, is free the incorporeal from meaning. The event is not meaning; it is that passage or path from the corporeal to the incorporeal. A word, for example, is both corporeal – the concrete, physical and material sound unit – but it also becomes more than this in being taken as meaningful or as the sign of something other than the word. The event is just this passage or creation of sense. This is what makes the event into a new series, and what makes it a break in the Platonic series. In *The Logic of Sense* Deleuze looks at the way the body's surface doubles itself and simulates, creates phantasms prior to meaning and intention. The voice for example is at once a corporeal organ but it also produces sounds and words, sounds that *then* become meaning. It is the passage from the corporeality of the material body to the incorporeality of sense that is given in the event. This means that sense is not a faithful double of what is (not a representation) but a cut, fissure, fibrillation or ungrounded difference – not a difference *from*, nor a difference *of*, but an event of difference. What the event presents us with, then, is a way of thinking the positivity of the incorporeal, and this will also move us beyond ontology. For the event is neither being nor non-being but 'extra-being'. The event is the way the actual or 'what is' affirms itself differentially, and each time as different:

> At the limit of dense bodies, an event is incorporeal (a metaphysical surface); on the surface of words and things, an incorporeal event is the *meaning* of a proposition (its logical dimension); in the thread of discourse, an incorporeal meaning-event is fastened to the verb (the infinitive point of the present). (Foucault 1998: 350)

This would then mean that the very idea of the subject or *logos* – as that point through which the world is disclosed or constituted – would be dispersed. We might still have to sustain the question of who speaks, and locate all discursive events in certain positions of force and decision. But these positions would not be the origins of the decision. It is through the *active* event of discursive procedures that positions or selves are effected. Examining the force and event of discourse exposes the selves or speaking positions produced. This is why Foucault speaks of abolishing the 'sovereignty of the signifier' (Foucault 1972a: 229). It is the notion of the signifier, as the simple double or re-presentation of some prior sense, that leads us to think of language as nothing more than a reflection of the world or the vehicle of sense. But language has its own active force. And it is this denial of language, this *logophobia*, that has subjected thought to some outside. Further, it is this notion of

language as the expression or representation of some transcendence
that has culminated in the 'anthropological sleep' of modernity. For it is
the idea of man – who can be investigated as the ground, horizon or
origin of sense – that has precluded us from thinking all those positive
discursive events that have produced man as an object. Thus for Foucault
anthropologism and transcendence are intertwined: only with the idea
of a being who is the site, point of view or ground for the world (man),
is thought *subjected* to some norm or image of thought. Whereas transcendence in the pre-modern period was understood to be the very
meaning or order of the world; it is in modernity and anthropologism
that transcendence takes the form of the human. The medium of truth
is man himself, produced through all those human sciences that view
man as an object to be discovered, recognised and represented in an
endless process of reactive self-objectification. Recognising the force of
discourse, on the other hand, will render thought *active*. No longer the
sign *of*, or recognition *of*, transcendence, thought will be an event itself.
There will be no normalising medium from which thought and discourse emerge; the challenge of immanence is thinking discourse as an
event in itself, without ground, and one that can neither be reduced to
thought nor thoroughly encompassed by thought (Foucault 1972a: 74).

Thought and discourse are not fully coterminous, and this explains
Foucault's insistence on incorporeal materialism. Discursive formations
are material. They are not the ideal expressions of sense, the simple
becoming of a *logos*. Discourse has a force. It produces possibilities and
exclusions. The discourse of sexuality, for example, actually orders bodies,
marks its pleasures and produces its truth. The discourse that speaks of
the criminal, the hysteric or the homosexual may be *incorporeal*; but
these discourses function materially or produce concrete effects. Unlike
pre-modern modes of power, discourse does not act directly on the
body – through incarceration, corporal punishment or medical inter-
vention. But the incorporeality of certain events – such as discursive
formations and relations of visibility – is nevertheless material. Bodies
are worked upon, disciplined and distribute their own pleasures through
discursive formations. And if this is so the self is not some autonomous
subject who precedes and represents a world, not some grounding
consciousness, but a point at which certain regularised procedures will
effect *modes of self-relation*. Modern discursive formations, for example,
produce the self through the ground or medium of life and sexuality.

The modern self inquires into itself in order to disclose, recognise, interpret and uncover its being. The self is formed as a *subject*: as a being to be known and not as an activity of knowing. And this modern production of subject is both material (in producing bodies in certain ways) and incorporeal (through discourse). But discourse is not the only incorporeal dimension of power. Once we think of power in this non-juridical way we have to acknowledge a wider logic of existence. The layout of prisons, the medical gaze, the disciplinary look of the schoolroom all effect the very being of bodies and demonstrate the productive character of power. In Foucault's most well-known example, it is through the visible distribution of the panopticon that an inner self or soul is effected. Because the gaze of power is possible, and is made possible by a viewing tower at the centre of the prison, the prisoner will become self-viewing. A visible relation – the possibility of a gaze – produces an incorporeal effect. The prisoner is no longer subject to corporal discipline; an incorporeal 'soul' or inner self is produced that incarcerates the self to its own being (Foucault 1979: 217). And in the nineteenth century the productive gaze of power will shift again; in the human sciences and the discourse of sexuality the self will no longer be observed from without but will examine and study itself.

The soul produced by the panopticon is one mode of anthropologism among others; and Foucault's history exposes both the persistence of anthropologism and its quite different manifestations. 'Man' is the effect of certain questions or games of truth. In the eighteenth century a new question produces a new being. What is the criminal? What grounds his inner being, psyche or intent? The criminal is now more than his actions, for these actions have been referred back to some subject (Foucault 1979: 18). But these questions that produce the soul of the prisoner are themselves effected through visible relations, such as the gaze of the panopticon and the point of view of the criminologist. Foucault's project of immanence will radically re-figure the problems of anthropologism and point of view. Like Kant and Heidegger, Foucault will refuse to locate a grounding subject or site of logic within the world. His work extends Kant's critique of anthropologism: man cannot operate as the ground of thought or logic because man is already a posited being and effected through logic. But whereas Kant will refer logic back to the transcendental subject, and Heidegger will reappropriate *logos* as the very sending of being, Foucault will attempt to think the logic of existence positively. Logic is not a general ground, nor the radically anterior site of an ungrounding. The logic of existence is immanent: effected through events of discourse, practices, spatial and visible relations, and bodily management. Power is positive and immanent: it issues in a multiplicity of effects and distributions. It is not an 'outside' or ground that might be disclosed, for any act of disclosure or interpretation would be another specific and located (power) event. After the event of power we might recognise a certain regularity or logic – such as the production of man – but it would be reactive to think man as the ground of that logic. In order to think *actively* thought must constantly engage in misrecognition: confronted with what we are or the point of view from where we speak, we must be compelled to think otherwise (Foucault 1986a). This would not demand an appeal to an outside or anteriority always belied by thought. Rather, thought must be understood as not at home with itself – as effected within a domain of difference and relations that includes the unthought (bodies, the visible, space, and the being of discourse).

REPRESENTATION

According to Foucault, then, the representationalism of the classical episteme is both a specific modality of the a priori – a specific way in which events are distributed – as well as being an instance of the Western 'refusal of positivity' (Foucault 1970: 371). The general history of *The Order of Things* takes up and extends Heidegger's critique of representation (targeting Heidegger's 'being' as one more effected transcendence that then comes to function as a prior ground [Foucault 1970: 325]). In many ways Foucault's history in *The Order of Things* mirrors Heidegger's critique of modernity, although there is an important difference. Foucault concentrates on how representationalism produces specific practices and systems of knowledge (in particular the eventual study of man as a representational animal). Heidegger's task of overcoming representation by thinking being more authentically is a return to thought's more appropriate dwelling. Foucault, on the other hand, seeks to unhouse thought and demonstrate that all its posited homes or origins are specific, contingent and continually undergoing reconfiguration and transformation. Furthermore, any site or space of knowledge that is posited as an origin of representation is an effect of the refraction or distribution of representation itself. This is one of the points made by Foucault's analysis of *Las Meninas*, the scene that opens *The Order of Things*. In his detailed description of Velásquez's painting Foucault describes the play of light, the distribution of gazes, a series of reflecting surfaces, and the way in which the framed painting situates a viewing subject. From this one can conclude that point of view is a positive effect (and not a transcendental horizon). There is no single perspective that exceeds experience in general; the point of the viewer is effected *within the visual field*. Nor is experience adequately described as *perspective* (a way of seeing, ideology or world-view). Perspectives and positions have *positive conditions*: systems of language, disciplinary boundaries, the distribution of bodies in space and the organisation of the visible. So we cannot think representation as the condition for thought; there is no single representational condition; there are a number of positive conditions of which the idea of representation is an effect.

The classical idea of knowledge as re-presentation presupposes *a world that only needs to be spoken*. Knowledge might then regard itself as an articulation of the world. This is why Foucault refers, in this period, to the world as a 'murmur' – not already articulate but thoroughly articulable. So there is at one and the same time a break with the Renaissance idea of an *already* meaningful world of resemblance alongside a retained sense of the world as on its way to being meaningful, requiring only representation: 'There must be, in the things represented, the insistent murmur of resemblance; there must be, in the representation, the perpetual possibility of imaginative recall' (Foucault 1970: 69; see also 120). The next period of modernity is one in which the murmur of things becomes a problem. There begins to be a question of the validity of the relation between logic (order) and ontology (what is).

This is why Kant is an important figure in the background of *The Order of Things*. Kant saw the natural sciences proceeding with happy certainty (confined to represented things) while philosophy appeared to be locked into unanswerable questions about God, the origin of the world, the infinite and so on. The answer? Kant showed that the certainty of the natural sciences was secured by their location within the categories of thought (representation); philosophy's task would then be to ask how such certainty was possible (that is, what is the condition for the possibility of representation). In so doing Kant at once adhered to the classical episteme of representation and constituted 'a new philosophical space' which was also *the limit of representation*:

> Inversely, a new philosophical space was to emerge in the place where the objects of Classical knowledge dissolved. The moment of attribution (as a form of judgement) and that of articulation (as a general patterning of beings) separated, and thus created the problem of the relations between a formal apophantics and a formal ontology; the moment of primitive designation and that of derivation through time also separated, opening up a space in which there arose the question of the relations between original meaning and history. Thus the two great forms of modern philosophic reflection were established. The first questions the relations between logic and ontology; it proceeds by the paths of formalization and encounters, in a new form, the problem of *mathesis*. The second questions the relations of signification and time; it undertakes an unveiling which is not and probably never can be completed, and it brings back into prominence the themes and methods of *interpretation*. (Foucault 1970: 207)

These 'two great forms' might be described as genesis and structure. The question of structure asks how systems of formal meaning (logic, geometry, mathematics, pure truth) relate to the world and how they are constituted. But the question of ideal structure has as its counterpart the 'second' form of knowledge which is that of genesis. Structures of knowledge cannot just be enclosed within a totality – history, psychology, formal systems or logic – they must have *emerged*. This is the problem of the opening of meaning, the origin or genesis of sense. It presents thought with the task of *interpreting* all its formal systems and inquiring into their origin or constitution. It is, essentially, Heidegger's question of *Ereignis*, as well as being Derrida's concern with the *arche*, trace or non-origin (Foucault 1972a: 121). It is the question of the origin of thought as meaning, the opening of structure. Heidegger's anti-representationalism can be understood as an insistence on the question of genesis, on how any logic or system opens. And Derrida's projection of deconstruction is a radicalisation of this 'question of the question'; for deconstruction will focus on those textual events that open the possibility of any scheme or structure. Derrida will attend to an 'untamed genesis' – a genesis that opens sense but that cannot itself be conceptualised. Derrida's quasi-transcendental method of attending to the opening of meaning that always exceeds the grasp of meaning could therefore be historically located within what Foucault describes as the 'empirico-transcendental' problematic. Here, thought locates its positivity or finitude within a transcendental horizon or ground.

Rather than short-circuit the transcendental question, Foucault aims to delimit the question of genesis and structure, the question of the origin of logic and recognition of conditions. Is thought condemned to retrace the limits of man, or is there a way beyond the anthropological sleep? The recognition of the *structure* of logic is the recognition of thought's own condition or limit. Like Derrida (1982a: 135), Foucault acknowledges that this recognition runs the risk of locating thought in its own home – the risk of anthropologism:

> [F]or the slightest deviation from these rigorously defined planes [philosophy and the natural sciences] sends thought tumbling over into the domain occupied by the human sciences: hence the danger of 'psychologism', of 'sociologism' – of what we might term, in a word, 'anthropologism' – which becomes a threat as soon as the relations of thought to formalization are not reflected upon correctly, for example, or as soon as the modes of being of life, labour, and language are incorrectly analysed. 'Anthopologi-zation' is the great internal threat to knowledge in our day. (Foucault 1970: 348)

However, the contrary movement to anthropologisation – the question of the origin or *genesis* of logic – runs the alternate risk of seeking some condition or emergence in a transcendental field. And it is this risk of anthropomorphism that Foucault labels the 'subjection to transcendence': the subjection to an outside that is posited as already present, transcendentally real. Foucault raises the possibility of a dis-engagement from these two forms of genesis and structure, forms which he sees as the very space in which *our own* thinking takes place. Structuralism, he insists, is not a break with classical thought but its continuation. And no break will be possible as long as the question of the relation between order/logic and some ground, being or presence is sustained. The problem of genesis or structure is a continuation of the classical problem of order and its ground:

> The essential problem of Classical thought lay in the relations between *name* and *order*: how to discover a *nomenclature* that would be a taxonomy, or again, how to establish a system of signs that would be transparent to the continuity of being: in the firmament of our reflection there reigns a discourse – a perhaps inaccessible discourse – which would at the same time be an ontology and a semantics. Structuralism is not a new method; it is the awakened and troubled consciousness of modern thought. (Foucault 1970: 208)

THE BEING OF LANGUAGE

Beyond structuralism and its 'logophobia' Foucault insists on the need to think the being of language positively, as a force or event in its own right and not as the expression of some pre-given or transcendent logic. This possibility of moving beyond representationalism and anthropologism emerges in the nineteenth century. In the nineteenth century, according to Foucault, discourse is no longer coterminous with thought or the world and words rediscover 'their ancient and enigmatic density' (Foucault 1970: 304). The nineteenth century marks a point of ambivalence in Foucault's history; for it both opens the possibility of an overcoming of representationalism alongside the culmination of representationalism in transcendental arguments. Indeed, literature has this important function precisely because all the other domains of knowledge have reduced language to signification. In nineteenth-century literature, however, words themselves become plays of light and darkness, revealing and concealing. Classicism had studied various modes of order, in life, labour and language. This order was revealed and available for reflection *as representation*; it was possible to study thought's own ordering power or logic. For Foucault, however, the nineteenth century came to recognise a certain 'density' in these phenomena of representation; there was a certain depth and opacity in modes of representation that *demanded interpretation*. Language was not a transparent medium but was regaining its status as a being with its own force and effect. (Hence the discourses of ideology, psychoanalysis and so on that will study language and other representational modes as ways in which thought is determined.) Language is no longer the innocent and transparent medium for a pure knowledge; knowledge will have its own positivity, density and being in language. The reflection on language in the nineteenth century will be, then, 'a transformation without residuum' (Foucault 1970: 305). For Foucault, this regaining of 'density' opens a possibility for both overcoming and intensifying anthropologism. On the one hand, it is in the knowledge and interpretation of language that thought will illuminate itself, by interpreting itself. Language – which is now other than us – will be that form of transcendence which is also us alone. The question will be of *who speaks* and the answer to this question will be self-revelation. Thus Nietzsche will be poised as an ambivalent figure whose manifest anti-humanism might still return all force-effects of language back to the ground of will or a speaking subject. On the other hand, the nineteenth century also produces Mallarmé, a writer who frees language from point of view, will and the human and presents language in its own being. The difference Foucault draws between Nietzsche and Mallarmé is between an approach in which speech might be attributed to a subject or will, as opposed to one in which thought is seen *in its being* as speaking. The second approach (of Mallarmé) is specifically literary:

> Whereas Nietzsche maintained his questioning as to who is speaking right up to the end, though forced, in the last resort, to irrupt into that questioning himself and to base it upon himself as the speaking and questioning subject: *Ecce homo*, Mallarmé was constantly effacing himself from his own language, to the point of not wishing to figure in it except as a executant in a pure ceremony of the Book in which the discourse would compose itself. (Foucault 1970: 306)

This raises the question of whether the current concern with language is a break in thought, enabling a 'multiple and re-illumined light' or merely a continuation of the eighteenth-century turn from order to its condition (Foucault 1970: 307). By attempting to make language visible in its entirety we are at one and the same time looking at thought's location as well as continuing the modern project of unveiling the unthought. The shift from (classical) discourse to (nine-teenth-century) language is one from thought as pure transparency to thought possessing a certain density in need of interpretation. Foucault's question about the study of language is whether this is a new form of thought, or whether we should be asking about thought at all (Foucault 1970: 386). Who is the absent thinking subject who reflects on knowledge? For Foucault, this is the problem of point of view and the problem of man.

THE ANTHROPOLOGICAL SLEEP

The problem of the study of language is not, then, man as an empirical object; but the very position of reflection upon this object: a lacuna, invisibility or 'space' that positively organises the visible and articulable. In the classical period humanity, as human *nature*, precludes a science of 'man' precisely because in classicism man *doubles the differences of nature*. Human nature can be studied as a natural being, and as one more way of revealing natural order (Foucault 1970: 309). 'Man', as opposed to human nature, is at once a recent invention of the eighteenth century but, according to Foucault, he is also there all along, for he exists as the general problem of the knowing subject: '[H]e had been waiting for thousands of years in the darkness for that moment of illumination in which he would finally be known' (Foucault 1970: 308). Indeed, Western thought has persistently been concerned with rendering the ground, a priori or site of knowledge present – as though thought might be returned to its origin or point of view. And this is why man, and then language, have been determined as the medium through which knowledge comes to itself. What the studies of life, labour and language sought to uncover was not an infinite order or logic that was *then* represented, but a *medium* that presents itself to itself and in so doing produces man:

> [A]nd he, as soon as he thinks, merely unveils himself to his own eyes in the form of a being who is already, in a necessarily subjacent density, in an irreducible anteriority, a living being, an instrument of production, a vehicle for words which exist before him. (Foucault 1970: 313)

Man as a positive, finite and dense animal produces the position or point of view of an infinite analysis of his *own* density: the analytic of finitude, 'when finitude was conceived in an interminable cross-reference with itself' (Foucault 1970: 318). The problem for Foucault is not just 'who speaks?' but, also, who is able to ask this question? How is this form of self-reflexivity established? It is whether we can escape this problem of point of view that *The Order of Things* seeks to question. Is it possible to free thought from its location in a ground or medium, and disperse thought into, and beyond, its positivity?

Any description of man as a positive or finite being has inevitably restored man to a single medium of the Same (Foucault 1970: 315) in which *truth resides in the very medium of man's own inquiry*. As Foucault insists, '[A] discourse attempting to be both empirical and critical cannot but be both positivist and eschatological; man appears within it as a truth both reduced and promised. Pre-critical naivete holds undivided rule' (Foucault 1970: 320). Psychoanalysis, for example, both studies man as an extrinsic object and determined being, but it does so by producing a field of recognition, for it is now the unconscious (its reading, decipherment and depth) that enables man to re-find himself. It is the 'pre-critical naivete' of such manoeuvres that sustains representationalism. What renders these manoeuvres 'naive' is their simple positing of a representational medium (such as language, the unconscious or culture). How this field of recognition or representation is itself effected is not questioned. This 'naivete' is the faith in the return of difference into the same. The very form of anthropologism is sustained. Man may have been decentred but a series of representational media (such as structure, the unconscious or language) function in his place (Foucault 1970: 385). Truth is located within the world and explained from the worldly being of man.

THE TASK OF A HISTORICAL 'A PRIORI'

Foucault does not, indeed cannot, simply assert some point outside the episteme of anthropologism. Rather, his genealogy is diagnostic. How is it that man came to be produced as a representational animal? *The Order of Things* is an archaeology of this question. Foucault's attempt to think a historical a priori can be seen as a project of active misrecognition, in line with Nietzsche's spirit of active forgetting.

When Foucault asks, 'But what is it impossible to think, and what kind of impossibility are we faced with here?' his question poses two problems (1970: xv). We must recognise that thought has a limit, that it is not *pure* possibility or consciousness but has a specific order, logic or distribution according to its historical location. This is the a priori. At the same time the a priori – *to be historical* – must differ. The a priori is itself discontinuous and not the immutable ground from which discontinuity emerges. The historical a priori describes a certain regularity or logic of different modes of difference, or various forms of 'fold' (Foucault 1970: 341). In the classical episteme difference is effected through procedures of ordering and taxonomy. In modernity difference is carved out, or folded, from man: difference is inscribed between man as an empirical being and the man who studies and represents that being. The historical a priori is not a ground that *then* undergoes history. The very notion of *historical* a priori attempts to think a history that becomes through different and shifting media – a history that differs historically. Modern history is a history of consciousness; but prior to modernity truth was disclosed through the history of things:

> This a priori is what, in a given period, delimits in the totality of experience a field of knowledge, *defines the mode of being of the objects that appear* in that field, provides man's everyday perception with theoretical powers, and defines the conditions in which he can sustain a discourse about things that is recognised to be true. (Foucault 1970: 158, emphasis added)

History is a series of differing grounds. Foucault's question will be whether it is possible to arrive at an epoch that will not ground itself, and he pursues this possibility both through the notion of the episteme and through an emphasis on dispersed positive conditions. This is what differentiates Foucault from historicism. By arguing that consciousness, man or spirit *is* history, conventional historicism ultimately includes thought within a single horizon, as the unfolding of consciousness to itself through time. Foucault's idea of the episteme is set against this emphasis on continuity. An episteme describes a series of foldings: the way selves question themselves, the ways in which being is questioned, the technical and discursive possibilities for different forms of question. An episteme is not a unified world-view or ideology. It is a series of positive conditions: spatial location, material constraints, methodology, practices, disciplinary boundaries and power relations. Furthermore, an episteme is not a general way of seeing. It operates as a regularity in disunity: in any episteme a series of questions and problems are posed with competing and conflicting arguments and methods. Foucault's history is both an attempt to think the radical discontinuity of different epistemes *and* an attempt to arrive at a methodology that would itself create an epistemic shift beyond representationalism and anthropologism.

Once classical knowledge granted the world a system and order, it became possible to question the knower of that order. This 'subject' of modernity was therefore the author of a certain 'logic'. The possibility of the world depended upon man as an economically, linguistically and historically representing being. Through this description of the emergence of representing man as an empirico-transcendental double, Foucault both intensifies and criticises Heidegger's *Destruktion* of metaphysics. Both Heidegger and Foucault tie the modern subject to a certain approach to logic. While the idea of a grounding logic characterises the Western episteme, it is in modernity that this logic is located within the mind of man and becomes an 'egology' or representationalism. For Heidegger, any 'logic' was effected through a more general *logos*, a comportment or relation to being that is only subsequently systematised and formalised. Heidegger's question was to ask how the 'logic' of representing man was itself possible. What is man such that he represents a world? And Heidegger's response was manifestly anti-anthropologistic: it is time as ec-stasis that then effects a man who comes to know a world. Time is not a 'logic' – a unified and measurable order – but a *logos* – a gathering, relation or existence-towards. For Foucault, however, Heideggerian phenomenology occupies the same episteme as modern representationalism (1970: xiv). The question of the opening between man and world, or Heidegger's insistence on maintaining the *problem* of anthropology, is only possible as a question through the delimitation of man as a representational animal. Only with the empirical objectification of man through certain practices of modernity is it possible to question man transcendentally, or to question the differential medium through which man becomes. Like Heidegger, but against Heidegger, Foucault's response is to think the difference between identity and difference. Heidegger's phenomenology operates through an empirico-transcendental episteme. For Heidegger, man as an ontic, inner-worldly or empirical being is the outcome of man as an ontological becoming or temporal ec-stasis. In contrast to the location of difference in the existence of *Dasein* or disclosure of being, Foucault will use the notion of the historical a priori to question any privileged medium of difference. In the case of Heidegger and phenomenology one might ask how time becomes a privileged differentiating or 'ec-static' horizon. Is it possible to think difference positively, not as the difference *of* or *from* some ground, and not as the difference *of* time or being? Whereas for Heidegger the differentiating power is *being* which sends itself through history, Foucault's thought of dispersion aims at a more radical thought of difference, a difference that would be subordinated neither to man, nor time, nor being: a difference that could not be thought as difference in general. There is not a being or Same that sends or disperses itself. Rather, thought is one mode of dispersion occurring alongside other modes of dispersal. And so Foucault's genealogies attend to various conflicting, overlapping and discontinuous modes of difference – differences between discursive regimes, the differences produced between a body and its moral coding, spatial differences and historical difference. Further, any outside or 'exteriority' to this field of dispersion is produced through the dispersion itself, so that any perceived 'ground' or a priori would be effected through those differences it seeks to explain: 'In the proposed analysis, instead of referring back to *the* synthesis or *the* unifying function of *a* subject, the various enunciative modalities manifest his dispersion' (Foucault 1972a: 55).

FOLDINGS OF THE VISIBLE

Rather than locating the logic of events in a single system or structure, Foucault's genealogies described inter-connected distributions through various media. These media of difference are not different forms of substance or presence that then differentiate or become; they are different modes of becoming that then effect certain exteriorities. Alongside spatial dynamics Foucault also describes discursive determinants and mutations, as well as varying modes of visibility. Indeed, it was Foucault's attention to the visible that played the most significant role in dispersing the logic of existence. Foucault's claim that the being of man and the being of language have never been thought together can be understood alongside a later remark in *The Order of Things* regarding the peculiar 'shining' of nineteenth-century language. At this point of the text Foucault extends his predominantly visual metaphorics to refer to language. If language can 'shine' this means that words are neither transparent nor are they contingent vehicles of communication. Rather, language has its own being, density or translucence. We can't view systems of language as 'ways of seeing' or as structures through which the world is viewed. Language itself is an event and this event needs to be thought in its specificity. To speak of language's own *shining* is to emphasise that the relation between thought and words is not representational; for there is also a relation *to words*. Words are not points of view, representational conditions or perspectives. Words themselves can be perceived or related to – and this of course occurs in literature, where the being and shining of language disrupt the representational sleep:

> [T]hroughout the nineteenth century, and right up to our own day – from Hölderlin to Mallarmé and on to Antonin Artaud – literature achieved autonomous existence, and separated itself from all other language with a deep scission, only by forming a sort of 'counter-discourse', and by finding its way back from the representative or signifying function of language to this raw being that had been forgotten since the sixteenth century. . . . Through literature, the being of language shines once more on the frontiers of Western culture – and at its centre – for it is what has been most foreign to that culture since the sixteenth century; but it has also, since this same century, been at the very centre of what Western culture has overlain. This is why literature is appearing more and more as that which must be thought; but equally, and for the same reason, as that which can never, in any circumstance, be thought in accordance with a theory of signification. (Foucault 1970: 43–4)

Foucault's insistence on language's density – a density that is disavowed in representationalism – places language as one mode of dispersion alongside the dispersion of the visible. Language is not the re-presentation of what is presented in seeing. The visible and the articulable have their own modes of difference, and neither is subordinated to the other. Language is not a way of seeing; and seeing is not reducible to the articulable.

The problem of the visible in Foucault's work is inextricably inter-twined with the task of disconnecting the putatively intimate connection between words and things. Recognising the positivity of the visible – its own peculiar differences – will free thought from its representational home. No longer determined by an already present logic, thought will be mobilised, propelled into a difference and discontinuity between a visible that never meets the articulable, and words that exceed what is given:

> It is not that words are imperfect, or that, when confronted by the visible, they prove insuperably inadequate. Neither can be reduced to the other's terms: it is in vain that we say what we see; what we see never resides in what we say. (Foucault 1970: 9)

The relation between knowledge and the visible is one of a folding: knowledge is at once a revealing and doubling of the visible, as well as being a series in its own right. Because speaking is *not* seeing, language is not representation. Language also has its own 'luminosity' and 'shining'; it is not a mirror but a space in which the visible is reconfig-ured. But this luminosity of language is at the limit of thought: '[W]e are so ill-equipped to conceive of the shining but crude being of language' (Foucault 1970: 339). Thinking this 'crude being' – as does Mallarmé – may effect a liberation from anthropologism. For it is in poetry that language is presented in its own force – as sound, rhythm and tone – and not as the passive repetition of a pre-linguistic, viewable and pristine real. Through poetry, Foucault argues, we 'once again' *see* lan-guage, as a force of dispersion that is not just a reaction to the visible but an event in itself. The late nineteenth century offers us the possi-bility of an end of man; for it is the force of language and the effective character of language that enables us to see the distribution of a logic that can not be enclosed within the human. It is possible that we may no longer recognise ourselves in the mirror of language; language's shining will distance us from any supposedly universal logic and render thought active. The visible is not just a pure presence that precedes articulation, awaiting a faithful mode of repetition in signs. The visible is itself looped with the invisible. What can be seen is enabled by a series of differences (such as the differences in space, light, practices, viewing apparatuses and discursive formations). It is this *unthought* differential folding that creates the event of thought. For Foucault, thinking the difference between what we see and what we say will preclude us from returning thought to some present ground – as though thought might step back from its viewpoint and discern its own logic.

Thought does not, then, have a single medium such as system or logic. Nor is thought at home with its ground – for language, visibility and embodiment have *positive* modes of difference that exceed thought and recognition. We can see the way in which thought is dispersed *beyond* itself – and not *within* some anthropological home – in the way that Foucault relates light to language. If we can treat words as events with their own 'shining' this is because language is always more than the medium or vehicle for thought. Language has a being of its own, or a *positivity*. Language is neither thought's condition, its limit nor its medium; words have an active and positive force. The Western tradition since Plato, Foucault argues, has been a 'profound logophobia' – always attempting to ground the being of language on some truth or presence. But this would only 'nullify' discourse (Foucault 1972a: 228). By referring to language's shining, and by granting language a luminosity, Foucault extends Heidegger's radicalisation or *Destruktion* of Western philosophy's dominant visual tropology. For Heidegger the representational schema of *logos* or 'idea' has its etymological origins in metaphors of looking. Rather than suggest that philosophy do away with this unfortunate and misleading trope, both Foucault and Heidegger radicalise this etymology. If the world is first disclosed though a looking, then the world is not an immediate presence but is disclosed through a relation, and in a particular way. If the apprehension of the world is what constitutes both the world and its knower (or point of view), then prior to any cognitive ordering there is a distance, relation or mode of disclosure. Prior to any presence there is a presencing, and this presencing takes place and in a determinate form (or according to a specific and located existence).

For Heidegger, then, recalling philosophy's origin in the gaze exposes a certain forgetting. The look that opens the world has always been thought in terms of a full self-presence, an immediate and simple re-presentation. But if we think this visual metaphor through, we are

compelled to recognise a necessary non-presence; the look relates to
what is not itself, and must do so by passing beyond itself. It is not a
look *from a subject to an object*, as though the look related two already
present terms. Presence is opened in the look. For Heidegger, then,
philosophy has forgotten the question or relation to being by determining being as that which is immediately present in the re-presentational
look. But thinking through this language of *theoria, eidos* and seeing
will also disclose that being is *given*, and that the look is *a look towards
and a look from*; the look is the relation, dwelling or proximity of being.
It is not the immediate presence or doubling of a mirror, but a shining.
Through this *Destruktion* of philosophy's dependence on the visible
Heidegger takes the consideration of being beyond standpoint, perspectivism, world-view or *Weltanschauung*. The look is not a point from
which the world is given; the look is that *relation* from which any
objectified notion of standpoint or point of view emerges.

   Foucault's considerations of the visible must be seen as similarly
more subtle and sophisticated than a sheer observation of perspective
or standpoint (for the very understanding of perspective is itself a
modality of the visible – conceivable only through certain historical
and discursive conditions). The description of *Las Meninas* that opens
The Order of Things refers to the various directions of light, reflection,
gazing and concealment. At its simplest, Foucault's attention to *Las
Meninas* is an observation of a representation of representation. The
painting is 'about' representation. It opens a representational scene,
allowing a thematisation of light, viewing, subjects and perspective.
The frame encloses an artist considering his subject and the light and
reflections around the artist's canvas, as well as the gaze of the included
subjects. (Just as earlier in *The Order of Things* when Foucault will direct
his attention to the *table* upon which dissection takes place, here his
attention is not to what is represented but the space across which representation is drawn.[1] This is the very figure of the historical a priori:
what space is unfolded such that certain questions are possible, and
certain objects made available?) In *Las Meninas* we only see the back of
the artist's canvas; the subjects to be painted are not included within
the scene except by way of reflection on another surface. It is as though
what is shown in the painting is the very opening of the possibility of
the question: who or what represents and is being represented? The
painter's gaze looks out at the viewer: 'we' are placed in the position of

both viewing subjects and the objects to be painted. But a reflection of the subjects to be painted in the far left of the frame reveals a discontinuity between the subject as viewer of the painting and the subject of the painting (the king and queen). To view this painting is to be in a field of light, reflections, looks, points of view and blind spots. Not only does *Las Meninas* open a question of representation; the painting itself is an event of visibility. Its visible relations are not ordered within a single representational site, and so *Las Meninas* is distinctly prior to the fall into the full anthropological sleep of representation. The *question* of the visible, the play of the visible is still possible here and is not yet enclosed within the standpoint or perspective of the human. *Las Meninas* disperses a seeing position through a proliferation of light, reflection and shining.

THE SPACE OF THOUGHT

Why open a genealogy of the human sciences with this painting and a consideration of light? In many ways Foucault's genealogy presents itself as the event of a *question*: how was man formed as the object/ subject of knowledge? *The Order of Things* is intense in its attempted refusal of an answer. We must not give yet one more anthropological ground, one more medium that might replace and revive the human as the locus of the question. Rather, we ask how man is formed through a certain type of question – the question of man's transcendental condition. And we do so both *through other questions* – what is unthinkable? – and in order *to arrive at other questions*. The hope of *The Order of Things* is that these new questions will not be reactive; they might no longer take the form of finding out conditions and grounds of thought. Such questions would be active: What can thought do? What might we become? The question of *The Order of Things*, the question of how man became a representational animal, already disrupts the logic of representation. For representational questions are precisely those that seek the ground, condition or origin of all questions. To question *this* form of question troubles the very modern and subjectivist value placed on man as that being who questions his being.

Is it possible that thinking might be neither a reflection nor a condition of the world but an event within the world? If this were the case then the problem of transcendence – how does thought relate to the world? – would have to be reformulated as a problem of thinking *within* a particular site, or series of sites. A history, such as Foucault's, that demonstrates the various modalities of thinking suggests that thought is not a radical origin, a transcendental horizon, but takes place only through regularities, carved out spaces, orders and differences. But Foucault, while questioning the force of the transcendental question, is not just content to assert its obverse. The point would be to think beyond the empirico-transcendental oscillation, or the oscillation between reducing thought to a worldly structure and elevating thought as a radical genesis. Thought is at once the event of a certain force and becoming, and so cannot be explained away as a given logic. Thought is also not just a thing in the world; for it does proliferate into a series of effects. At the same time, thought is not a pure and radical genesis; thought is marked, determined and limited by non-ideal conditions. In Foucault's history thought continually encounters its limit, only then to know, recuperate and interpret that limit. Thought is just this act of encounter with its own thought and unthought limits. *The Order of Things* is a history of the events of thought, its various encounters with the 'unthought': its engagement with visibility, articulation, space and the body:

> How can a thought melt away before anything other than itself? Generally speaking, what does it mean, no longer being able to think a certain thought? Or to introduce a new thought?
>
> Discontinuity – the fact that within the space of a few years a culture sometimes ceases to think as it had been thinking up till then and begins to think other things in a new way – probably begins with an erosion from outside, from that space which is, for thought, on the other side, but in which it has never ceased to think from the very beginning. Ultimately, the problem that presents itself is that of the relations between thought and culture: how is it that thought has a place in the space of the world, that it has its origin there, and that it never ceases, in this place or that, to begin anew? But perhaps it is not yet time to pose this problem; perhaps we should wait until the archaeology of thought has been established more firmly, until it is better able to gauge what it is capable of describing directly and positively, until it has defined the particular systems and internal connections it has to deal with,

before attempting to encompass thought and to investigate how it contrives to escape itself. For the moment, then, let it suffice that we accept these discontinuities in the simultaneously manifest and obscure empirical order wherever they posit themselves. (Foucault 1970: 51)

Like Heidegger, then, thinking for Foucault is a simultaneous revealing and concealing. However, for Foucault, thought's play of visibility and articulation is not located on a *single* clearing (of being) but on a series of overlaid planes. And it is this series of planes that *The Order of Things* sets out to disrupt by 'breaking up all the ordered surfaces and all the planes with which we are accustomed to tame the wild profusion of existing things' (xv). Most importantly, Foucault endeavours to open a space for the unthought not located *within* man: the unthought is not the density of a language or unconscious that might be continually revealed. This is why Foucault sets himself against the empirico-transcendental space of *man*, a space that produces what is other than thought as *thought's own exterior*:

> The modern *cogito* (and this is why it is not so much the discovery of an evident truth as a ceaseless task constantly to be taken afresh) must traverse, duplicate, and reactivate in an explicit form the articulation of thought on everything within it, around it, and beneath it which is not yet thought, yet which is nevertheless not foreign to thought, in the sense of an irreducible, an insuperable exteriority. In this form, the *cogito* will not therefore be the sudden and illuminating discovery that all thought is thought, but the constantly renewed interrogation as to how thought can reside elsewhere than here, and yet so very close to itself; how it can *be* in the forms of non-thinking. The modern *cogito* does not reduce the whole of being of things to thought without ramifying the being of thought right down to the inert network of what does not think. (Foucault 1970: 324)

The modern task of providing a foundation for knowledge through the transcendental question demands that any description of the human be located within its condition of possibility. The question of truth in general, a truth independent of any particular will or motivation, characterises the Western episteme (1970: xxii). This is what Foucault refers to in *The Archaeology of Knowledge* as the 'subjection to transcendence' (1972a: 203): truth is seen not as an act of becoming but as the submission to some already given (or transcendent) ground. But it is in the modern normalisation of the human subject as the locus of truth that this subjection reaches its extreme decadence. If, in the pre-modern episteme, the question of truth was directed towards a world to be known, then there was still, Foucault argues, some room for thought; there was still some difference between words and things. And it is this difference between words and things, so emphasised by Foucault, that allows for the disruption or de-reification of any general logic and the shattering of anthropologism (Foucault 1972a: 49). For if words are not the simple repetition of things then we have to give up the idea of man as a representational mirror and 'logic' as a correct scheme of the world. Once the thought of the *being* of language returns we can start to think of the *force* of our statements, what language *does*, and the *act* of knowledge. Knowledge will no longer be the simple re-presentation of what is in the mind of man: 'Ought we not to admit that, since language is here once more, man will return to that serene non-existence in which he was formerly maintained by the imperious unity of discourse?' (Foucault 1970: 386). If the world is not already meaningful, and if there is a gap between what we see and what we say, then any act of speaking or meaning will be an event of force, power, or will. Thinking the being of language and overcoming our 'logophobia' will provide us with an exit from anthropologism and the normalising stupor of subjectivism.

BETWEEN NIETZSCHE AND MALLARMÉ

How to overcome the reactive character of the anthropological sleep and how to activate thought by overcoming its subjection to a logic given in advance are questions that haunt the shifting character of Foucault's corpus. As early as *The Order of Things* Foucault is unclear as to whether the death of man is still a viable possibility. This possibility is poised between Nietzsche and Mallarmé, and between whether we must still ask the question of who speaks or whether language might be freed from point of view. In his earlier work, and in his near utopian appeal to the literary, Foucault imagines a moment when language is its own shining, not subjected to the ground of the human and continually mobilised by the dynamism of the visible:

> Literature is not language approaching itself until it reaches the point of its fiery manifestation; it is, rather, language getting as far away from itself as possible. And if, in this setting 'outside of itself,' it unveils its own being, the sudden clarity reveals not a folding-back but a gap, not a turning back of signs upon themselves but a dispersion. The 'subject' of literature (what speaks in it and what it speaks about) is less language in its positivity than the void that language takes as its space when it articulates itself in the nakedness of 'I speak'. (Foucault 1998: 149)

This thought of literature presents a possibility for language in general and a new mode of existence. In the density, force and event of literary language we see language not as a representation subordinated to some ground and not as the logic *of* some speaking subject or transcendental order. There is no normalising or humanising ground (such as life, sexuality or man), but the differential event and dispersion of discourse. In this conception of language, thought is a singular event, not subordinated to some pre-given structure or logic but occurring with the specificity and force of its particular discursive acts.

Unlike Heidegger, Foucault will not appeal to a more radical origin of the human – time or the sending of being. Rather, he will suggest certain modes of writing that can decentre the human, without appealing to some pre-human or transcendental condition. These modes of writing will be found in the work of Mallarmé, Roussel, and Borges, and other forms of speech that are disowned from point of view. Rather than a speech which is the speech *of* a subject, there is the event of speech or discourse itself *from which* certain subject positions might be discerned. This means that 'man' or the subject are not grounds of speech or language but effects of a certain way of speaking; and speaking is itself the effect of discursive formations. But even in this appeal to a possible overcoming of man, representationalism and subjectivism, Foucault is also aware of the risk of anthropomorphism. If we do not ask the question of who speaks, if we do not recognise a certain regularity of a logic of speaking positions, then thought loses its critical edge. Alongside Mallarmé and the being of language we also have to think just how language and difference produce a logic and produce selves, how a logic is effected after the event. The dream of liberating ourselves from 'man' must be set against the continual reappearance of the self, of the site of practices, speaking, viewing and becoming. The hope of overcoming all those illusions of autonomy, self-authoring and subjectivism through an appeal to dispersion is tempered by the recognition of a logic of existence. The pure becoming and difference of power is never pure; it takes place through positive sites, practices, and locations, and creates autonomy effects. Indeed rather than imagine a reign of absolute dispersal beyond all point of view and locatedness, Foucault also remains aware of the persistence of recognition and representation. His emphasis on the self, rather than the subject, in the later volumes of *The History of Sexuality* modifies what will remain as a continual utopianism in his work. On the one hand is the dream of a difference or effect that is immanent, not subjected to the ground of the human or the normalisation of some general logic. On the other hand Foucault sustains a critical recognition that thought always takes place and always recognises and regulates itself. This is the very project of genealogy; given where we are and the regularity and normativity of how we think, is it possibile to disown our thought and think otherwise? This can only be examined through a new form of the question of the self and the question of who thinks. We ask about our origin and our being, not to recognise who we are and the inevitability of what we have become, but in order to render what appears as the unquestionable ground or cause of our existence as an effect of what we don't recognise. This is why Foucault traces all the discourses of the human sciences – moral discourses of reform, normalisation, self-recognition and cure – back to their inhuman causes. The modern discourse of sexual self-discovery is a mutation of the Christian confessional, which is itself the moralisation of Ancient practices of bodily and household management. The human sciences are *ad hoc* developments of a series of events including the creation of objects such as the criminal, the homosexual and the insane – and these objects of knowledge are themselves effects. The reforming prison is the accidental outgrowth of procedures of punishment that have nothing to do with the moral development of man. It is from the spectacle and force of punishment that the discourse of reform and self-regulation will emerge. What genealogy does, then, is work against the recognition of anthropologism – that what we are is the effect of our own self-origination and understanding. And it does this not by appealing to a pre-human outside, but by tracing the continual muta-tions of the human, and the *different ways in which the question of who we are has enabled what we might become*. In Ancient Greece these ethi-cal questions were formulated in terms of what a body might do and how it might manage its pleasures. In modernity these forms of self-questioning become representational and hermeneutic: not, what can a body do, but what does this body represent, what is its deeper, sexu-al *meaning*? (Foucault 1981: 155)

CRITICAL ETHICS AND THE POST-HUMAN

Genealogy remains faithful to the general project of immanence by attempting to overcome representationalism. Thought is not the repre-sentation of some presence, as though the point of view of subjects preceded what was to be thought. Rather, point of view, self, position and 'who speaks' are effects of distribution. One can think this distrib-ution critically and genealogically: from the logic, positions, selves or regularities it effects. But one can also sustain a more speculative dimension: is it possible to free dispersal from logic, to avoid point of view and speaking positions? Rather than just recognise that transcen-dence is the effect of a posited outside, is it possible to remain within immanence? Foucault's appeal to certain modes of literary writing sug-gested that more than a critical or genealogical manoeuvre could be undertaken. His appeal to Ancient Greek modes of ethics also has a certain utopian dimension. Foucault's analysis is, for the most part, critical and genealogical. Ancient Greece can demonstrate that ques-tions of the self and ethics do not necessarily involve a general ground or logic; questions need not appeal to the good or law in general but might involve the specificity of bodies and pleasures. This would not be a freedom from all norms and regulations; there would still be a discipline, regularity and order to practices. But this formation of selves would be *active*; it would form its rules, norms and procedures without subordinating that formation to some general ground, such as human nature, the soul, the moral law or inner sexuality.

But the critical dimension of Foucault's history is also accompanied by an anthropomorphic dream of non-autonomy. The self might no

longer recognise itself as a thing within the world, subjected to a logic
not its own. The desire for an *active* ethics is one in which the self
remains as a question, a game of truth, a procedure and an event –
never reified into the normality of its being. Not subordinated to a
world, presence or ground, this self is freed from the scar of representation. Not a self who re-presents, nor a presence that can then be
represented, Foucault's self in formation is ideally nothing other than
the event of its own becoming. The logic of existence would not be a
system to be recognised but an ever-shifting dynamism, becoming and
dispersion of the post-human. Attention to this radically dispersed logic
or power is precisely what will awaken us from the anthropological
sleep and the burden of representation.

Foucault remained vigilant regarding the continual autonomy-effects
of this dispersed and pre-human logic, suggesting that the event of
dispersion would inevitably fall back into some form of human recognition. There will always be the active formation or regularity of selves
and practices. And these formations ceaselessly fall into the reactive:
rather than seeing the self as the effect of a certain event or act, the self
posits itself as the ground, subject or author of the event. There is a
continual positing of transcendence, a perpetual inability to think
power in its radical anonymity. And this is why *The Order of Things*
charts the various ways in which thought forms itself by understanding
its own ground, never fully able to remain as pure activity unhoused
from any location in the human. Foucault's work suggests a certain
inevitability to this reaction, such that thought will continually recognise
itself. This is why, he insists, we need genealogy as a continual project of
misrecognition. Any posited home or ground of thought can be disclosed – through genealogy – as one of thought's own representations.

It is the anti-genealogical project of Gilles Deleuze, describing itself
as a *geology*, that intensifies the project of immanence. Rather than a
continual and critical demystification of all our posited grounds and
sites of recognition, Deleuze suggests a project of transcendental
empiricism. Here, there will be nothing other than the given. The given
will not be the gift *of* being, nor will the given be given *to* some subject.
The given – the empirical – is not the real. The given is that event or
becoming from which a real, or a transcendence, is imagined. For
Deleuze, we need to think the given as transcendental, such that
there just is the event of giving from which any real or subject is then

projected. Transcendental empiricism, or radical empiricism, is the culmination of the project of immanence. If there is not some being that *then* gives, or some subject who then receives the given, then there is just one univocal plane of giving, with no outside, no ground and no point of view. This univocal givenness exceeds the human, being, the subject and the real – for all these are effects of the given. The question – *the question* – is whether the given *can* be thought as immanence, freed from the subjection to transcendence, freed from all those illusions of being, presence or the human which are effects of the given.

NOTE

1. The 'Preface' to *The Order of Things* cites Borges's fictional 'Chinese encyclopaedia'. This encyclopaedia lists a thoroughly unthinkable and impossible logic. According to Foucault, the effect of imagining this *impossible* order is that it 'does away with the *site*, the mute ground upon which it is possible for entities to be juxtaposed' (Foucault 1970: xvii). There is an 'operating table' upon which dissection takes place; but the table is itself effected in thought's specific operations. This table, that is not a mute ground but that nevertheless carves out a space through which thought can 'operate upon the entities of our world', might be compared to Deleuze and Guattari's 'plane of immanence' (1994). Both Foucault's table and Deleuze's plane are forms of a 'positive unconscious' – ways of thinking thought's ground or condition without positing some *prior* and general transcendental presence. Like Derrida, Foucault will also refer to some pre-human *syntax* – a distribution or dissection that opens an intersection between language and space (Foucault 1970: xvii). This syntax is not a general logic given in advance but 'that less apparent syntax which causes words and things (next to and also opposite one another) to "hold together"' (xviii).

CONCLUSION:
THE RISK OF ANTHROPOMORPHISM

———◦◦———

It is not always easy to be Heideggerian. (Deleuze and Guattari 1994: 108)

DELEUZE: BEYOND TEMPORALITY AND VIEWPOINT

There are two distinct readings of the world: one invites us to think difference from the standpoint of a previous similitude or identity; whereas the other invites us to think similitude and even identity as the product of a deep disparity. The first reading precisely defines the world of copies and representations; it posits the world as icon. The second, contrary to the first, defines the world of simulacra; it posits the world itself as phantasm. . . . So 'to reverse Platonism' means to make the simulacra rise and to affirm their rights among icons and copies. (Deleuze 1990: 261–2)

Discussing the work of Levinas, Derrida refers to empiricism as philosophy's constitutive gesture (Derrida 1978: 151). It is in the ideal of pure empiricism – that there might be an unmediated encounter with alterity – that philosophy disavows the necessary factical disclosure of the real. The idea that there might be a thought of being not determined by the specificity of human existence – the dream of overcoming human locatedness (in short, anti-anthropologism) – is perhaps the driving force of speculative anthropomorphism. In an attempt to overcome anthropologism philosophy has presented itself as an

anthropomorphism: the leap to a site beyond where we are, a speculative dream of some ethics or law beyond the human. And it is in
adopting such an apocalyptic tone of pure presence that the *articulation*
of existence is forgotten. Any theory of being as system, or structure, is
already the effect of a way of looking, an openness of the look, a point
of view which is never given as the pure presence of a point but is
always dispersed through disclosure. The illusion of anthropomorphism
can therefore only be countered with an anthropology – a location of
theory or thought in the finitude of human existence. But such an
anthropologism cannot replace anthropomorphism as another ground.
On the contrary, the 'there' of the human is neither ground nor
grounded, but the dispersed opening of the difference between the
two.

The condition for any ontology, Heidegger argues, is the pre-
ontological event of transcendence: a directedness-towards a world.
But this temporal 'going-out-towards' of transcendence, as the opening
of *logos*, or as 'saying-gathering,' is neither a *relation* of knowledge nor
a *correspondence* of judgement. Both relation and correspondence suggest two entities that are then connected through an act of perception.
Transcendence, however, is the factical, existential, determined, located
and positive opening upon which a judgement or knowing is founded.
For Heidegger, the fact that the *prior* or *primordial* status of this temporal going-out-towards is itself expressed in temporal terms does *not*
indicate that the origin is misrepresented or corrupted by being
explained through the very terms (of temporality) that it is meant to
ground. The 'circularity' of this reasoning demonstrates this: that any
explanation of the point of view of experience itself takes place from a
point of view. To privilege *temporality* as the generation or origin of
this point is not to miss the pure self-presence of the origin. For the
origin – like the a priori, primordiality, presence – is nothing outside the
determination of time. If the point of view which explains temporality
is constituted only after the event of the temporal itself then we are
forced to recognise a radical anteriority that remains *as anterior* from
the point of view of a temporality which can never step outside itself.
We might regard the position of transcendental inquiry as one of
impossible closure: any explanation of the origin of experience must take
place from the point of view of experience itself. The determination of
our point of view can only represent an outside *negatively*: as that *from*

which point of view emerges. (And this negativity would, therefore, always be marked, determined or contaminated by the positivity of the point of view from which the non-finite was determined.) The pure self-presence of the origin can only be *thought as origin* once the non-originality of temporal locatedness has taken place.

This recognition of point of view – which might be described as tragic – acknowledges its finitude and locatedness by positing the essential impossibility of grasping what lies beyond the finite. Any infinite, origin or presence is determined as primordial only after the event of a finite point of view. The tragic predicament of this position can be understood in two ways. It is possible to *locate* the point of view of temporal determination within some non-temporal real (and thereby emphasise the inherent non-correspondence of point of view and the unattainability of the absolute). Alternatively, what is other than point of view can be seen as an effect of point of view's own self-positing (such that the absolute is an effect of finite thought). If point of view is located *within* some pre-temporal field, then it makes sense to think beyond point of view, beyond temporality, beyond the punctuality of selfhood to a pre-personal spatiality – a space that is not effected from the human. In broad terms we might characterise Deleuze's project of transcendental empiricism as just such a project of overcoming the subjectivism and perspectivism of point of view (Deleuze 1990: 173; 260).

According to Deleuze, if philosophy were to ask a question other than that of 'who speaks' (Deleuze 1990: 107), if thought were to think what is other than thought itself, then philosophy might be something other than a transcendental idealism, and might do so without being a transcendental realism. Deleuze's 'transcendental empiricism' demands to be thought in this way: not as an overcoming of the transcendental tradition but as its affirmative fulfilment (Deleuze 1990: 105). Kant's transcendental idealism acknowledges that the world *as given* – the empirical world – must always be determined by the way in which it is given. The very givenness of the world demands a recognition of transcendental ideality: the representational ground of thought *to which* the given is given. The 'thing in itself' can only be thought after the appearance of the thing as given, as an abstraction from the finitude of an intuiting point of view. The thing in itself may be presupposed but never intuited. Transcendental idealism, like Deleuze's transcendental empiricism, sets itself against a philosophical project that attempts to *know* what lies outside the given. The difference between transcendental idealism and transcendental empiricism is a subtle one. Firstly, Deleuze's transcendental *empiricism* (like transcendental idealism) remains within the given. This is what makes it an empiricism and not a realism. There is not a real that is then given; any 'real' is thought from and effected from a certain event of giving. But *transcendental* empiricism does not locate the given *within* the subject (ideality). Empiricism, for Deleuze, goes all the way done. And this is why the subject – contra Kant – is an effect of the given and not some site within which the given might be located (Deleuze 1991: 29). Indeed, the given exceeds the subject. Hence it is the *empirical* (the given world) which is transcendental and not the *thought* of the given (idealism). Deleuze imagines a 'pre-personal field of singularities': modes of givenness that surpass the human (Deleuze 1990: 297). This explains Deleuze's interest in all those forms of writing, information and codings which are neither meaningful nor human (genetic codes, pre-historic stratifications, animal becomings and machines).

In contrast, Kantian transcendental idealism, by locating the given as *given to* a subject (a site of ideality) may preclude *knowledge* of what is not given; but it nevertheless presupposes that the given must be differentiated from that which gives, the thing in itself. Transcendental idealism sees the given as within an unbounded realm of the supersensible. While we cannot intuit what transcends the subject's representations, there is still an absolute outside or transcendence. Seen in these terms it is not surprising that Deleuze refers to Kantianism as a dualism, and sets his own project of immanence against the location of the given *within* thought (Deleuze 1988: 86). For any location of the given, or attribution to point of view, results in an 'outside'. Deleuze's philosophy presents itself as the project of thinking the given without positing some transcendent 'plane' within which the given is ordered (Deleuze and Guattari 1994: 47; 59). The possibility of such a philosophy depends upon overcoming what Deleuze has identified as philosophy's perennial question: 'Who Speaks?' For it is this question that has always referred the event of sense or becoming of the world *to* some position; and this position has itself always been determined as the ground or 'good image' of thought. Thought, Deleuze insists, is not a thing to be recognised and represented, as though thought were either one more given thing or some ground of the given (Deleuze and Guattari 1994:

197). By re-thinking the given beyond representation we might free thought from point of view, logic and the human and arrive at the given as a *pre-personal* field of singularities (Deleuze 1990: 297).

THE REPRESENTATION OF THOUGHT

In *The Order of Things* Foucault diagnoses modernity through the combined symptoms of anthropologism and representation. And Foucault is neither the first, nor the last, to be critical of modernity's fall into representation. The idea that the mind is a passive mirror that re-presents some external reality was attacked at least as early as Hegel's criticism of Kant. What Hegel found so abhorrent in Kantianism was the isolation and alienation of mind in relation to some inert outside world (Hegel 1977: 95). And a similar attack on the reification of mind and world (as representer and represented) is repeated as recently as Richard Rorty's *Philosophy and the Mirror of Nature* (1980), Deleuze's *Difference and Repetition* (1994) and Lyotard's *Libidinal Economy* (1993). What Hegel and the later anti-representationalists share is a criticism of the subjugation of mind to some unattainable outside or presence, as though mind were merely the passive and separate reflection of an external world. In opposition to the presence/representation divide, then, these thinkers have sought to render the logic of existence dynamic, fluid and ungrounded, as though difference might occur *immanently*: not a difference imposed through some representational scheme or judging logic, but a difference neither determined nor bounded by anything other than itself. Rather than the objective existence of a logic of categories, logic is deemed to be the outcome of an immanent movement. Rather than a subject who represents the world through some vehicle of logic, logic just is that process that allows subject and object to be differentiated. Representation is therefore targeted as the illusion of an unquestioning subjectivism or anthropologism. Only in the paradigm of a separate subject or 'man' who then encounters a world is representation required as a way of uniting thinking substance with external matter. It is in the error of anthropologism or subjectivism that thought (mis)recognises itself as a *thing*, as a determinate type of being with a given logic, and with a logic that then determines what is. In the anthropological sleep, mind, man or subject are used as the explanatory grounds that re-present the world. The status of this ground is, however, left out of question.

This error of positing mind or subject as a thing within the world that also represents the world is usually located as the hallmark of modernity, and all the incriminating evidence seems to lead back to Descartes. From Heidegger and Husserl through to contemporary feminism, Descartes's *cogito*, as thinking stuff or *res extensa*, is symptomatic of the prison of modern existence.[1] It is this grounding *res cogitans* or 'soul' that incarcerates the body and life (Foucault 1979: 29–30). (And Kant had already described the ethical horrors of Cartesianism; if we make the mistake of thinking of the subject as a type of *substance* then there is no room for freedom [Kant [1787] 1933: 470]. Against Descartes, we must recognise that the subject cannot be a thing, for the subject is nothing other than the very possibility for thinking of things.) Only with the idea of the subject as a representing animal are we able to establish the human being as the ground for all being. But while Kant's attempt to establish the subject as a procedure of representation and not as a represented thing aims to avert anthropologism, it also invites the very risk of anthropologism. It becomes increasingly difficult to avoid taking the transcendental condition of representation as itself a thing to be represented. This is the very problem of finally arriving at the representational threshold of modernity. Is it possible to think the possibility of representation without positing a *man who represents*? Anthropologism returns insistently, and does so by returning all those sites of difference, dispersion and becoming to the recognised ground of man.

And so Kant is the first to raise a series of critiques of Cartesianism that will extend to contemporary pragmatism, feminism and post-structuralism. The mind is not a screen, mirror or theatre; it cannot be unproblematically posited in this anthropologistic manner. Cartesianism is targeted as the reification and ossification of what should be properly considered as a movement or procedure, rather than a thing or substance. However, the persistent refusal *and return* of the subject as substance should lead us to question the exemplary status of Cartesian doubt. Descartes functions as the synecdoche for the modern scar of representation. It is Cartesianism that is held responsible for isolating the subject as a presence which then represents another presence, and since Descartes there has been no shortage of pre-subjective or transcendental analyses that have attempted to see subject and presence as effects of a more general movement, syntax, differentiation or logic. The question that we might direct to all these anti-Cartesian and anti-anthropologistic endeavours is whether the fall into representation is an accident and whether the event of the post- (or pre-) human can ever be achieved. Today the horrors of Cartesianism are identified in a variety of domains: in the patriarchal phobia that resists the unified and lived body that precedes subject/object boundaries (Grosz 1994); in the domination of a Western reason that can know no other but determines all being in its own image (Adorno and Horkheimer [1944] 1979); and in the ascendancy of a cultural studies that simply assumes a disembodied and rationalising system of representation without a question of who speaks or owns such a system (Hartman 1997). What is at stake in the overcoming of Cartesianism and representation? In such a post-human world thought would be freed from reification, and logic would be the dynamism of movement and difference, rather than a determining system. Thought would no longer be subjected to some grounding representation (such as the human, the rational, or even *Dasein*), but will be the possibility of representation in general.

The first and most persuasive attack on anthropologism was that undertaken by Kant, an attack mobilised by the idea of representation. It makes no sense, Kant argued, to explain the origin of knowledge by referring to a being *within* the world. Descartes's subject is another type of substance; to posit this substance as the site within which the world is represented forecloses the question of how this substance itself would be known. Thus Kant insists that knowledge cannot be accounted for by locating representation within an empirical site, such as man. The representing subject is not a worldly being but a representational condition for the world. This is why Kant insists on a *transcendental* logic. In order to *have* a world there must be some givenness or giving of the world. But it is erroneous to conclude from this givenness that the world is *given* to some other thing, site or point within the world. Kant's transcendental logic does not describe a being *to whom* the world is given, but general conditions for givenness. It is through this logic of the given that a subject is then presupposed. The subject describes nothing other than the way in which the world is given. This process of the giving of the world includes the determining concept of substance. The subject is not itself a substance but that which determines being as substance. Only through the synthesising power of the subject is the world given as substance. The subject is, then, known only as it represents the world and not as a representation.

The same can be said of the political subject of modernity as described through contemporary liberal theory. The representational power of the subject is an ideal of procedure (and not a given set of norms). This is why liberal theory places right – the possibility of determination – before the good (a concrete, determined and normative understanding of goods). Even those communitarians who object to this idea of the pure and neutral proceduralism *of the individual* do so, not by grounding the political on this or that specific good or value, but by arguing for a more 'holist' or 'shared' understanding of procedure and representation.[2] Neither liberals nor communitarians argue for some founding concept of human nature; it is precisely because of the openness of human life that we can argue for the liberal conception of self-representing subjects or the communitarian conception of collective self-formation or imagined communities. It is not that the subject possesses certain moral truths or a moral sense that it will then articulate through political representation (as though representation were a feature added to the subject's already given morality). On the contrary, the political subject is just this capacity for representation. Because the subject is not a worldly thing who possesses immutable norms for action, subjects are bound to processes of representation. For it is through representation that the subject establishes itself, not as a determined being with values, but as a value-inaugurating being. Political representation is not the expression *of* autonomy – as though the subject pre-existed the process of representation in the manner of a self-contained thing. Political representation is the *institution* of autonomy. In the act of representation the subject is established as a point of view, as the effect of decision, as the locale or determinateness of autonomy. As self-representing, subjects cannot legitimately appeal to a *worldly* ground for their being – neither human nature, nor moral sense, nor their identity or subjectivity – for subject and identity are effected through a relation to the world, and are not things within the world. As in the transcendental and epistemological project of representation, this political sense of representation sustains the attempt to overcome the notion of man as a represented thing. To represent man – as does anthropologism – is to close the *question* of man's being. But this question can only be opened by arriving at representation, such that man is not a represented (or representing) thing but a power of representation.

Despite Kant's insistence on the subject's *transcendental* nature – such that the subject is the way the world is given and not a worldly thing – it was Kant's argument for representational conditions that was later attacked as still too human, or too anthropologistic. How could a transcendental logic, as a representational condition, not fail to function as yet another version of man? How is it that Kant can criticise the error of anthropologism and its assumption that it can know the being of the subject, yet nevertheless go on to describe a transcendental logic that is still subjective? Following Kant, German idealism set itself the task of freeing logic, or representational conditions, from the human or the point of view of the subject. Logic and representation were not subjective activities but the very being of the world. (This is why Hegel writes a *Logic*, for logic is not an order imposed on the world, nor a set of forms existing in another world; there is nothing other than logic or the order of the world's own becoming.) The world is a process of representation. The subject – as a point of view within which representation takes place – is the effect of a more general process of representation, and not the condition of representation.

This radical anti-Kantian anti-anthropologism was not confined to German idealism. Indeed, this extension of representation beyond the human might be one of the most tempting manoeuvres of post-Kantian anti-subjectivism. Heidegger's 'Es Gibt', Rorty's language games without subjects, structuralism's systems that effect speaking positions, and all those radically anterior notions of *différance*, becoming and syntax, are attempts to think that representation which is not one. Not a subject who then re-presents some present world, but a representation without a grounding presence – an 'it speaks' without point of view. This brings us to the limit of the motif of representation. When feminist theorists like Teresa de Lauretis (1987) argue that gender is not some thing to be represented but is 'always already a representation' we are really no longer speaking of *re*-presentation in its classical (and widely condemned) sense. Indeed, the very idea of *re*-presentation is undermined by the claim that there is nothing other than representation.

What needs to be recalled, however, is that in his critique of anthropologism and the idea of the subject as a representational animal, Kant had already anticipated a problem with a tendency to think outside of the point of view of knowledge altogether. It was this error that he identified as anthropomorphism: the failure to recognise that if something is to be known it must be given, and must be given to some point of view (or finite site of receptivity). While it is illegitimate to hypostatise this point of view as in itself a thing, whatever is *known* will still be conditioned by the necessity of its being represented – not intuited immediately but *appearing*. We therefore have to consider the site of representational conditions. Failure to think of the point of view of representation creates the illusion that we experience things immediately and in themselves, and so we fail to recognise the contribution or difference of thinking. In the error of anthropomorphism all thought's contributions – its concepts and forms – are taken as real. Thus a logic is located *in* the world; we think of the world possessing its own forms and concepts, as though the world itself owned a grammar of substance and attributes, of cause and effect, of time and space. It is this anthropomorphic forgetting of our own contribution that leads to the height of philosophical irresponsibility. Thought simply claims to have 'found' its ideas and concepts; it subjects itself to a logic it 'discovers' and in so doing dis-owns its own representational and *decisive* power. To refer to a transcendentally real logic or system of representation is to forget how or where such a system is itself represented.

It is through both these errors – of anthropologism *and* anthropomorphism – that representation comes to function as the scar and threshold of modernity. Representation acts as a scar precisely because of the persistence of anthropologism. Any attempt to resist positing or representing a worldly ground for knowledge – by referring to a representational condition such as the subject, logic, language, structure or difference – can always be represented as one more thing within the world, a represented thing that grounds the represented world in general.

TRANSCENDENTAL VIEWPOINTS

Kant's definition of the subject in opposition to anthropologism defines his Copernican turn, a turn away from the empirical point of view – the viewing of *things* – to the transcendental point of view: a view that is no longer the view *of* things, but the possibility of viewpoint in general. From this Copernican turn back to the point of the subject it can make no sense to see the subject as a represented thing within the world. When we examine the very idea of a *world* we recognise that concepts are already in play; the subject, or point of view, is already effected. The 'world' is meaningfully given as an external existence in time and space, subject to causality and thought of as a substance with attributes. Any such possible world is already conceptual, and is therefore the outcome of representation or, in Kant's terms, the outcome of a transcendental logic. By establishing representation as the condition for any possible world, Kant brings philosophy to critical responsibility, and sets his own work against groundless speculation. If the world is only *as given*, or as represented, then one cannot ground or explain the world, and certainly not by appealing to some supersensible realm beyond the given. The supersensible can only be thought *from* the given, from the very possibility of the sensible, receptive or finite point of view. For if things appear or are received, then they are received by some other finite point. From this recognition of the necessarily sensible or receptive character of knowledge, we can think the supersensible not as a thing that itself might be received or sensed, but as the very condition of the sensible or given. For this reason, the transcendental turn is not a step outside or 'flight' from the given, but a turning back upon the given, a *Copernican* turn that does not discover another site but recognises where we have been all along (Kant [1787] 1933: 533–4).

The representational turn thereby establishes the proper point of view of modernity as enlightenment. And this process of enlightenment expresses itself politically and epistemologically, with both politics and knowledge being liberated through the autonomy of representation. To argue that logic cannot be found within the world, but is the condition for a world, is to recognise thought's contribution. Epistemological enlightenment abandons the project of knowing a first cause outside all experience, or of determining the ultimate character of substance. Causality and substance are *ideal* determinations: ways in which the world is represented as a world. Such concepts cannot therefore be applied to some point beyond our world. But this epistemological enlightenment is inextricably intertwined with political enlightenment. If man is not a being within the world but a representational condition, then man *is* only in so far as he represents himself. Man is appealed to, not as some *given* ground for law, but as a capacity to be self-grounding. And this capacity for self-representation occurs through the recognition of point of view. If knowledge is finite, located and receptive, then no trans-finite or unconditioned ground can determine human being in general. It is because of the finite point of view of the subject – any possible subject – that there can be no appeal to a divine or pre-subjective ground of law. No *law* (as unconditioned and universal) can be *given*, for to be given is to already be located, finite and conditioned. And so if no pre-subjective or unconditioned law can be *given*, one must give a law to oneself. Political autonomy is the consequence and predicament of this representational condition. In both the political and epistemological recognition of representational conditions, representation is not a given set of rules but an activity or movement of autonomy. This can be traced back to Kant's idea of a transcendental logic, but also to more general ideals of the formality and universality of logic. Transcendental logic is not a set of psychological predicates or a mental fiction imposed on the world; rather, it is the very form of the world. Representation cannot be grasped in itself as a thing, but only reflectively as that procedure that enables us to think things in general.

The recognition of representation, discovered in the power of thought to give itself a world and a law, constitutes the threshold of enlightenment. But this threshold is constantly forced to assert itself in the face of a persistent anthropologism, where man appears not so much as a procedure for representing a law or a world, but as a lawful thing within a world with its own laws. Against anthropologism and foundationalism, Kant and his later anti-anthropologist critics attempt to think an autonomous capacity for representation that is not reduced to yet one more represented thing. However, this striving for the recognition of representation as the possibility of autonomy is continually thwarted and precluded by the scar of representation, the representation *of* the representational possibility. For, *once represented*, possibility becomes determined and no longer a pure formality or openness. This second sense of representation is no longer the recognition of one's self as a pure capacity; for it is *as represented* – as man, humanity, the subject – that one is subjected to representation. One submits to a representation *of* the human, the subject or logic – forgetting that these concepts are effects of representation. Here, representation appears as an imposed or external scheme, a scar that precludes autonomy and the transparency of self-recognition.

When Kant adopted Aristotle's categories as the very form of experience, he did so in order to demonstrate that logic was not an external order in the world. Rather, logic is the way that thought has a world. The world is given *as* temporal, spatial, causally determined, measurable, quantifiable, delimited and substantial. But these features of the world are features of thought's synthesising power and ought not be mistaken as things in themselves, or 'in' the world. But while Kant rendered logic transcendental, and thus situated the subject as a condition for the world rather than a worldly being, Heidegger and phenomenology nevertheless criticised Kant for a residual subjectivism, representation-alism and anthropologism. Kant still understood logic as a 'subjective' representation, and separated this representation from a world in itself. Heidegger took logic that one step further. Before any subject who owned a logic, there was a synthesis or 'gathering' – a *logos* – that then effected the subject. This subject was not the pure condition for representing a world but a comportment, dwelling or projectedness-towards a world. And so Heidegger concluded that the very concept of the subject would need to be done away with or radically modified. For Heidegger, the subject – that which grounds or underlies – is the effect of an un-grounding, a movement or transcendence. Prior to any 'subject' with a 'logic' there is, for Heidegger, a *logos*: a 'saying-gathering' or way of being that 'gives' a world. *Logos* is, then, not a 'logic' but a pre-human, pre-subjective gathering, synthesis or temporalising.

DISPERSING LOGIC BEYOND THE HUMAN

But even this phenomenological appeal to time by Heidegger was later to be criticised as both representational and anthropological by Foucault (and others). For Foucault, Heidegger's appeal to the transcendental horizon of time was yet one more movement of 'man'. In modernity, in fact, man had been nothing other than an empirico-transcendental double: a finite being who grasps his condition – such as time or history – as the unified ground of his own becoming. Against a Heideggerian appeal to an authentic and pre-subjective *logos*, Foucault asserts *positivity*: all those features that remain irreducible to thought and the human. Foucault's analysis concerns itself with a logic, regularity or 'positive unconscious', a logic that exceeds the ideality of the point of view of the subject (Foucault 1970: xi). More than a history of ideas, Foucault concerns himself with a logic of spaces (architecture, institutions, bodily practices), a logic of the visible (the organisation of gazes, the technologies of viewing, the distribution of light and the refraction of surfaces), and a logic of bodies (practices of diet, punishment, erotics and discipline). Furthermore, Foucault insists on a *historical* a priori. As Heidegger had already argued, the very concept of 'a priori' invokes time, for the a priori is what is 'prior' or lies beforehand (Heidegger

1996). This suggests that time is more than a transcendental/logical condition; it is the very possibility of thinking *conditions*. Foucault's challenge to Heidegger's privileging of temporality is undertaken through the notions of the *historical* a priori and the fold. *The Order of Things* refers quite explicitly to conditions of thought. But not only do these conditions exceed the ideal medium of temporality – by including institutions, spaces, practices and material determinations – the very logic of conditions differs historically. For Foucault, Heidegger's understanding that *Dasein'is'*, only in the extent to which *Dasein* thinks itself through time, is *one* form or modality of folding – one way in which thought questions itself to become itself. The very idea of the a priori – the idea of a formal ground that then gives itself a world – is the particular fold of modern existence. *The Order of Things* concerns itself with examining the various canvases, dissecting tables or spaces across which knowledge is drawn. The 'positive unconscious' is just this 'outside', ground or medium that is constituted by the relations of any particular episteme. There is not a ground to knowledge in general – whether of history, man or being. Grounds are effected through the specific and particular relations of an episteme. In modernity this is exemplified in the practices of the human sciences. Here, the medium of truth and knowledge is man, and this medium is the effect of certain distributions (the formation of prisons and hospitals, the discourses of sexuality, and the very idea of truth as the unveiling of man's transcendental 'density'.) Foucault's history of Ancient Greek ethics describes another folding; questions of truth are not given through interpreting the cause of man's being and knowledge but are concerned with what one ought to do, the efficacy of practices, and the management of one's self (Foucault 1988). Truth is folded through a different mode of relation, a different form of difference: not the relation between 'man' and the transcendental condition, but the relation between a body and its pleasures. Foucault's idea of the 'fold' is an attempt to free thought once and for all from anthropologism and representationalism. There is not a being that then discloses itself. Rather, there are events of disclosure or foldings that are not self-enclosed, events that form an *ad hoc* regularity that is subsequently recognised as *being*. Domains of objects are produced through a dispersion, a dispersion that has no general form and no single locale. For Foucault, thought does not disperse *itself*; nor can thought attend to some prior or proximate *being*. Thought is the effect of specific, positive and determinate ways of being – effected through various foldings that are not the foldings *of* some being in general. The way to overcome a general logic of man – a logic in which a part of the world functions to explain the world in general – is to confront and resist all those specific ways in which a general ground is constituted. For the most part this will entail addressing all those different modalities of point of view, *the various ways in which selves or points of view are effected by specific knowledge practices*. Foucault's entire career might be understood as a tireless campaign against the privileging of man or thought as a general condition. This explains his persistent anti-anthropologism and anti-representationalism. The world is not given through representational conditions or a logic. Logic just is the perceived regularity of existence after the event of its dispersion. Logic is not a medium or order that sustains itself above and beyond the various events of existence. Rather, the order of things is the effect of a series of interconnected, differing and conflicting foldings – relations among bodies, spaces, discourses, visible fields and practices.

If, as Foucault insists, there is no man in general, then a genealogical position will ultimately be *critical*. What appears as our ground, the a priori, or the very medium of our being is precisely what ought to be subject to question, rather than recognised as our own representational condition (Foucault 1986b). It is in this idea that Foucault's thought at once issues in the culmination and the crisis of modern representationalism. The *condition* of thought must not be understood as some recognisable or pre-given ground, but must be accounted for according to how any such condition is known. Even the structuralist endeavour to think the condition of thought in the inhuman medium of language or system is one more displaced anthropologism, one more attempt to locate thought within a recognisable locale. Foucault's attempt to unground the logic and conditions of existence by extending distribution beyond thought's *own* conditions and recognition is an intense anti-anthropologism. But as his own career made so clear, all those attempts to unground thought did so in the face of a persistent re-recognition of grounds. His concepts of power, history and discourse were taken as themselves transcendental conditions. Judith Butler, for example, has criticised the limitations of Foucault's concept of discourse by arguing that we need to consider that which exceeds discourse. In so doing she returns discourse to a representationalist logic, such that discourse is seen as the discourse *of* some more general logic (Butler 1993: 35). Habermas also interprets Foucault's use of history as yet one more transcendental horizon (Habermas 1987: 254). And in the early uptake of 'power' in literary–critical uses of Foucault power was not seen as an immanent domain with no outside, but as the power *of* certain selves and institutions (Greenblatt 1980). The point is not to correct these 'misreadings' of Foucault, but to question whether a correct reading is at all possible. Can we think discourse, power or history immanently, without positing a general or grounding logic?

This is the risk of any anti-anthropologism. Any appeal to the inhuman can function as one more real within which the human point of view is located. The appeal to a post-human and differential domain of immanence with no ground and no outside is a striving for a freedom from *reaction*. In such a post-representational utopia thought would no longer be a determinate thing or substance relating to some presence, but the pure movement of difference. The problem, of course, is that in such an overcoming of representation the *thought* of the inhuman disavows its own location, positivity and point of view. The other-than-human, the thought of the event or becoming, is never a pure and immediate becoming but is always given in some way; whatever is posited as in- or pre-human bears the character of that human determination which it seeks to overcome.

For this reason the post-representational and post-human moment of modernity never arrives: the moment in which no general logic would be accepted as given, the moment in which thought would remain in a perpetual question without reification and without the self-recognition of its *own point of view* – without the predicament of autonomy (the effected lawfulness of the self). Man never arrives at the representational threshold, the point at which any general logic or medium would be recognised as the effect of *our* representational power. (For this very appeal to 'our' power or the power *of thought* reconstitutes a double of man; 'we' recognise ourselves as those beings open to question.) The demand of modernity is a recognition that any representational ground be seen as the effect of thought's representational capacity. Thought must not subject itself to, or recognise itself in, such a ground. Rather, thought must recognise itself as *nothing* other than this capacity of grounding. Once thought accepts *a representation of itself as an image of thought* (Deleuze 1994: 131), the passage to enlightenment is halted. What precludes the full recognition and enlightenment of the representational condition is the scar of representation. Rather than being the radicalisation of its capacity to think or represent, thought subjects itself to a representation. (And this subjection includes all those representations of representation: the mind as a mirror, theatre, screen, or *tabula rasa*.) The outcome of this perpetual resistance to anthropologism is an intense anti-representationalism. Thought must not be defined either as the representation *of* some given substance, nor as fully defined through any effected representation – such as the human, being, language, culture or structure.

For even a pre-human differential logic – such as the dispersal of power, or the event of difference – can be accepted and recognised as the ground of 'our' being. The task would appear to be to think these notions beyond thought, beyond recognition, beyond concepts and beyond all possible representation. To what extent, in pursuing this path beyond anthropologism, is thought led into anthropomorphism? Led into thinking a domain of the transcendentally real, a real that is not owned by any point of view?

THE UNREPRESENTABLE

Against the positing of a condition that can be represented and recognised, post-Kantian anti-anthropologism has attempted to think the unrepresentable. How can thought be freed from representation, from the idea that there is a subject who thinks by relating to a present world? Kant had inserted the logic of representation into modernity by arguing that any world is a world *for* some representing point of view. Representation, therefore, and its concomitant anthropologism, would seem to be surmountable only by liberating thought from point of view. Rather than seeing thought as issuing from some being within the world who has a logic, logic might be dispersed into a radically pre- (or post-) human eternal return. Kant had already opened the way for this overcoming of the human point of view. The Kantian subject is effected through the givenness of being, and is not itself a being among beings. The subject is not a presence or thing that encounters the world in order to re-present that world in some mental space.

Knowledge is not the relation between two present things or substances, but the determination of things or substances by a logic. Kant had insisted that empirical realism, the experience of the world *as real*, necessarily and legitimately generated a transcendental idealism. The only way in which a world can be given *as real* is if it is *given*, and therefore it must be given to some point of view or subject. The subject is nothing other than the event of this finite giving, the synthesising of the given as a world.

After Kant, however, the attempt to overcome point of view has issued in the dream of an empiricism that will not generate an idealism: the idea of a *giving* without location in a point, subject or logic. This has inspired a plethora of projects through which modernity's representational recognition will finally be both achieved and overcome. (The event of representation will no longer be subordinated to a presence, no longer be a re-presentation.) In this ideal or idea of non-presence, beyond all ontology, there is not a presence (neither subject nor being) that precedes or owns representation. The idea of overcoming a metaphysics of presence relies on freeing thought from point of view, freeing representation from thought, and imagining a giving, writing, sending, coding, marking, *semiosis* or tracing that is not the giving or writing *of* – but writing itself. The logic of representation will be challenged by another *logos*: not a thought that attends to, or thinks of, some presence. This 'other logos' will be other than ontology. It will declare itself as a grammatology, a pragmatism, a project of immanence, or a transcendental empiricism: a givenness, event or act not subjected to either a real or a subject. A givenness that is transcendental does not subordinate the given *to* some point of view (idealism), nor does it see the given as the given *of* some being. There is just giving – a giving that is transcendental, unconditioned, ungrounded and not located within some presence or real.

This notion of a radically pre-human givenness extends the boundary of force or effect beyond the human, and therefore beyond the traditional domain of autonomy. What distinguishes Deleuze's transcendental empiricism from deconstruction comes out most clearly in the direct confrontations of the relation between ethics and philosophy. For Deleuze philosophy, as the affirmation of *what is*, is an ethics; any question, concept or act of philosophy is itself one more affirmation of the given (and not a ground or justification of the given) (Deleuze

1990: 149; Deleuze and Guattari 1994: 159). For Derrida, however, ethics is (at least) a double movement: both the affirmation of philosophy's capacity to extend beyond the given (with the concepts of truth, reason and so on) *and* the recognition of the inherent violence of this extension, for such philosophical concepts *decide* the singularity of the given according to some idea of presence (Derrida 1978: 128). While Derrida recognises a certain ethical necessity to this violence of the idea of pure presence, he has also raised the possibility of another modality of ethics. We can imagine philosophy as non-autonomous, not as a *question* that places itself outside all representation. If philosophy is not the pure opening and autonomous beginning of the question, it might be a passive listening, or allowing to be heard, of that which gives itself. This non-autonomous philosophy would dismantle logocentric representationalism: the idea that representation is the representation *of* some being by a subject who owns an adequate logic. Against an owned or autonomous representation, philosophy would free itself from the self-enclosure of point of view and imagine itself given over to what is neither known nor knowable, but which nevertheless affects. Thinking beyond autonomy and point of view liberates thought from its parochial anthropologism. But it does so by appealing to a philosophy to come: a philosophy not yet imaginable precisely because of the representational illusion. If this philosophy to come is to be achieved, though, we need to re-think writing, play and representation:

> To think play radically the ontological and transcendental problem-atics must first be seriously *exhausted*; the question of the meaning of being, the being of the entity and of the transcendental origin of the world – of the world-ness of the world – must be patiently and rigorously worked through, the critical movement of the Husserlian and Heideggerian questions must be effectively followed to the very end, and their effectiveness and legibility must be conserved. Even if it were crossed out, without it the concepts of play and writing to which I shall have recourse will remain caught within regional limits and an empiricist, positivist, or metaphysical discourse. The counter-move that the holders of such a discourse would oppose to the precritical tradition and to metaphysical speculation would be nothing but the worldly representation of their own operation. It is therefore *the game of*

the world that must first be thought; before attempting to understand all the forms of play in the world. (Derrida 1974: 50)

If play is the 'game of the world' then play cannot be contained within a logic, as it would be by logocentrism. Play is not a differential
structure imposed upon presence. For in Derrida's sense of play the
very idea of logic and ontology are radically displaced. It is not that
there is being that is then differentiated or thought through a logic; the
idea of presence or being is already the effect of play. Further, this play
is not a play within a logic or structure. Logic or structure are effects of
a play that is so pre-human it is the very play of the world. Thought in
this way, play liberates writing from logic and opens the possibility of
a difference or trace that exceeds the subject, autonomy and presence.
Two questions need to be asked. Is such a freedom from logic possible?
And is such a non-autonomy desirable? In terms of possibility, the
question might be approached historically and logically. If writing has
been determined as the representation of presence – throughout the
Western *logos* – then can this illusion be taken as avoidable? Is it not
the case that any attempt to free syntax, play, representation or writing
from the ground of sense will always be returned to some ground? And
this leads us to the question of logical possibility, and whether anthropologism can be overturned by locating representation beyond all
autonomy and point of view.

If autonomy is defined as some already given point within the world
that owns and authors sense and representation, then Derrida's
examination of the logic of sense will rightly preclude autonomy. For
the very possibility of sense and representation is that it must still hold
force and recognition beyond any single point of view or intending
subject. The subject does not give itself a law, but is placed within law.
But subjectivity is nevertheless effected through a certain lawfulness
or regularity of syntax. And so autonomy might be thought, not as
the self-presence of the subject, but just as that persistence, regularity
or constancy of a specific mode of logic. The dream of a difference or
syntax beyond all point of view, is necessarily belied by the point of
view from which any such syntax must be thought. This is to say not
only that there is never a difference in general, but that the *ways in
which this difference is unthinkable, the ways in which thought arrives at
its limit constitute a specific point of view*. Point of view is not the

self-inaugurating logic of the world, and autonomy is not groundless self-authorship. Point of view and autonomy are predicaments of representation. In recognising that we do not think writing in general, but always think writing as the writing *of* some presence, then we are compelled to own the *ways* in which we pass beyond, or transcend ourselves, to this presence. This ownership or recognition awakens thought to its inevitable parochialism and anthropologism; any dream of a writing beyond point of view is still 'our' dream. And the ways in which we figure this 'beyond' of point of view is precisely what places us in a point of view and produces an autonomy – not an autonomy of self-becoming, but an autonomy that is the effect of recognising our becoming after the event.

AUTONOMY

Consider, in this regard, Irigaray's notion of sexual difference, where autonomy is not understood as the property or pure self-becoming of a subject. Autonomy is just the recognition that the way in which a subject relates to what is not itself, is a *specific* way of relating and not a pure difference in general. This allows, as Irigaray insists, for different modalities of difference, different ways of transcendence. The subject is neither an already given essence nor the pure and neutral becoming of existence; the subject's becoming is always the becoming *of* this specific and embodied being and a becoming towards another embodied being. Autonomy is not, then, a pure self-projection whereby one give's a law to oneself. Seen within a relation of sexual difference, autonomy is the recognition of the character of a subject's becoming, a character that is only disclosed in relation to *another* becoming. Irigaray sees *sexual* difference as the first possibility for thinking an autonomy that *owns* its mode of transcendence, and does so by recognising the character of transcendence. If, following Heidegger's reading of Kant, it is necessary to have a metaphysical comportment if one is to go beyond oneself and think another *being*, it is also necessary that this act of transcendence is inflected by the specific mode of its becoming. The aim of metaphysics would not, then, be to arrive at a syntax of pure becoming in general, but to recognise the ways in which any such syntax takes place – the specific, located, embodied and different modes of this syntax.

Irigaray's ethics of sexual difference needs to be read as the opening to autonomy rather than a ground from which autonomy might be determined. The thought of sexual difference provides a way of thinking different modes of difference, not just the difference between a subject and object, but a difference between two self-differing subjects. But this ought not mean that sexual difference can exhaust the horizon of modalities of difference. For if the character or specificity of the way in which difference is effected were halted at the logic of sexual difference we would have fallen back into anthropologism and representationalism: as though the difference that effects autonomy and point of view could be determined as the difference between two (sexed) beings. What sexual difference raises, though, is the positivity of difference – a difference that is the difference *of* this being, a being that differs in relation *to* another differentiating being. The question is whether this positivity of difference, if it is not exhausted by the differentiation of sexed beings, can be entirely dispersed beyond the human. Is it possible to think the specific differences or becomings of beings in a world freed from all anthropologism?

If Derrida locates *différance* in a non-autonomous logic of the *gramme*, then he does so by moving beyond being. And he does so at the risk of a certain anthropomorphism. But this risk in Derrida's thought is continually tempered by his own recognition of the question of point of view. Metaphysics opens with the *idea* of a truth that would exceed finite conditions, determination and location; but this idea is at once belied and contaminated in its specific articulation. The *idea* of truth in general is never given *in general*, but is always articulated through a specific articulation (an articulation that aims to exempt itself from the particular point of its own writing). This double movement of any metaphysics depends upon accepting truth as the idea of the 'in general', and defining philosophy as the hyperbolic question that exceeds all particular truth claims. At the same time Derrida also indicates a possibility of going beyond this question, and this issues in the anti-representational and utopian aspects of grammatology. This entails forgoing ontology and autonomy, for both these notions locate the logic of difference, either as the difference *of* being or the difference *of* a subject. The fulfilment of this idea of a logic of difference that is not subordinated to anything other than itself may always be impeded as long as we sustain the language of writing, representation and metaphysics. A more speculative attempt to free thought from representation would need to move beyond the traditional grammar of metaphysics. More than critical, such a project would have to affirm difference itself, rather than regarding difference as a pre-conceptual and continually reified excess at the limit of metaphysics.

On the one hand, then, Derrida's project of deconstruction takes a primarily *critical* form, locating excess, the *gramme* and the trace at the limit of truth and sense. On the other hand Derrida also makes an affirmative and 'messianic' movement beyond critique, a movement that would transform philosophy and would do so by attending to all those movements, effects, tracings and markings that exceed presence, representation and recognition but nevertheless have a certain force. This affirmative or messianic aspect of Derrida's work is, however, insistently and tirelessly tempered by the critical attention to the necessary contamination and violence of any gesture beyond a given totality. Deleuze, however, puts forward a more startling provocation to metaphysics, moving beyond the question of who speaks, beyond the 'in general', and beyond point of view. If Irigaray will insist on different modes of difference, she will do so by arguing that difference takes place and is embodied. There are *genres* of difference. Sexual difference is neither the difference of some identity, nor a difference in general, but the difference of different bodies. But how is a body itself differentiated? For Derrida this question would lead us back, reflectively, to the thought of *différance*, a difference that is not the positive difference *of* this or that being, but difference as an event in itself. Deleuze, on the other hand, will at once sustain the project of thinking difference positively, and not as a quasi-transcendental condition. Deleuze examines sites and zones of difference; the difference of bodies, of genetic codings, of semiotic systems, of spaces and visible effects. For Deleuze, difference is both empirical and transcendental. Difference is empirical because what is given, lived or experienced is difference itself (such that difference is not a condition of experience or the given; it is experienced). But difference is also transcendental. There is not some ground or presence outside difference that is then given through difference. Difference goes all the way down; there is no beyond to difference; no plane within which difference is located. Difference is not a condition that gives being; being is differential. (And this is why it is perhaps no longer appropriate to talk of 'being' here.)

DELEUZE'S TRANSCENDENTAL EMPIRICISM

The 'I think' is the most general principle of representation – in other words, the source of these elements and of the unity of all these faculties: I conceive, I judge, I imagine, I remember and I perceive – as though these were the four branches of the Cogito. On precisely these branches difference is crucified. They form quadripartite fetters under which only that which is identical, similar, analogous or opposed can be considered different. . . . For this reason, the world of representation is characterised by its inability to conceive of difference in itself. (Deleuze 1994: 138)

In quite different ways Deleuze has attempted to overcome philosophy's twin spectres of representationalism and subjectivism, and has done so by dislocating the given from point of view. Deleuze presents a number of utopian possibilities that would free thought from its subjection to representation. Part of Deleuze's project is diagnostic, examining the ways in which philosophy has subordinated itself to representations. The aim of this diagnosis is to think philosophy differently. After examining the ways in which philosophy has continually disavowed its own *activity*, Deleuze will raise the question of whether an active metaphysics is possible. Like Nietzsche, Deleuze describes the way in which philosophers create concepts from life: concepts such as being, truth, existence, reason and so on (Deleuze 1983: 1; Deleuze and Guattari 1994: 18). Nietzsche, however, accused metaphysics of a necessary reactivism. Metaphysics takes an event of life – such as the concept of the good – and then uses this concept to judge or justify life. In this reactivism a created effect (a concept) has mistaken itself as a cause; the concept is taken as the reason or order to which life ought to submit. Deleuze, on the other hand, puts forward the possibility of an active philosophy, a philosophy adequate to life, a philosophy that will not ground life through some general logic. For it has been the history of a *reactive* metaphysics that has taken the effects of life and then used them to judge life. Concepts – which are for Deleuze responses to the given – are used to ground or explain the given. Through this reactivism thought never fully owns its own power. But Deleuze does not, in response to this reactivism, want to establish the act of thought as the true ground of becoming. Thought is an event in a field of the given, a given that extends well beyond thought's own comprehension.

Deleuze describes the history of philosophy as the construction of a series of planes of immanence, such that the given has always appeared as given *to* some site (Deleuze and Guattari 1994: 51). Deleuze therefore rejects the notion that the Copernican turn to the subject really was such a radical move in philosophy:

> It is frequently said that philosophy throughout its history has changed its center of perspective, substituting the point of view of the finite self for that of the infinite divine substance. Kant would stand at the turning point. Is this change, however, as important as it is claimed to be? As long as we maintain the formal identity of the self, doesn't the self remain subject to a divine order and to a unique God who is its foundation? (Deleuze 1990: 294)

Like Heidegger, Deleuze sees the modern subject as just one more way of thinking what is according to some general ground. In order to think the given *transcendentally – not* as given *to* or given *from* – philosophy needs to be freed from the question of 'Who speaks?'. Only in a freedom from the attribution of sense to subjects can philosophy affirm and activate what is. Any idea of a grounding subject, or any empiricism subordinated to ideality or thought, nullifies the event of the given, negates its force and domesticates the possibility of philosophy to some pre-given image. For Deleuze, freeing the event of philosophy from the question of who speaks will demand attention to speaking 'assemblages' and to a voice that comes from 'elsewhere' or 'on high' (Deleuze 1990: 193). Speech will no longer be located within point of view and point of view will no longer function as the ground of the given.

In his diagnosis of philosophy, Deleuze describes the ways in which the active event of thinking has been subordinated to point of view. Two imperatives follow from this diagnosis. The first is not to see thought or the given as immanent to some plane. Rather than the given being given *to* some subject, the given needs to be thought transcendentally. This issues in the project of thinking 'givings' that exceed the subject and the human: genetic codings, geological stratifications, intensities, sensibility, animal becomings, machinic movements, and cinematic effects. This expansion of the given challenges the very logic of representation. Thought is not the representation of some real – for the given is not the given *of* the real *to* the subject. Deleuze's monism attempts to affirm 'what is' as a plurality of givings (Deleuze 1994: 4). So no particular given or image should act as the ground for any other given or image. Thought, therefore, is one mode of the givenness of the given among others; it is neither the ground of the given nor the representation of the given. Thought is itself an event and not a replica or representation of the real. Further, the features so often used to define thought – its incorporeality, its virtuality, its sense or meaning – are not the privileged attributes of thought. There are movements of sense, virtuality or incorporeal transformations that lie beyond thought or concepts. Deleuze is interested in all those areas of the virtual that exceed the ideal domain of human mind, such as the sense and virtual effects of machines, computers, and cinematic apparatuses. It then follows that if what lies beyond thought can also be understood as the active becoming of the given, then thought is not the ground of the given but a response within the given. The given cannot be located within a plane, ground or presence. So, in response to the history of philosophy's construction of planes, Deleuze suggests that we not only recognise this series of constructions but also attempt to think beyond any grounding plane, or plane of transcendence. This would demand thinking THE plane of immanence as such (Deleuze and Guattari 1994: 59). This plane is pre-philosophical (37). There is already a 'dispersion' or 'distribution' that enables thinking to take place, and from this dispersion various philosophies operate with accepted images of thought. But what needs to be understood is the violent and involuntary aspect of thought (Deleuze 1994: 139). Thought is not the representation of some presence, nor some process of self-recognition. Thinking is difference, disruption and encounter. In recognising this 'heterogenesis' of thought, philosophy might then affirm itself, and move beyond the recognition or representation of an outside, in favour of thinking the very movement that 'gives' the outside. And this means that thought would be active repetition: each time there is thought there is the renewal, affirmation and transformation of difference (Deleuze 1994: 136). Thinking THE plane of immanence is Deleuze's answer to a true or authentic transcendentalism (Deleuze and Guattari 1994: 59). The transcendental ought not be traced back from what we already know. Rather, from where we are we need to think the most absurd possibilities, the most audacious imaginings. Thinking is not a representable being but an event of difference. THE plane of immanence is just this perpetual possibility of re-differentiation. Metaphysics becomes merely reactive when this plane of immanence is subjected to a plane of transcendence: when thought is represented, grounded or recognised through some image of thought.

THE STYLE OF IMMANENCE AND
THE IMMANENCE OF STYLE

Deleuze's second response to his diagnosis of philosophy as a subjection of thought to some pre-given or transcendent image moves further than redefining a philosophy that is no longer subjected to ontology. This second aspect of Deleuze's project of immanence lies in redefining thought. To think differently will demand a new grammar and a new style, and in order to understand what is demanded of such a grammar we need to diagnose the style of philosophy so far. Philosophy has always offered itself as the recognition of thought, as though thought could be both represented and understood in its proper representational capacities (Deleuze 1994: 135). Both the unquestioned grounding of the given on a plane of transcendence and the recognition of thought as the good subject of philosophy are targeted by Deleuze as illusions of anthropologism. Rather than accept an 'image of thought' Deleuze suggests that we might imagine 'thought without an image' (Deleuze 1994: 276). Rather than establishing some new plane or point from which thought takes place, or to which experience is given, Deleuze suggests that we embrace a nomadology. Here, thought would be freed from point of view, freed from an image of thought, freed from recognition, logic and the question of 'Who speaks?'. Thought would be the affirmation of an event or movement, not a represented or representing being but an effective force. Philosophy's grammar has always led thought away from this active possibility.

Our subject/predicate structures, or the very form of our logic, lead us to think of a being, substance or ground that *then* bears some predicate.[3] And, as Heidegger pointed out, this subsuming of *what is* under its form of being known, has foreclosed the very event of being. Heidegger thought that the response to this inclusion of being within the self-presence of the *logos* was best dealt with by thinking the difference between being and thinking, or the opening of being through thinking. And in many ways this project is sustained in Foucault's attempt to recall the difference between words and things, or the visible and the articulable. Deleuze's response, on the other hand, is to think a new grammar or logic rather than the difference between logic and *what is*. Indeed, Deleuze explicitly differentiates his project from what he sees to be Foucault's sustained Kantian dualism (Deleuze 1988: 86). Deleuze's new grammar of philosophy will be a new movement of thinking; and because thinking is an event within the given and not a representation of the given, a new grammar of thinking will also be a new event as such. That is, the event of thinking, grammar, writing, tracing or moving is not an event *in relation to being*. There is not a being that is then represented, a subject that bears predicates, or a substance that has perceivable quantities. Against this separation of representational logic Deleuze will put forward the possibility of a logic of *immanence*: where the event of the given is nothing other than itself, and not the givenness *of* some presence. How will this logic be achieved? Well, if it is the case that the idea of a substance or ground that underlies our predications is an accident of grammar then we will have to write philosophy differently. Certain styles of writing, such as free-indirect style, will be offered by Deleuze not as more correct ways of representing being, but of being and thinking non-representationally. Here, there will be no radical difference between thinking and being – neither is subordinate to the other. In a transcendental empiricism there is just the difference of events. Free-indirect style, to take one example favoured by Deleuze and Guattari, is not a picture, proposition or representation of what is; it is a way of being in itself (Deleuze and Guattari 1987: 84). Deleuze's appeal to style, then, is not aesthetic. It refuses to think of writing as the effective laid over the actual. If actuality is nothing other than its effects then *style will itself be a mode of being* (Deleuze 1997: 113).

Consider the following instance of free-indirect style that opens D. H. Lawrence's 'The Ladybird':

How many swords had Lady Beveridge in her pierced heart! Yet there always seemed room for another. Since she had determined that her heart of pity and kindness should never die. If it had not been for this determination she herself might have died of sheer agony, in the years 1916 and 1917, when her boys were killed, and her brother, and death seemed to be mowing with wide swaths through her family. But let us forget.

> Lady Beveridge loved humanity, and come what might, she would continue to love it. Nay, in the human sense, she would love her enemies. (Lawrence [1923] 1960: 9)

If we ask the question of 'who speaks?' with regard to the above quotation we are presented with an equivocation or dislocation of voice. The passage is not in quotation marks, but it expresses an embrace of humanism that the narrative of Lawrence's novella contradicts. (Lady Beveridge's humanism is depicted as otiose, and this negation of life is inscribed in her physiognomy: she is 'a little, frail, bird-like woman' with a 'long, pale, rather worn face, and . . . nervous gestures' who speaks 'with a thin, English intonation' [Lawrence [1923] 1960: 10].) Lawrence's use of free-indirect style creates a distance from humanism without establishing another point or voice. It is not *Lawrence* who is speaking in the opening of the novella, for the style of the speech is that of Lady Beveridge herself. The hyperbole, mawkish sentimentality and *psychological* inwardness of the language is in direct opposition to the novella's subsequent technique that describes characters through their physiognomy. (Count Dionys is dark and 'aboriginal' while Daphne is described through a 'splendid frame, and . . . lovely, long, strong, legs' [13].) Lawrence's story acts as a diagnosis or symptomatology of the very style of humanist pity. Rather than being 'owned' by the voice of a character or located in an authorial point of view, the language of humanism – of charity, pity, self abnegation and feeling – is seen for what it *does*. In free-indirect style, characters or points of view are produced through ways of speaking. Lawrence's despised humanists repeat a voice that comes from elsewhere, a voice that is not created by any subject but is already spoken. Voice is not a becoming grounded in an autonomous subject; the subject is the effect of voice (Deleuze 1990: 248). In Lawrence's novella it is the clichés and banalities of humanism that effect certain subject positions. Further, we are also given the thoroughly *inhuman* character of human voice in all those places in the novella where there is 'speaking' without a located voice. In the above quotation the phrase 'But let us forget' might be attributed to Lady Beveridge's slavish effacement before her clichéd ideals. But the following paragraph opens with an instance of what Deleuze describes as the 'collective assemblage' nature of all speech: 'Somebody had called her the soul of England.' Lawrence is freeing language from voice, showing the ways in which phrases repeat themselves, produce moral positions and operate apart from any inner intent or human decision.

Deleuze's attention to style is, however, an affirmation rather than a critique. Rather than arguing that any point of view will raise the question of the ground from which a point of view emerges, Deleuze aims to think a style that troubles the attributive and critical force of point of view. What is so difficult in free-indirect style is not just the answer to the question of 'who is speaking?', but also the very possibility of this question. Free-indirect speech is the very wandering or nomadics of style, dislocated from a speaking subject, producing a multiplicity of positions, a collage of voices or an assemblage. In free-indirect style, law or logic are reactions or interpretations that come after the event of voice, speech, tracing or wandering. And if *meaning* is just the reactive effect of certain ways of speaking, then we will only overcome our reactive submission to meaning and the law if we regard speaking not as the vehicle of sense but as a movement or event alongside other events. In their reading of Kafka, Deleuze and Guattari will activate the very force of Kafka's texts. Kafka is so often read as a writer who will set Law essentially beyond all the labyrinths and corridors of any particular or institutional law, as though Law were some unattainable presence beyond all acts of speech (Brod 1960). Deleuze and Guattari will demonstrate the reactive nature of this logic by re-reading Kafka (Deleuze and Guattari 1986). The father, Law or negativity is the reactive effect of all those movements celebrated and effected in Kafka's texts: movements of animals burrowing, of passages and corridors, or wanderings and journeys without end. There is just this event or wandering of texts, just the metamorphoses of animals, hunger artists and insects – forms of becoming that cannot be reduced to the proper becoming *of* the law or *from* the father. What Kafka's texts disclose is the event of style itself, the striation of space through style, and movements that exceed any intending subjects. Law is not the ground of what is but the reactive result of positing some father behind our metamorphoses, some punisher behind the limits of our bodies, some meaning behind our signs, and some order behind the chaos of our logic (Deleuze and Guattari 1986: 45). Whereas free-indirect style is a way of thinking the writing of voice that is not the voice owned by a subject, Kafka's texts take writing beyond voice – to space, inscription, animal wanderings and machines. And a similar claim is also made for the writing of

Beckett, Lawrence, Melville, Woolf and other high modernists, a writing freed from law, the proper and the good: a writing that affirms the event, the machine, the body and all those aspects of existence that are irreducible to sense and recognition: 'The affects of language here become the object of an indirect effectuation, and yet they remain close to those that are made directly, when there are no characters other than the words themselves' (Deleuze 1997: 108).

Freeing thought from its subjection to transcendence demands a new way of thinking about voice and speaking; speech is not the speech of some point of view or subject. There just are events of speech and from this certain regularities, such as located speakers, are effected. And it is this event that is affirmed in free-indirect style. But what do other styles do? How can Deleuze account for the overwhelming Western corpus of literature and philosophy that deploys a representational grammar? If 'what is' is *not* a presence there to be represented, how did we come to think and speak in this way? Deleuze and Guattari's reading of Kafka offers some answer to this problem. Even those great texts of the Law and the father can be *activated*. What their reading of Kafka's text does is not ask what it *means*. Rather they ask how texts *work*: how laws are effected, subject positions carved out, desires instituted, and ideas of presence and ground produced through textual events and questions. There is, then, a two-fold tactic. First, we need to affirm a style that is adequate to life. Free-indirect style is not the style *of* some being; it is existence or language *speaking itself*, a way of being effected through style. Secondly, we need to read in such a way that all those texts of Law are not taken as *representations* of law, but as ways of speaking, moving and writing that then effect a law they supposedly represent. And there is also a third tactic for thinking the plane of immanence; this is more than a tactic of writing and reading. It is the very grammar of being: the infinitive (Deleuze 1990: 221).

Think of the ambiguity in the notion of subject; it is both a form of grammar (subject/predicate) and that which underlies or grounds thought (the subject as *hypokeimenon*).[4] Anti-representationalism, from Heidegger on, has also been a persistent anti-subjectivism for just this reason. For Deleuze and Guattari, if 'what is' is nothing other than its becoming, then there can be no appeal to a more *proper* grammar. For grammar just is this movement of becoming. But one can demand that we move beyond the grammar of the subject precisely because it is a grammar that disavows the force of grammar. The subject–predicate structure issues in an ontology precisely because the idea of a subject is a grammatical form that posits the 'pre-grammatical'. Through the logic of the subject, it is as though there is what is, and then grammar comes to express it. A certain grammar gives a certain movement to thought. The subject–predicate grammar presents itself as grounded *on* some pre-grammatical subject, rather than affirming its own movement as that which effects the subject. In contrast to this, a mode of grammar that affirms itself *as grammar* is the infinitive (Deleuze 1990: 221). Here, there is just the unattributed and unlocated movement of a verb form: 'to think', 'to dance', 'to write'. Rather than saying that 's is p' or 's does p', we think the movement of grammar without it being the movement *of* a subject, and without it being a movement located *in* time. Rather, it is this movement itself that effects various 'striations' of time and space:

> The Verb is the univocity of language, in the form of an undetermined infinitive, without person, without present, without any diversity of voice. It is poetry itself. As it expresses in language all events in one, the infinitive verb expresses the event of language – language being a unique event which merges now with that which renders it possible. (Deleuze 1990: 185)

FROM ANTI-REPRESENTATIONALISM
TO ANTHROPOMORPHISM

Both Deleuze and Derrida imagine future philosophies that will overcome representation in its epistemological sense, and this is achieved by moving beyond ontology. If there is not a being that is then represented, then there can also be no subject who remains as the privileged site, screen, theatre or mirror of representations. The outcomes of this project in terms of the language and writing of philosophy are manifold, and include the yearning for new modes of writing, new grammars and the destruction of the distinctions between philosophy and literature. This does not mean that philosophy will just be a 'kind of writing', for this would still leave writing as rhetoric, effect or ornament. The very idea of writing must be transformed. No longer the representation of a real we have banished (as in Rorty), writing will be the very nature of a real that 'is' just dispersion, *différance* or sending. The metaphysical imperative has become an aesthetic imperative.

Kant had argued that the transcendental subject already possessed pure concepts in order to experience the world, and this is extended in Heidegger's insight that the understanding of being is not something abstracted by philosophers but must be in place in order to exist, or have a world. But this metaphysical imperative might be seen to rely – even in Heidegger – on a certain mode of representation, or a certain *aesthetic decision*. For Heidegger, the privileging of the visual is *both* a symptom of philosophy's fall into forgetting *and* its possibility of redemption. The idea that being is already present and there to be represented is epitomised in the language of 'theory', 'idea', 'idealism' and 'intuition' – all of which, Heidegger argues, have a visual origin. This demonstrates an original subjectivism in philosophy's way of speaking. The subject is the onlooker, perceiver or distanced observer, and this belies the *proximity* of the subject with being. For Heidegger, *Dasein* is not a separate, viewing and distanced point. *Dasein* dwells with being; and whatever *Dasein is* is effected through this existence. When philosophy becomes idealism – in Schelling – it merely fulfils its subjectivist trajectory. All that 'is' is determined through the idea, and all being is just this representing of itself in the idea. It is not just that human looking has pervaded being; the problem is not just anthropomorphism. It is also that the human has been determined, unquestioningly, as a looker. This means that philosophy's relation to language has two tasks.

The first will be to overcome the visual and subjective bias by thinking *language*. The world is not just apprehended or looked at by a separate subject but is disclosed through language. Poetry will become so important for Heidegger precisely because it recalls this disclosure, a disclosure not of a separate and distanced look but of the saying–gathering of language. And when Heidegger *does* refer to the visual arts – as in his famous discussion of Van Gogh's painting of a pair of shoes – he will discuss the painting, not in terms of its visual form, but in terms of its capacity to disclose a *meaningful* world (Heidegger 1971: 36). Against the idea that there is a world that is then seen or represented, poetry recalls the *being* of language. Language is not the medium or representation of a world already seen; all seeing is meaningful, *already* existing in a world. The world is not an object to be viewed from a single point. The world is a disclosed world that is given through language, and poetry just is this dwelling of world and word. Thus Heidegger's use of poetry as the exemplary mode of the aesthetic is also a decision regarding what it is to think. Thinking is not the separate representation of the world – as though the mind were a canvas upon which the world were printed. Thinking is a proximity with being, and this proximity is exemplified in the listening, speaking and *dialogic* character of poetry.[5]

Heidegger, and those who follow his attack on subjectivism, not only turn to art practices that disrupt the primacy of the disinterested or separated viewer; the visual itself is also redefined and used to radicalise the relation between logic and existence. This is where philosophy's dependence on the visual is radicalised rather than overturned. Is it possible to think a look, image or visuality that is not the look *of* some point of view? If it is the case that, as Heidegger insisted, our notions of 'idea' and 'idealism' recall an original relation of looking, then this also shows that the world is not a separate presence but is given through a relation, appearing or apprehending. Heidegger's use of metaphors of light, shining and illumination stress the *relation* of looking, its locatedness and specificity. This extension of viewing and looking beyond the self-presence of the subject is intensified in Foucault's dislocation of the visible from the viewing subject. His celebrated example of the panopticon demonstrates the ways in which the visible is effected through positive conditions: the distributions of bodies, architecture and discourse (Foucault 1979: 217). This means that the visible is not the vision *of* some subject. (In the case of the panopticon the visible *relation* of the central viewing tower produces a surveillance detached from any person or viewer.) Further, Foucault also intensifies the difference of visibility that cannot be reduced to sense or cognition. If language has its own shining or luminosity then it can also be seen as *positive*, as having effects and a force that exceeds intent. Derrida and Deleuze have also radicalised the Western metaphorics of light and optics. If light has traditionally been employed to figure the self-illumination of reason, then the dispersion of light and its dependence on apparatuses, media, surfaces and screens, takes us beyond point of view and frees difference from the *logos*. If light is distributed through space, and no longer subordinated to the self-presence of the look, then philosophy and thought might be able to move beyond the anthropologism of self-definition.

AN ETHICS BEYOND AUTONOMY

For Derrida the ethical and political consequences of re-thinking representation beyond anthropologism issues in an ethics of non-autonomy. Only abandoning the location of a *logos* within a subject or site of ownness will allow for the full responsibility of the force of *différance*. To include *différance* within the self-presence of a subject would be to reduce, silence and violently appropriate the given that lies beyond thought or knowledge. The concept must therefore be re-conceived: not as the ownness or self-presence of meaning, but as the anonymous effect of a promise. And with regard to political theory this also leads to a democracy thought beyond representation. Rather than affirming the democratic *polis* as the active outcome of a self-representing subject, Derrida attempts to think a *polis* bound by passive philiations: connections beyond the logic of calculation and equal exchange. This would challenge the very notion of democracy as representative or deliberative. For Derrida, this promised democracy-to-come is the utopia where responsibility is freed from knowledge (Derrida 1997: 69), and where the concept of the political moves beyond a calculation of the proper (64) to a perpetual openness of the 'perhaps' (67). Representation would only scar this new democracy with the violence of anthropologism; for it is in representational democracies that what one wills is also the will of all, issuing in an imagined moment of unity, consensus, agreement and the overcoming of difference.

   Although Deleuze is less explicit about the political consequences of transcendental empiricism, the anti-anthropologistic fervour of his work would also preclude any straightforward democratic representationalism. His most political works, the anti-Oedipal tracts penned with Félix Guattari, sustain a post-Marxist attempt to dislodge thought from a good self-authoring subject in order to explain the 'micro-fascism' of desire: all those ways in which desire turns against itself, subordinates itself and engineers its own oppression. The political force of *Anti-Oedipus* does not lie in freeing the individual from the force of oppression, but in freeing force from any individual representation. If one imagines oneself as adequately represented by the Oedipal image of desire, then one has merely submitted to the analyst's story. In some ways, then, Deleuze and Guattari's 'schizoanalysis' fulfils the representational demand of modernity: no law can be given from without, for any *law* that is given is necessarily finite, conditioned and subject to question and legitimation. Rather than recognising the force of a given law, *Anti-Oedipus* intensifies the affirmation of force itself, or that which issues in law. But if this affirmation of force is regarded as (or contained within) the proper end of the human, then it is once more subordinated to something other than itself. Schizoanalysis is, therefore, a perpetual disconnection or pulverisation of the effects of force. If an event of desire institutes a point of view or subject who desires, then the response ought not be to recognise this subject, nor to demand representation. On the contrary, such recognition could only enslave or reverse the force of desire. Desire, force and becoming *must*, therefore, be freed from any reactive representation. Desire must not be seen as the desire *of* some desiring being, nor must desire submit itself to any representation – such as Oedipus, sexuality, man or the subject. It is through the subjection to one of its own effects that desire becomes other than itself, shifts from being active to reactive. (In this way, Deleuze and Guattari explain the possibility of oppression without having to posit some essential human subject to be emancipated, nor some punishing external power.) Desire just is this force of its own becoming, a force that is disavowed or evacuated of force when desire is seen as an effect of something other than itself.

This can also be explained through the anti-dialectic of Nietzsche's logic of nihilism. By positing some ground *behind* will and appearance, we subordinate appearance to one of its own effects. When we subsequently fail to uncover that ground we fall into a reactive nihilism, lamenting that we are condemned to mere representations (Nietzsche 1968). But Deleuze's simulacrum and image reverses this reaction; the ground itself is an image, and the simulacrum is not located in a series that leads from being to its copy (Deleuze 1990: 259). The simulacrum is a *different* series: the eternal affirmation of difference. For if difference is *eternal* then it neither begins from, nor arrives at, some presence. What 'is' is just a repeated affirmation of difference. And in terms of political theory this means that force is that which, *affirmed as force*, refuses to arrive at law and refuses to remain within any general representation (or 'molar' identity). On the contrary, the nature of a political movement, as a movement, is its 'molecular' becoming: a continual affirmation of itself as an act, desire or force (Deleuze and Guattari 1987).

Further, it is the very logic of representation that enslaves desire through an economy of exchange and equivalence. Capitalism is the outgrowth of a history of recognition. It is in capitalism that desire is given a token – recognised, measured and subordinated to a general code or logic. This is what links capitalism and Oedipus. On the one hand, both capitalism and psychoanalysis promise the thought of a logic beyond representation: in capitalism, value is given through exchange itself and not based on use value or the value of any single or grounding substance. In psychoanalysis it is the distribution of energy or desire that then forms itself into organised bodies and invested objects. The promise of these theories of economy is belied, however, when they become representational: when they present themselves as the grounding value and code of all other codes. It is when psychoanalysis translates all manifestations of desire into versions of Oedipus, or when capitalism only recognises the exchange of work and profit, that the pure openness of difference is frozen or reified into the representation *of* some grounding code. The political response to this ossification is, therefore, to resist codings. Rather than interpretation or demystification, schizoanalysis offers itself as further production: the proliferation of codes and not their taming.

Desire or force must become radically anti-anthropologistic, freed from any proper site or point of derivation. The good polity will not enslave itself to a vision of man but will sustain the perpetual non-recognition of itself. To a certain extent, then, Deleuze and Guattari's anti-anthropologism is compatible with modern representationalism. In a representative democracy what is willed is not my being – my own interests, my particular desires, my partial concerns – but will itself. Representative democracy is justified by appealing to the self-constituting or un-grounded character of human reason. If no law is given or imposed from without, then I am compelled to will a law. And this law should also be consistent with a self-willed nature. In keeping with the affirmation of will that underpinned enlightenment emancipation, Deleuze and Guattari oppose themselves to any law or code that appears as simply given. What needs to be activated, *Anti-Oedipus* argues, is the force or will of laws and codes. The analyst must not be seen as one who occupies some point of view outside the whole, with his laws of interpretation functioning as a privileged code. Oedipus is one possible coding among others. In opposition to an Oedipal psychoanalysis that would merely represent some meaning, schizoanalysis decodes. This means that it goes further than the self-willing of enlightenment political theory, and this because of an intensified anti-anthropologism. It is not just that subjects must not accept an interpretation of themselves that is imposed from without. It is not just that the human ought not be seen as the basis or ground for what is appropriately willed. Even a self-willed identity is a negation of the will that is its true event. The willing *of identity* is a reactive willing. To give oneself a law is precisely the reactive political effect that *Anti-Oedipus* sets out to pull apart. A truly active will does not will *itself*, decide itself or recognise itself. Active willing is a flight from identity, a continual dispersion, wandering or becoming.

Against the recognition of will in a speaking subject, *Anti-Oedipus* emphasises the distribution of a moving body-machine. This is why Deleuze and Guattari write of the 'consumption of pure intensities' (Deleuze and Guattari 1984: 20). Consumption is not the effect of some system of capital. There is an initial pre-human intensive state or series from which subjects and systems are formed. This is why we need to begin with the machine, without meaning, centre or telos. And we need to see the ideal level of Oedipus and the signifier as the effect of the real and material productions of desire, not their ground or cause. But rather than simply dismiss the Oedipal reversal of Freudian psychoanalysis *Anti-Oedipus* also diagnoses its advent. How is it that desire enslaves itself? How can we think the falling back of desire in a philosophy of immanence? The first step in a philosophy of immanence is not to place desire in some ideal or fantasmatic plane in opposition to the real. Desire is material production (Deleuze and Guattari 1984: 30) and what desire produces is the real; thus the real is defined not as presence, or what is, but as *both* the actual and the virtual. The movement that establishes Oedipus and capitalism as tyrannical is also the very movement that (extended and affirmed beyond the dialectic) will re-affirm the flow of desire. Both desire and production begin as 'machinic' connections. Thus it is the very character of the real to become, or to pass from the actual to the virtual. But a certain mode of connection – the Oedipal triangle or the law of profit – establishes itself as the law of all connection. All codes are reduced to a grand code. What needs to be recognised in both capital and desire is not some grounding lack or need through which all difference passes, but the fact that desire and capital *can* produce lack as one of their virtual moments. The subject is one mode of gap, difference or break among others – part of a general and material flow of desire and production. Capitalism and psychoanalysis open modernity by thinking law as a law of difference, as a regulation that is immanent rather than transcendent. But this immanence is lost sight of or halted when it is re-coded by one of its virtual moments – profit or the phallus. For in such re-codings a certain movement of difference comes to govern difference and exchange in general.

For Deleuze and Guattari, Oedipus is the prevalence of a single code, a single image of desire that speaks for desire in general. There are several moves that need to be made to extend Oedipus beyond the code. The first is to see the Oedipal connection as one connection among others. The second is to recognise the reactive and dialectical nature of this connection. From an image, fantasy or virtual movement of desire – the maternal object, the Oedipal dyad – one retroactively assumes a ground or presence *from which* this difference emerged (a presence that is held in the law or the phallus). But this origin *of difference* is one of difference's own movements. One mode of desire – the desire of the father or the analyst – acts as the code of desire in general. The desire of the capitalist – profit – codes production in general. But these grand hermeneutic codes are effects, and not grounds, of a field of intensities, connections and singularities. Any totality is the effect, and not the origin, of a field of singularities or a multiplicity (Deleuze and Guattari 1984: 74–5).

Not subjecting itself to an image of thought or some transcendent ground, Deleuze's transcendental analysis takes thought to its 'nth' power, and asks what dispersions or distributions are possible (Deleuze 1994: 140). Philosophy is continually (eternally) affirmed, not in representing or copying thought, but in thinking *again*. Politically and ethically, this means that philosophy is itself an affirmation (*amor fati*): not subordinating the given to a representation or ground but continually affirming thought itself as an event of the given (Deleuze and Guattari 1994: 159). And this affirmation will also demand a new grammar and style of philosophy; for philosophy realises itself, not by recognising itself through a model of good sense, but in creating new concepts, instituting new planes and avowing the event of its own writing (Deleuze and Guattari 1994: 197).

Deleuze's overcoming of representationalism will be fulfilled when words no longer function as signifiers or tokens of meaning, but act as effects, events and productions. Language will not be located within a point of view, nor seen as the expression of a prior will. Language is not the crowning essence of man as a representational animal; language is a differential event coterminous with multiple planes of difference. Semiosis for Deleuze goes all the way down: plants, animals and life in general perpetually will, differentiate and affirm. This givenness ought not, therefore, be subordinated to some representational screen or subject. Transcendental empiricism is *transcendental* precisely in its refusal of some transcendent ground. Empiricism is the event or encounter of the given, grounded on neither a subject (idealism) nor an object (realism). Empiricism carries the difference of the given beyond any ground. Similarly, as expressed in *Anti-Oedipus*, schizoanalysis insists that desires are not reducible to a single economy; nor are they exchanged for higher goods. Desire is active when it is desire itself. Economies of desire do not exchange equivalent values; what is desired is the flow of exchange itself, and each flow is *singular* (not a sign, equivalent or substitute for something other than itself). In a libidinal economy one invests in exchange itself, and not what that exchange might represent. If one regards capital as one flow of exchange among others (and not the code of all codes), then one no longer subordinates desire to some general economy. Indeed, economy moves from being a system that represents, equalises and quantifies some presence, to being the circulation, mobility and exchange that is only retroactively (and reactively) taken as the representation *of* some proper ground.

Deleuze's expansion of the sense of economy also frees political critique from ideology and representationalism. One might imagine ideology, most crudely, as misrepresentation. If this were so then capitalist ideology could be translated, de-coded or de-mystified with regard to some real or disavowed value, such as labour. The idea of a point of the real that grounds an economy – whether that be the labour value of Marxism or the libido of psychoanalysis – is radically reversed by schizoanalysis:

It is true that reality has ceased to be a principle. According to such a principle, the reality of the real was posed as a divisible abstract quantity, whereas the real was divided up into qualified unities, into distinct qualitative forms. But now the real is a product that envelops the distances within intensive quantities. (Deleuze and Guattari 1984: 87)

It is not that there is a medium or quantity (being or the real) that is then distributed, exchanged or represented. It is no longer the case that exchange and economy can be recognised as the exchange and economy *of* some grounding presence. On the contrary, in the beginning is exchange, flow, difference, desire and becoming. In a reactive movement (of ideology or illusion) this circulation is taken as the sign *of* some other thing: labour, the phallus, meaning, being.

Traditional Marxism had criticised capitalism precisely because the original presence of man's relation to the world – an original and self-defining proximity – had fallen into exchange for its own sake. What begins as a movement of liberation from nature and servitude – the freedom to exchange one's labour – is alienated from its ground to the point where exchange itself governs human existence. The exchange that begins as human action is then alienated into an external and implacable logic. Thus Marxism is ultimately an anthropologism: the return of all system to its proper ground and point of origin. Indeed, Marx's criticism of Hegel depends on just this point: what Hegel saw as the *absolute* movement of spirit must be re-grounded in human labour and man's concrete relation to the world. Against Marx's anthropologism, Deleuze and Guattari define capital not as a misrecognised abstraction from man's life and being, but as a still too human coding of all exchange according to a single value. Their aim, then, is not to return capital to the recognition of a non-alienated human subject, but to intensify flow, exchange, distribution and economy beyond any grounding. Only in this move will political critique be active: not subordinating itself to a being or value and not restricting economy to the exchange or equivalence of some presence or substance. For it is not as though there is an actuality – being – that is then overlaid by the virtual – representation, ideology or sense. Rather, what *is* is itself both actual and virtual, continually imaging itself, becoming, signifying, connecting, moving and dispersing. The problem of politics is not an imposed ideology on a proper presence. The problem is one of *reaction*: taking one event of the virtual – one becoming – as the ground or reality

of all becomings. This is how psychoanalysis has functioned: a particular event of sense (the Oedipal narrative) functions as the ground of
all other narratives.

The point then is not to give a more accurate account of desire but to
free desire from a single code, to intensify a multiplicity of investments
and to refuse the idea that all acts of desire stand in for, are exchanged
or substituted for some originally prohibited loss. The schizoanalytic
utopia does not only free desire from the Oedipal narrative or the
psychoanalyst's point of view. Desire is extended beyond point of view
altogether, and beyond the boundary of the human. The ideas of the
machine and becoming-animal serve to de-anthropologise the realm
of difference. The world is not a presence to be re-presented in the
signifying mind of man. Sense, difference and logic extend beyond the
human. In contrast to the divide between presence (world) and representation (man), Deleuze and Guattari posit a univocal realm. Freed
from its re-presentation in a located point of view, speech and images
are dispersed in collective assemblages. Embodiment extends beyond
organisms, and becoming is effected in the animal, the machine, the
voice from nowhere, and the 'mechanosphere' (Deleuze and Guattari
1987).

THE ANTHROPOMORPHIC RETURN

From this it would follow that beyond the scar of representation – the
location of the world as given *to* man – there is simply the given: an
economy or system of exchange that is not the exchange *of* some being.
The idea of being, presence or substance is a reactive effect whereby
becoming is taken as the becoming *of* some ground, or where the given
is taken as the gift *of* being, or where the given is given *to* some privileged site.

In *The Politics of Friendship* Derrida directly engages with the motif of
responsibility beyond its enclosure within knowledge and representation, and this is done by appealing to heteronomy or a 'law before the
law'. This law is not a law that gives itself to itself once foundations
have been dismantled. It is a law that *gives*. 'Prior' to any coherence,
recognition or self-determination, *différance* disperses. We cannot even
say that *différance* disperses itself, for there is not yet self, *autos* or point
of apprehension. We might say, then, using Derrida's own language,

that if philosophy has always been the dream of an empiricism – a dream of a given that is apprehended without interference, loss or mediation – then this dream will be fulfilled and overcome in the utopia of grammatology and non-autonomy. What impedes a pure empiricism is the *thought* of the subject, whereby the given is not immediately apprehended but is re-presented according to a certain logic. In order to achieve a pure empiricism, one could either see the subject as thoroughly adequate to, or proximate with, the given. In this case the given would not be given *to* some other site; the given would be nothing other than its subjective representation. (It is this 'representationalism' that Heidegger (1987) diagnoses in Nietzsche's 'will to power' and that Derrida criticises as logocentrism, the inclusion of all that is within the domain of the representable.) If a pure empiricism that encloses all that is within the experience of a subject can be criticised for its forgetting of being, one could think empiricism beyond subjective determination, and beyond reification into a logically given world. In so doing one would achieve the overcoming of representationalism, but would do so at the cost of anthropomorphism. Such a move would disown knowledge through an appeal to a pre-human anteriority. To posit a givenness or absolute beyond the subject, beyond knowledge or beyond human experience is, as Deleuze insists, a more radical transcendentalism. Whereas Kant traced the transcendental from the empirical, Deleuze's transcendentalism takes empiricism beyond the subject (Deleuze 1994: 135). In this regard, Deleuze celebrates his own project as a more profound transcendentalism, against the reactive horrors of representationalism and against the enslavement to anthropologism. For Deleuze transcendental analysis extends us beyond what is represented – not to some *metaphysical* beyond, outside, or *transcendent* 'plane' – but to the unimaginable, eternal or 'nth' power of the given (Deleuze 1994: 143).

Derridian deconstruction, on the other hand, ceaselessly regulates against the risk of resting with the transcendental, and continually recognises that any description of the outside of metaphysics remains metaphysical (Derrida 1982a: xii). Nevertheless, thinking the *non*-autonomy of responsibility relies upon taking the domain of the given beyond the self, beyond knowledge and beyond the point of view of experience. Derrida's notions of *différance*, the trace, *écriture*, *envois*, the *gramme* and other 'quasi-transcendentals' are mobilised in order to think what lies beyond representation and the decision of the subject.

The ideal of autonomy, or a subject that is self-authoring, is surmounted through the inscription of what lies beyond, or what effects, the limit of the subject. But this inscription is itself also determined, effected and limited. The description of this excess can only be a *quasi*-transcendental, never fully exempted from the field it attempts to explain. Derrida's quasi-transcendentalism amplifies a long tradition of anti-anthropologism. No event within the world – neither man, nor subjectivity, nor structure – can enclose or exhaustively account for the world in general. One needs to think play or writing, not as grounding conditions, and not as the play *of* some being. Consequently, one begins from the transcendental question, but does so in order to lead to a consideration of a power that lies beyond the power of the question, beyond the subject and beyond comprehension:

> It is to escape falling back into this naïve objectivism that I refer here to a transcendentality that I elsewhere call into question. It is because I believe that there is a short-of and a beyond of transcendental criticism. To see to it that the beyond does not return to the within is to recognize in the contortion the necessity of a pathway [*parcours*]. . . . the value of the transcendental arche [*archie*] must make its necessity felt before letting itself be erased. The concept of the arche-trace must comply with both that necessity and that erasure. It is in fact contradictory and not acceptable within the logic of identity. The trace is not only the disappearance of origin – within the discourse that we sustain and according to the path that we follow it means that the origin did not even disappear, that it was never constituted except reciprocally by a nonorigin, the trace, which thus becomes the origin of the origin. From then on, to wrench the concept of the trace from the classical scheme, which would derive it from a presence or from an originary nontrace and which would make of it an empirical mark, one must indeed speak of an originary trace or arche-trace. Yet we know that that concept destroys its name and that, if all begins with the trace, there is above all no originary trace. (Derrida 1974: 61)

POLITICS BEYOND AUTONOMY

In addition to his critical recognition of the limits of philosophy, Derrida also offers some possibilities for re-thinking the *logos*: no longer as the grounding condition of what is, but as that which exceeds all recognition, comprehension and representation. If this non-origin is thought not as the writing *of* some presence, the gift *of* some being, the exchange *of* some value, but as *différance* itself, then it is possible that philosophy might re-define itself through a new ethics. This ethics, in thinking the beyond of autonomy, will be poised between the violence of determining that 'beyond' and the silence of awaiting a 'beyond' that can never present itself. This opens the way for a political theory of a democracy-to-come and a justice-to-come. For Derrida, the *concepts* of democracy and justice are at once determinations – meaningful and limited concepts – at the same time as they indicate a necessary 'beyond': the very meaning of justice is a law that would not be contaminated by particular determinations; the very meaning of democracy aims at freedom from imposed determination and closed structures of recognition. Thought in this way, democracy will no longer be based on recognition and a relation to others who remain proximate to, akin to, or symmetrical with oneself. If one thinks the structurality of structure, or the non-autonomous opening of alterity, then one might have to conceive democracy beyond representation. One's being or identity is already the effect of a *différance* that exceeds decision. Politics will also therefore not be contained *within* the point of view of the subject. The political – the relations to others – will extend beyond the knowable and representable. And this also means that democracy is no longer the representation *of* some proper human reason, nor the creation of autonomy through representation. Democracy now concerns the unrepresentable: all those traces, movements and differences that are effective, if not affective.

Deleuze and Guattari also argue that the political precedes being and they, too, create a new 'series' for political theory. The State does not stem from interests; nor does the State exist to tame and curb interests. Prior to the State and 'coded' interests – those interests that are represented and representative – there is the movement and production of desires. From this movement of desire the State is formed as a 'territory' or coding; and *from this territory* certain desires are coded as the interests of subjects. (The mistake has been to think of the subject as the origin of represented interests; the subject is the effect of coding certain desires as interests.) For Deleuze, unlike Derrida, the post-structuralist challenge of thinking a writing or tracing that exceeds the known and human structures of language or system is directed, not to a law before all law, nor to a passive listening to that which exceeds the self. For Deleuze, the notions of eternal return, active becoming and *amor fati* are directed beyond recognition and beyond autonomy. For what the eternal return affirms is the power of difference to sustain differentiation, to not remain content within any recognised identity or representation. To affirm difference eternally is to take difference beyond representation. Any *represented* difference has fallen into identity; any difference as a difference *of* or difference *from* has been subordinated to an identity, and thus difference is no longer eternal. Eternal difference differentiates without ground, without end and without subordination to logic, decision or the point of view of the subject.

One has to ask, however, whether such a utopian non-autonomy is either possible, desirable or consistent with an affirmatory ethics. There are several ways in which this question might be broached. The first is to consider the degree to which all these dreams of a beyond to autonomy take the utopian form of a diagnosis of representation. Derrida's explicit reflections on representation acknowledge the impossibility of a simple escape or cure. To think of philosophy as defined by the concept of representation is to already deploy representational logic. The past is organised into an epoch, with 'representation' functioning as its defining or grounding concept (Derrida 1982b). Rather than imagine a future freed from representation, Derrida pulverises representation into a plurality of *envois*. There is no origin that has been reified, totalised or belied by representation; there is no 'fall' into a representational logic at the cost of the lived immediacy of existence. Derrida does not seek a return to the pre-representational, nor an overcoming of the system of representation. Rather, he re-figures representation. No longer representation *of* some given, but as a 'giving' or sending that is plural, disseminated and dispersed, representation will undo itself beyond all location within epoch, presence or subject. But the question arises as to whether this plurality of *envois*, the freeing of representation from any site or presence, does not repeat the anthropomorphic illusion. For surely any beyond to presence, point of view and recognition will be a *determined* beyond. Derrida himself is vigilant with regard to any pure outside to metaphysics; but the idea of a 'responsibility without autonomy' does signal an attempt to give the unrepresentable a crucial ethical function. We might acknowledge that an autonomy of self-presence is essentially impossible: to give oneself a law is already both to differ from oneself and to rely on a 'law before the law' (structures, syntax and differences that allow a particular law to constitute itself as law). But does this exhaust the possibility of autonomy?

Think of what precludes or impedes the dream of a Derridian grammatology or a Deleuzian philosophy of immanence, or even a Foucaultian art of existence where the self would not be subjected *to* a logic but would effect that logic through existence. What hinders this project of arriving at a post-representational utopia is the seeming inevitability of *reaction* (in the Nietzschean sense). Actions are seen as actions *of*; signs are taken as signs *of*; what appears is seen as the appearance *of* (some transcendence); and what is asserted as true is taken as true beyond the force of the utterance, event or practice. To recognise the force of reaction is to recognise the persistent return of representation, point of view and logic. It might be illusory to posit logic as the ground of events, for any logic will be the outcome of events. There might be a responsibility in recognising the differential movement within which thought is located, a movement that is subsequently (and reactively) recognised as a logic or determined as a re-presentation. And there might also be a responsibility in recognising that any supposed autonomy is never self-present: the subject is effected through that which exceeds representation. But there might be a further responsibility in acknowledging the *autonomy-effects* of logic. These autonomy-effects follow from both sides of the representational antinomy. To take what is as a representation is to recognise thought's contribution to the world: the world is never given in itself, but *as given* is always given in a certain way or according to a logic. To place this logic within the subject is the error of anthropologism: taking a particular being or a part of the world as the ground for the world in general. To place this logic beyond subjectivity is the error of anthropomorphism: forgetting the ways in which our world is determined as 'our' world (even if this 'our' is effected coterminously with the world and is not the outcome of a pre-determining subject). In many ways, the dream of non-autonomy, the dream of a system that exceeds the self, that exceeds recognition and logic, is the final moment of modernity's dream of overcoming the scar of representation.

Representation, therefore, presents two challenges. If our world is a represented world then thought must not seek some real in itself, nor imagine thought as some given that might be known immediately. This is not to say that thought is a picture of the real; it is just to acknowledge that the very notion and possibility of the *real* is a gap, separation, distance or difference between what is given as present and its site of experience, or re-presentation. Thought is located within representation or some logic of existence (the mode in which the given is given). But any attempt to describe this logic, site of representation or point of view risks an anthropologism: we start to think of 'logic' as a thing that represents some presence, whereas logic is just that regularity or persistence of that form which gives the world as present. Ideas of the subject, man, structure, conceptual scheme or culture sustain the anthropologistic and Cartesian illusion that representation might be described as a mirror, screen or theatre for the world. And so any notion of an autonomous subject in the Cartesian sense must be resisted; for the 'logic' that gives the world cannot be a thing within the world. It is this anti-Cartesian emphasis which refuses to reify logic and which refuses to remain with any image of thought that issues in the critiques of logocentrism, phallocentrism, representationalism, normalisation and a host of other anthropologisms. But what is lost if we forget the concomitant error of anthropomorphism? Can responsibility be adequately accounted for by appealing to a writing beyond subjectivity or a tracing beyond recognition?

What is lost in this dream of non-autonomy or anti-subjectivism? The answer may well be that the attempt to overcome the horrors of man induces an anthropomorphic sleep. The dream of the 'beyond' or the post-human holds such allure that we remain naive in relation to the dream work. Any 'beyond' of the human will not only be given and determined in a certain way; it is also the beyond *of the human* – determined, in part, by the risk of anthropologism. It is not just that any 'beyond' of being and presence will be taken as *being*, and will be recognised. It is also that the departure to this beyond is motivated by the dominance of a quite specific terror: the terror of Cartesianism where man is determined as a thing within the world, where logic is a lifeless system and the world is represented as a separate object rather than lived pre-ontologically. The thought of the inhuman will always be taken from a determinate notion of the human. The dream of non-autonomy, post-representationalism, anti-subjectivism, homelessness, anteriority and liberation from point of view cannot be fulfilled by the debunking of the Cartesian subject alone. It may make no sense to posit a subject – as substance – that explains all other substance. And it may make no more sense to posit a representing animal as the ground of all representation. Both these moves do beg the question of the grounding substance. But, despite the incoherence of anthropologism, the post-structuralist endeavour has shown the persistence of the Cartesian illusion. Any demystification of a grounding substance, such as man or the subject, tends to result in the positing of yet one more ground: language, the unconscious, structure or difference. Any ground is, then, not a thing to be represented but is only given in the process of representation; but this recognition of representation as that which precludes grounding is a threshold that never arrives. The ungrounding term becomes one more representation of a ground: terms like difference, structure or desire replace 'man' as a being that explains all being. The thought of non-autonomy gestures to a utopia where thought will no longer ground itself in a representation, when there will be no reified logic that is recognised as the order of existence, and when existence will free itself from the imposition of its own images. But this affirmation of an ungrounding without being, presence or *autos* fails to recognise the inevitability of point of view, the return of representation and the persistence of recognition. And this predicament of point of view endures even in the notion of the pre-personal, the singular or the anterior; for those very styles that are used to dislocate the point of view of the subject nevertheless produce a stylistic regularity or, to use Foucault's phrase, an art of existence.

The persistence of anthropologism suggests that rather than rid thought of its illusions of a grounding subject, one ought to recognise and be responsible for the mode of one's self-grounding. In the face of the failure to overcome anthropologism we are required to own certain autonomy effects: all the ways in which the logic of existence is lived as the ordered logic of some being. Thus autonomy would be not just a responsibility for a structure that exceeds recognition, but a responsibility for the ways in which this 'beyond' of recognition is continually domesticated, owned, recognised and represented.

Accordingly, we might describe the first imperative of autonomy as the recognition of the structural illusion of anthropologism. Our experience is taken as *our* experience (even if the 'our' is effected through experience); experience is therefore owned, located and subjected to a logic. Secondly, we might see a second imperative of autonomy through the responsibility of resisting anthropomorphism. How could any pre-human, anterior or unrepresentable difference or non-presence be known or lived? The thought of what exceeds our representation will always be *our* excess: given in certain ways and effected beyond certain limits. And this will be so no matter how vigilantly we guard against any naive subjectivism or humanism. The autonomy that issues from recognising the illusion of anthropomorphism is not some pre-experiential point of decision; autonomy is, rather, the effected point, regularity or ownness constituted through experience. But autonomy would also not be a self-questioning subject who determines their world and who must then 'own' any logic of this world. Considered in terms of the illusion of anthropomorphism, autonomy would recognise that as *responsible*, thought is a *response to* some being. The hope for a writing without prior presence or without an intending subject aims for difference as such, beyond subordination to a ground. But this impersonality occludes thought's nature as response *to* some being, the essential separation of thought as experience. The subject is not a substance prior to experience, but experience is (as experience *of*) just this separation: just this positioning of the subject, its delimitation, its finitude and ownness. To recognise autonomy is to recognise the given as given *to* some point, locus or way of being (even if this point is co-determined through the giving of the given). This is to recognise a certain logic of the given: not a logic that precedes and exceeds the particular givings of the world but a logic that is effected as a certain regularity, representability or ownness of the world. Autonomy may be refuted if it is defined in the sense of a substance who, present to himself, gives himself his own proper law through a process freed from all determination that is not self-determination. But to think of difference in general as non-autonomy is to displace, rather than confront, the predicament of autonomy. For the idea of a pre-human structurality is in many ways akin to a law that gives itself, without ground, presence, being or locus. And this is to suggest that so many of those post-modern dreams of the post-human extend and fulfil, rather than overturn, enlightenment goals of a pure self-determination without opacity, positivity or limit. What precludes self-present autonomy in the Cartesian sense is autonomy as an irreducible procedure and effect. Because the subject is not a substance, but is effected through the givenness of the given, autonomy occurs after the event – effected through decisions, practices, regularities and ways of being. Autonomy is not self-present, not fully transparent to itself. Rather, autonomy signals a knot, opacity or locus – a certain recognised or represented *ethos* – that impedes the absolute, anterior and multiple play of difference. It is this recognition of the predicament of autonomy that might lead us to think of an ethics focusing on both representational illusions of anthropologism and anthropomorphism.

Thought can never rest assured with any representation of itself as a thinking thing, for this anthropologistic error would preclude the *question* of the logic that allowed any such represented thing itself to be given. Such a representationalism would assume that thought might know, delimit and comprehend its ownness. Nor could thought simply disown all logic and locate itself as nothing more than an effect of the pre-human, as though thought itself bore no character or made no contribution. Any such pre-human or inhuman would always be determined by the point of view of what it means to be human. An ethics of a redefined or procedural autonomy will be poised between these two illusions of representation: the illusion that thought is a representable thing, a self to be known or a substance to be perceived (anthropologism) *and* the illusion that there is an inhuman real that might be lived immediately to deliver thought from its representational limit (anthropomorphism).

Consider the significance of this antinomy as it is played out beyond the domain of philosophy in arguments surrounding representation and identity. On the one hand, it is argued, representation is a violence done to my being. To be subordinated to representation is to suffer from stereotypes, alienated images, or normalising models of the human. Versions of modern anti-anthropologism have been sustained in popular and contemporary criticisms of the beauty industry, colonialism, the mass media, pornography and ideology. To accept an image of oneself that is imposed from without is to take a representation as a thing in itself; it is to forgo my own subjective autonomy and responsibility. And this reification of the self through representation explains a host of contemporary ills, from male violence and women's oppression to capitalism and imperialism. For in such cases, the subject is determined by a representation that effaces its nature as representation and presents itself as natural, immutable and given. Externalised representation scars the self, limits its being, and subjects life to a logic that is not its own. At the same time, this reification of representation in alienated images is countered by a demand *for representation* in the political–ethical sense – the demand that images not be imposed from without but be autonomous or authentic. Such supposedly more authentic representations are grounded in subjects, intentions and decisions rather than the dehumanised and alien machines of representation that dominate the mass media.

As long as we remain within a Cartesian sense of autonomy, however, such autonomous representation will be a contradiction. And this contradiction extends to the iconic status that surrounds the myth of Descartes. On the one hand, Descartes is marked as the very fall into modernity: the point at which the subject becomes a representing screen set over against an inert and present world. On the other hand, the anxiety regarding representation relies on the desire for a Cartesian subjective purity. If one is submitted to a regime of representation, then the self will not be fully autonomous. By submitting to representation one takes oneself as a thing, a *res extensa* rather than the separated spontaneity and non-being of pure thought. The desire to overcome autonomy and representation is a hyper-Cartesianism directed against Descartes (Bray and Colebrook 1998). *Res cogitans* is still too thing-like, too human – and the same goes for any *represented* site of thought, including autonomy. We will only have arrived at the threshold of modernity when thought no longer labours under the anthropological illusion, when it no longer recognises itself, owns itself, or locates itself as an autonomous point in relation to being. But doing away with the *being* of the self, if it is to be persistent and rigorous, has culminated in the doing away of *being* altogether. The move 'beyond ontology' overcomes the scar of representation. There is not a present world of being that is then re-presented. Rather than the being *for* a subject, there is just difference, sending, life, or the eternal return of existence affirming itself.

However, autonomous representation can be re-thought in the sense opened by Irigaray's account of autonomy. Autonomy is not the self-grounding or self-origination of the subject, but an owning of one's being, even if that owning is never fully transparent or present. Autonomy is a recognition that one is never a *pure* becoming, but always the becoming from some point and towards some transcendence.

This predicament of autonomy is fleshed out in the representational antinomy. One acknowledges that the world is a represented world, and so one is responsible for the point of view of knowledge. This constitutes autonomy as the site to which the world is given, as well as acknowledging – if not knowing – the positivity or contribution of that site. On this side of the antinomy, autonomy works against anthropomorphism, for it is only through autonomy that we recognise the world as *our world* and do not take our own representational logic as some immutable thing in itself. But the represented world is still a *world* and hence is other than knowledge, and so one is responsible. This responsibility exceeds, but does not annihilate, autonomy. On this side of the antinomy, responsibility is the necessary but endless labour against anthropologism. For through responsibility, as a *response to* what is other than the self, thought recalls that any recognised ground or ownness is always itself grounded and is therefore never adequate to itself. Through the representational antinomy we are not just supplementing responsibility with autonomy; we are recognising their essential nonseparation and their essential tension. For the claim to autonomy, or the recognition that thought *takes place*, is always belied and dispersed by those essential conditions that exceed the self. (And so any anthropologism or self-recognition is brought to consider the inhuman and what enables, but is not included within, recognition.) But the call to responsibility, as response to the world, is always contained, limited or marked by some modality of response. (And so any anthropomorphism, or striving to think what is beyond 'our' human purview, is mobilised from that very site of the human it seeks to erase.)

The idea of autonomous representation is, perhaps, an oxymoron. To represent oneself is to submit to a trans-individual system of language, signification or representation. But any such representational scheme can never be fully disowned, rendered anonymous, collective, inhuman or fully dispersed beyond all subjectivity. Rather the act of representation institutes autonomy, or places a self in a point of view. Autonomy ought not be defined in the terms of a being that is then expressed. Rather, the procedure of autonomy is a recognition that there is no foundational being other than its continual institution through a representation that dislocates itself from a prior presence. If we do not recognise that representation effects an autonomy that it can then be seen to belie, if we try to overcome this scar of representation, then we do so at the expense of forgetting what it is to think. In short, we attack the error of anthropologism – the idea of a general human subject who represents us all – with the error of anthropomorphism: the idea of a world that is fully and adequately given, without representation, separation or the contribution of thought.

NOTES

1. The clearest examples are: Heidegger's reading of Descartes in *What is a Thing?* (Heidegger 1967); Husserl's critique of Descartes in *Cartesian Meditations* ([1931] 1960); and Irigaray's re-reading of Descartes in *Speculum of the Other Woman* (1985a). For more contemporary criticisms of Descartes and the fall into representation see Rosi Braidotti's description of 'Cartesian Orphans' in *Patterns of Dissonance* (1991); Susan Bordo's 'The Cartesian Masculinisation of Thought' (1986); and Teresa Brennan's *History After Lacan* (1993).

2. Both Charles Taylor and Michael J. Sandel have recently objected to the over-simplification of the communitarian–liberal division, a division in which authors such as John Rawls, Ronald Dworkin and Robert Nozick are set over against Taylor, Sandel, Michael Walzer and Alastair MacIntyre. What both Sandel's and Taylor's arguments capture is that communitarianism has been unjustly targeted as a theory that simply asserts a set of shared values. Rather, according to Taylor, we can only explain the existence of individuals if we have some 'holist' explanation of their social formation (Taylor 1995 181–203). But Taylor, no less than his supposed liberal opponents, advocates deliberation, question, reason and self-representation. According to Sandel, who objects to being called a communitarian, it is a process of judgement, rather than shared values, that needs to be the basis of political theory (Sandel 1998: xi)

3. 'A quantum of force is equivalent to a quantum of drive, will, effect – more, it is nothing other than precisely this very driving, willing, effecting, and only owing to the seduction of language (and of the fundamental errors of reason that are petrified in it) which conceives and misconceives all effects as conditioned by something that causes effects, by a "subject", can it appear otherwise. For just as the popular mind separates the lightning from its flash and takes the latter for an *action*, for the operation of a subject called lightning, so popular morality also separates strength from expressions of strength, as if there were a neutral substratum behind the strong man, which was *free* to express strength or not to do so. But there is no such substratum; there is no 'being' behind doing,

effecting, becoming; 'the doer' is merely a fiction added to the deed – the deed is everything' (Nietzsche [1887] 1967: 45).

4. Derrida has regarded this movement beyond the grammar of subjectivism as crucial to his own project: 'How can we get away from this contract between the grammar of the subject or substantive and the ontology of substance or subject?' (Derrida 1995a: 262).

5. The tradition of taking thinking and existing as 'dialogic' that follows from Heideggerian hermeneutics is most clearly represented by Gadamer (1995) but does have a wider currency in the post-Heideggerian literary theory that views all literature through notions of engagement, community interaction and world-constitution. (Habermas [1987] will see literature primarily as world-disclosive, and reader response theorists, from Wolfgang Iser (1978) and Hans Robert Jauss (1982) to Stanley Fish (1980), will also insist that a text is rendered meaningful through a reader's own hermeneutic community and horizon.)

REFERENCES

For most twentieth-century writers, such as Derrida, Deleuze, Foucault and Heidegger, publication dates are those of the editions cited. For most pre-twentieth-century texts, original publication dates are given in square brackets.

Adorno and Horkheimer [1944] (1979), *Dialectic of Enlightenment*, trans. John Cumming, London: Verso.

Allison, Henry (1990), *Kant's Theory of Freedom*, Cambridge: Cambridge University Press.

Althusser, Louis (1984), *Essays on Ideology*, London: Verso.

Baudrillard, Jean (1993), *Symbolic Exchange and Death*, trans. Iain Hamilton Grant, London: Sage.

Belsey, Catherine (1980), *Critical Practice*, London: Methuen.

Benhabib, Seyla (1992), *Situating the Self: Gender, Community and Postmodernism in Contemporary Ethics*, Cambridge: Polity.

Bernstein, J. M. (1992), *The Fate of Art: Aesthetic Alienation from Kant to Derrida and Adorno*, Cambridge: Polity.

Bhabha, Homi K. (1983), 'The Other Question: Homi K. Bhabha Reconsiders the Stereotype and Colonial Discourse', *Screen* 24.6 (1983), pp. 18-36.

Blake William (1966), *Complete Writings*, Geoffrey Keynes (ed.), Oxford: Oxford University Press.

Bordo, Susan (1986), 'The Cartesian Masculinisation of Thought', *Signs: Journal of Women in Culture and Society*, 11.3, pp. 439–56.

Bowie, Andrew (1990), *Aesthetics and Subjectivity from Kant to Nietzsche*, Manchester: Manchester University Press.

Braidotti, Rosi (1991), *Patterns of Dissonance*, Cambridge: Polity.

Bray, Abigail and Claire Colebrook (1998), 'The Haunted Flesh: Corporeal Feminism and the Poetics of Disembodiment', *Signs: Journal of Women in Culture and Society*, 24.1, pp. 35–67.

Brennan, Teresa (1993), *History After Lacan*, London: Routledge.

Brod, Max (1960), *Franz Kafka: A Biography*, trans. G. Humphreys Roberts and Richard Winston, New York: Schoken Books.

Burke, Edmund [1790] (1910), *Reflections on the French Revolution*, A. J. Grieve (ed.), London: Dent.

Butler, Judith (1993), *Bodies That Matter: On the Discursive Limits of 'Sex'*, New York: Routledge.

Butler, Judith (1997), *The Psychic Life of Power: Theories in Subjection*, Stanford: Stanford University Press.

Cohen, Joshua (1989), 'Deliberation and Democratic Legitimacy' in *The Good Polity: Normative Analysis of the State*, Alan Hamlin and Philip Petitt (eds), Oxford: Basil Blackwell.

Colebrook, Claire (1997), 'The Trope of Economy and Representational Thinking: Heidegger, Derrida and Irigaray', *Journal of the British Society for Phenomenology*, 28.2, pp. 178–91.

Cornell, Drucilla (1991), *Beyond Accommodation: Ethical Feminism, Deconstruction and the Law*, New York: Routledge, 1991.

Coward, Rosalind and John Ellis (1977), *Language and Materialism*, London: Routledge and Kegan Paul.

Culler, Jonathan (1974), *Flaubert: The Uses of Uncertainty*, Ithaca: Cornell University Press.

Davidson, Arnold I. (1997), 'Structures and Strategies of Discourse', in *Foucault and His Interlocutors*, Arnold I. Davidson (ed.), Chicago: University of Chicago Press, pp. 1–17.

Davidson, Donald (1984), *Inquiries into Truth and Interpretation*, Oxford: Clarendon Press.

De Lauretis, Teresa (1987), *Technologies of Gender: Essays on Theory, Film and Fiction*, Bloomington: Indiana University Press.

Deleuze, Gilles (1983), *Nietzsche and Philosophy*, trans. Hugh Tomlinson, New York: Columbia University Press.

Deleuze, Gilles (1988), *Foucault*, trans. Sean Hand, Minneapolis: University of Minnesota Press.

Deleuze, Gilles (1990), *The Logic of Sense*, Constantin V. Boundas (ed.), trans. Mark Lester, New York: Columbia University Press.

Deleuze, Gilles (1991), *Empiricism and Subjectivity: An Essay on Hume's Theory of Human Nature*, trans. Constantin V. Boundas, New York: Columbia.

Deleuze, Gilles (1994), *Difference and Repetition*, trans. Paul Patton, Columbia University Press.

Deleuze, Gilles (1995), *Negotiations: 1972–1990*, trans. Martin Joughin, New York: Columbia University Press.

Deleuze, Gilles (1997), *Essays: Critical and Clinical*, trans. Daniel W. Smith and

Michael A. Greco, Minneapolis: University of Minnesota Press.

Deleuze, Gilles and Félix Guattari (1984), *Anti-Oedipus: Capitalism and Schizophrenia*, trans. Robert Hurley, Mark Seem and Helen R. Lane, London: Athlone.

Deleuze, Gilles and Félix Guattari (1986), *Kafka: Toward a Minor Literature*, trans. Dana Polan, Minneapolis: University of Minnesota Press.

Deleuze, Gilles and Félix Guattari (1987), *A Thousand Plateaus: Capitalism and Schizophrenia*, trans. Brian Massumi, Minneapolis: University of Minnesota Press.

Deleuze, Gilles and Félix Guattari (1994), *What is Philosophy?* trans. Hugh Tomlinson and Graham Burchill, London: Verso.

Derrida, Jacques (1974), *Of Grammatology*, trans. Gayatri Chakravorty Spivak, Baltimore: Johns Hopkins.

Derrida, Jacques (1978), *Writing and Difference*, trans. Alan Bass, London: Routledge and Kegan Paul.

Derrida, Jacques (1981a), *Dissemination*, trans. Barbara Johnson, Chicago: University of Chicago.

Derrida, Jacques (1981b), 'Economimesis', trans. R. Klein, *Diacritics: A Review of Contemporary Criticism*, 11.2, pp. 3–25.

Derrida, Jacques (1982a), *Margins of Philosophy*, trans. Alan Bass, Sussex: Harvester.

Derrida, Jacques (1982b), 'Sending: On Representation', *Social Research* 49.2, pp. 294–326.

Derrida, Jacques (1987a), *The Truth in Painting*, trans. Geoff Bennington and Ian McLeod, Chicago: University of Chicago Press.

Derrida, Jacques (1987b), *The Post Card: From Socrates to Freud and Beyond*, trans. Alan Bass, Chicago: University of Chicago Press.

Derrida, Jacques (1988), *Limited Inc.*, Evanston: Northwestern University Press.

Derrida, Jacques (1989), *Of Spirit: Heidegger and the Question*, trans. Geoffrey Bennington and Rachel Bowlby, Chicago: University of Chicago Press.

Derrida, Jacques (1992), *Given Time: I. Counterfeit Money*, trans. Peggy Kamuf, Chicago: University of Chicago Press.

Derrida, Jacques (1994), *Specters of Marx: The State of Debt, the Work of Mourning and the New International*, trans. Peggy Kamuf. New York: Routledge.

Derrida, Jacques (1995a), *Points . . . : Interviews, 1974–1994*, Elisabeth Weber (ed.), trans. Peggy Kamuf et al., Stanford: Stanford University Press.

Derrida, Jacques (1995b), *The Gift of Death*, trans. David Wills, Chicago: University of Chicago Press.

Derrida, Jacques (1996), *Archive Fever: A Freudian Impression*, trans. Eric Prenowitz, Chicago: University of Chicago Press.

Derrida, Jacques (1997), *Politics of Friendship*, trans. George Collins, London: Verso.

Descombes, Vincent (1993), *The Barometer of Modern Reason: On the Philosophies of Current Events*, trans. Stephen Adam Schwartz, Oxford: Oxford University Press.

Detienne, Marcel (1996), *The Masters of Truth in Archaic Greece*, trans. Janet Lloyd, New York: Zone Books.

Dumont, Louis, (1977), *Essays in Individualism: Modern Ideology in Anthropological Perspective*, Chicago: Chicago University Press.

Fish, Stanley E. (1980), *Is There a Text in this Class?: The Authority of Interpretive Communities*, Cambridge, Mass.: Harvard University Press, 1980.

Foucault, Michel (1970), *The Order of Things*, London: Tavistock.

Foucault, Michel (1972a), *The Archaeology of Knowledge and the Discourse on Language*, trans. A. M. Sheridan Smith, New York: Pantheon.

Foucault, Michel (1972b), 'Preface', Gilles Deleuze and Félix Guattari, *Anti-Oedipus: Capitalism and Schizophrenia*, trans. Robert Hurley, Mark Seem and Helen R. Lane, London: Athlone, pp. xi–xiv.

Foucault, Michel [1965] (1973), *Madness and Civilization: A History of Insanity in the Age of Reason*, trans. Richard Howard, New York: Pantheon Books.

Foucault, Michel (1979), *Discipline and Punish: The Birth of the Prison*, trans. Alan Sheridan, Harmondsworth: Penguin.

Foucault, Michel (1981), *The History of Sexuality, Volume 1: An Introduction*, trans. Robert Hurley, Harmondsworth: Penguin.

Foucault, Michel (1986a), 'What is Enlightenment?' in *The Foucault Reader*, Paul Rabinow (ed.), Harmondsworth: Penguin, pp. 32–50.

Foucault, Michel (1986b), *Death and the Labyrinth: The Work of Raymond Roussel*, trans. Charles Ruas, intro. John Ashbery, London: Athlone.

Foucault, Michel (1987), 'Maurice Blanchot: The Thought from Outside', in *Foucault/Blanchot*, trans. Jeffrey Mehlman and Brian Massumi, New York: Zone Books.

Foucault, Michel (1988), *The Use of Pleasure: The History of Sexuality, Volume 2*, trans. Robert Hurley, Harmondsworth: Penguin.

Foucault, Michel (1993), 'About the Beginning of the Hermeneutics of the Self: Two Lectures at Dartmouth', trans. Mark Blasius, *Political Theory* 21.2 (May 1993), pp. 198–227.

Foucault, Michel (1998), *Aesthetics, Method and Epistemology*, James D. Faubion (ed.), *Essential Works of Michel Foucault 1954–1984*, Paul Rabinow (ed.), New York: The New Press.

Freud, Sigmund (1925), 'Negation' in *The Standard Edition of the Complete Psychological Works of Sigmund Freud, Volume XIX (1923–1935)*, trans. James Strachey, London: Hogarth, pp. 235–9.

Gadamer, Hans-Georg (1995), *Truth and Method*, 2nd edn, trans. Joel Weinsheimer and Donald G. Marshall, New York: Continuum.

Gilson, Etienne (1961), *The Christian Philosophy of Saint Augustine*, trans. L. E. M. Lynch, London: Victor Gollancz.

Godwin, William (1985), *Enquiry Concerning Political Justice*, Harmondsworth: Penguin.

Goldsmith, Steven (1993), *Unbuilding Jerusalem: Apocalypse and Romantic Representation*, Ithaca: Cornell University Press.

Greenblatt, Stephen (1980), *Renaissance Self-Fashioning: From More to Shakespeare*, Chicago: University of Chicago Press.

Grosz, Elizabeth (1989), *Sexual Subversions: Three French Feminists*, Sydney: Allen and Unwin.

Grosz, Elizabeth (1994), *Volatile Bodies: Toward a Corporeal Feminism*, Sydney: Allen and Unwin.

Habermas, Jurgen (1971), *Knowledge and Human Interests*, trans. Jeremy J. Shapiro, Boston: Beacon Press.

Habermas, Jurgen (1985), 'Modernity – An Incomplete Project', trans. Seyla Benhabib, in *Postmodern Culture*, Hal Foster (ed.), London: Pluto, pp. 3–15.

Habermas, Jurgen (1987), *The Philosophical Discourse of Modernity: Twelve Lectures*, trans. Frederick Lawrence, Cambridge: Cambridge University Press.

Habermas, Jurgen (1989), *The Structural Transformation of the Public Sphere: An Inquiry into a Category of Bourgeois Society*, trans. Thomas Burger with the assistance of Frederick Lawrence, Cambridge, Mass.: MIT Press.

Habermas, Jurgen (1992), *Postmetaphysical Thinking: Philosophical Essays*, trans. William Mark Hohengarten, Cambridge, Mass.: MIT Press.

Habermas, Jurgen (1993), *Justification and Application: Remarks on Discourse Ethics*, trans. Ciaran P. Cronin, Cambridge, Mass.: MIT Press.

Hacking, Ian (1975), *Why Does Language Matter to Philosophy?* Cambridge: Cambridge University Press.

Hadot, Pierre (1995), *Philosophy as a Way of Life: Spiritual Exercises from Socrates to Foucault*, Arnold I. Davidson (ed.), Oxford: Blackwell.

Hartman, Geoffrey (1997), *The Fateful Question of Culture*, New York: Columbia University Press.

Hegel, G. W. F. [1807] (1977), *The Phenomenology of Spirit*, trans. A.V. Miller, Oxford: Oxford University Press.

Hegel, G. W. F. [1825] (1995), *Lectures on the History of Philosophy: 1 Greek Philosophy to Plato*, trans. E. S. Haldane, Lincoln: University of Nebraska Press.

Heidegger, Martin (1959), *An Introduction to Metaphysics*, trans. Ralph Manheim, New Haven: Yale University Press.

Heidegger, Martin (1967), *What is a Thing?* trans. W. B. Barton, Jr and Vera Deutsch, Lanham: University Press of America.

Heidegger, Martin (1968), *What is Called Thinking?* trans. J. Glenn Gray, New York: Harper and Row.

Heidegger, Martin (1969), *Identity and Difference*, trans. Joan Stambaugh, New York: Harper and Row.

Heidegger, Martin (1971), *Poetry, Language, Thought*, trans. Albert Hofstadter, New York: Harper and Row.

Heidegger, Martin (1979), *Nietzsche: The Will to Power as Art*, trans. David Farrell Krell, New York: Harper and Row.

Heidegger, Martin (1982), *On the Way to Language*, trans. Peter D. Hertz, San Francisco: Harper and Row.

Heidegger, Martin (1984), *Early Greek Thinking*, trans. David Farrell Krell and Frank A. Capuzzi, New York: Harper and Row.

Heidegger, Martin (1985), *Schelling's Treatise on the Essence of Human Freedom*, trans. Joan Stambaugh, Athens: Ohio University Press.

Heidegger, Martin (1987), *Nietzsche, Volume III: The Will to Power as Knowledge and Metaphysics*, trans. Joan Stambaugh, David Farrell Krell and Frank A. Capuzzi, San Francisco: Harper and Row.

Heidegger, Martin (1988), *Hegel's Phenomenology of Spirit*, trans. Parvis Emad and Kenneth Maly, Bloomington: Indiana University Press.

Heidegger, Martin (1990), *Kant and the Problem of Metaphysics*, 4th edn, trans. Richard Taft, Bloomington: Indiana University Press.

Heidegger, Martin (1991), *The Principle of Reason*, trans. Reginald Lilly, Bloomington: Indiana University Press.

Heidegger, Martin (1992), *The Metaphysical Foundations of Logic*, trans. Michael Heim, Bloomington: Indiana University Press.

Heidegger, Martin (1996), *Being and Time*, trans. Joan Stambaugh, Albany: State University of New York Press.

Heidegger, Martin (1998), *Pathmarks*, William McNeill (ed.), Cambridge: Cambridge University Press.

Husserl, Edmund (1929), *Formale und Transzendentale Logik*, Halle.

Husserl, Edmund [1931] (1960), *Cartesian Meditations: An Introduction to Phenomenology*, trans. Dorian Cairns, The Hague: Martinus Nijhoff.

Husserl, Edmund [1954] (1970), *The Crisis of European Sciences and Transcendental Phenomenology: An Introduction to Phenomenological Philosophy*, trans. David Carr, Evanston: Northwestern University Press.

Irigaray, Luce (1985a), *Speculum of the Other Woman*, trans. Gillian C. Gill, Ithaca: Cornell University Press.

Irigaray, Luce (1985b), *This Sex Which is Not One*, trans. Catherine Porter, Ithaca: Cornell University Press.

Irigaray, Luce (1991), *Marine Lover of Friedrich Nietzsche*, trans. Gillian C. Gill, New York: Columbia University Press.

Irigaray, Luce (1993), *An Ethics of Sexual Difference*, trans. Carolyn Burke and Gillian C. Gill, Ithaca: Cornell University Press.

Irigaray, Luce (1994), *Thinking the Difference: For a Peaceful Revolution*, trans. Karin Montin, London: Athlone.

Irigaray, Luce (1995), 'The Question of the Other', trans. Noak Guynn, *Yale French Studies* 87, pp. 7–19.

Irigaray, Luce (1996), *I Love to You: Sketch of a Possible Felicity in History*, trans. Alison Martin, New York: Routledge.

Iser, Wolfgang (1978), *The Act of Reading: A Theory of Aesthetic Response*, London: Routledge.

Jauss, Hans Robert (1982), *Toward an Aesthetics of Reception*, trans. T. Bahti, Minneapolis: University of Minnesota Press.

Joyce, James (1977), *The Essential James Joyce*, London: Granada.

Kant, Immanuel [1783] (1950), *Prolegomena to Any Future Metaphysics*, trans. Carus, revised Lewis White Beck, Indianapolis: Bobbs-Merrill.

Kant, Immanuel [1785] (1959), *Foundations of the Metaphysics of Morals and What is Enlightenment?* trans. Lewis White Beck, Indianapolis: Bobbs-Merrill, The Library of Liberal Arts.

Kant, Immanuel [1787] (1933), *Immanuel Kant's Critique of Pure Reason*, trans. Norman Kemp Smith, London: Macmillan.

Kant, Immanuel [1788] (1993a), *Critique of Practical Reason*, trans. Lewis White Beck, 3rd edn, New York: Macmillan.

Kant, Immanuel [1790] (1987), *Critique of Judgment*, trans. Werner S. Pluhar, Indianapolis: Hackett Publishing.

Kant, Immanuel (1993b), 'On a Newly Arisen Superior Tone in Philosophy,' in *Raising the Tone of Philosophy: Late Essays by Immanuel Kant, Transformative Critique by Jacques Derrida*, Peter Fenves (ed.), Baltimore: Johns Hopkins.

Lacan, Jacques (1977), *Écrits: A Selection*, trans. Alan Sheridan, New York: Norton.

Lacan, Jacques (1982), and the école freudienne, *Feminine Sexuality*, Juliet Mitchell and Jacqueline Rose (eds), trans. Jacqueline Rose, London: Macmillan.

Lacan, Jacques (1992), *The Ethics of Psychoanalysis: 1959–1960. The Seminar of Jacques Lacan*, Book VII, trans. Dennis Porter, ed. Jacques-Alain Miller, London: Routledge.

Laclau, Ernesto (1996), *Emancipation(s)*, London: Verso.

Lacoue-Labarthe, Philippe (1990), *Heidegger, Art and Politics: The Fiction of the Political*, trans. Chris Turner, Oxford: Basil Blackwell.

Lawrence, D. H. [1923] (1960), *Three Novellas: The Fox, The Ladybird and The Captain's Doll*, Harmondsworth: Penguin.
Lovejoy, Arthur O. (1936), *The Great Chain of Being: A Study of the History of an Idea*, Cambridge, Mass.: Harvard University Press.
Lyotard, Jean-Francois (1993), *Libidinal Economy*, trans. Iain Hamilton Grant, London: Athlone.
Macdonell, Diane (1986), *Theories of Discourse: An Introduction*, Oxford: Basil Blackwell.
MacIntyre, Alastair (1984), *After Virtue: A Study in Moral Theory*, 2nd edn, Indiana: Indiana University Press.
MacIntyre, Alastair (1990), *Three Rival Versions of Moral Enquiry: Encyclopaedia, Genealogy and Tradition*, London: Duckworth.
MacKinnon, Catharine A. (1987), *Feminism Unmodified: Discourses on Life and Law*, Cambridge, Mass.: Harvard University Press.
MacPherson, C. B. (1962), *The Political Theory of Possessive Individualism: Hobbes to Locke*, Oxford: Oxford University Press.
Manent, Pierre (1994), *An Intellectual History of Liberalism*, trans. Rebecca Balinski, Princeton: Princeton University Press.
Merleau-Ponty, Maurice (1962), *The Phenomenology of Perception*, trans. Colin Smith, London: Routledge and Kegan Paul.
Merleau-Ponty, Maurice (1964), *Signs*, trans. Richard C. McCleary, Evanston: Northwestern University Press.
Milton, John (1971), *Paradise Lost*, Alastair Fowler (ed.), London: Longman.
Milton, John (1982), *Complete Prose Works of John Milton*, Vol. 3, Don M. Wolfe et al. (eds), New Haven: Yale University Press.
Mohanty, Chandra T. (1991), 'Under Western Eyes: Feminist Scholarship and Colonial Discourses', in *Third World Women and the Politics of Feminism*, Chandra T. Mohanty, Anne Russo and Lourdes Torrens (eds), Indiana: Indiana University Press, pp. 51–80.
Nancy, Jean-Luc (1997), *The Sense of the World*, trans. Jeffrey S. Librett, Minneapolis: University of Minnesota Press.
Nietzsche, Friedrich [1887] (1967), *On the Genealogy of Morals and Ecce Homo*, Walter Kauffman (ed.), trans. Walter Kaufmann and R. J. Hollingdale, New York: Vintage.
Nietzsche, Friedrich (1968), *The Will to Power*, trans. Walter Kaufmann and R. J. Hollingdale, New York: Vintage.
Nussbaum, Martha C. (1994), *The Therapy of Desire: Theory and Practice in Hellenistic Ethics*, Princeton: Princeton University Press.
O'Neill, Onora (1989), *Constructions of Reason: Explorations of Kant's Practical Philosophy*, Cambridge: Cambridge University Press.
Paine, Thomas [1791–2] (1985), *The Rights of Man*, Harmondsworth: Penguin.

Plato (1961), *The Collected Dialogues of Plato*, Edith Hamilton and Huntington Cairns (eds), Princeton: Princeton University Press.

Rawls, John (1972), *A Theory of Justice*, Oxford: Oxford University Press.

Rawls, John (1993),'The Law of Peoples', *On Human Rights: The Oxford Amnesty Lectures 1993*, Stephen Shute and Susan Hurley (eds), New York: Basic Books.

Rawls, John (1996), *Political Liberalism*, New York: Columbia University Press.

Rorty, Richard (1980), *Philosophy and the Mirror of Nature*, Oxford: Basil Blackwell.

Rorty, Richard (1982), *Consequences of Pragmatism: Essays: 1972–1980*, Minneapolis: University of Minnesota Press, 1982.

Rousseau, Jean Jacques (1968), *The Social Contract*, trans. Maurice Cranston, Harmondsworth: Penguin.

Sandel, Michael J. (1998), *Liberalism and the Limits of Justice*, 2nd edn, Cambridge: Cambridge University Press.

Spivak, Gayatri Chakravorty (1990), *The Post-Colonial Critic: Interviews, Strategies, Dialogues*, Sarah Harasym (ed.), New York: Routledge.

Taylor, Charles (1995), *Philosophical Arguments*, Cambridge, Mass.: Harvard University Press.

Vernant, Jean-Pierre (1991), *Mortals and Immortals: Collected Essays*, Froma I. Zeitlin (ed.), Princeton: Princeton University Press.

Watt, Ian (1957), *The Rise of the Novel: Studies in Defoe, Richardson and Fielding*, London: Chatto and Windus.

Weber, Max [1904] (1976), *The Protestant Ethics and the Spirit of Capitalism*, trans. Talcott Parsons, London: Allen and Unwin.

White, Hayden (1973), *Metahistory: The Historical Imagination in Nineteenth-Century Europe*, Baltimore: Johns Hopkins.

Wollstonecraft, Mary [1792] (1985), *Vindication of the Rights of Woman*, Miriam Brody Kramnick (ed.), Harmondsworth: Penguin.

INDEX